Seven Steps to Success for Sales Managers

Seven Steps to Success for Sales Managers

A Strategic Guide to Creating a Winning Sales Team Through Collaboration

Max Cates

Publisher: Paul Boger
Editor-in-Chief: Amy Neidlinger
Acquisitions Editor: Charlotte Maiorana
Operations Specialist: Jodi Kemper
Cover Designer: Chuti Prasertsith
Managing Editor: Kristy Hart
Project Editor: Elaine Wiley
Copy Editor: Cheri Clark
Proofreader: Laura Hernandez
Senior Indexer: Cheryl Lenser
Senior Compositor: Gloria Schurick
Manufacturing Buyer: Dan Uhrig

© 2015 by Max Cates

For information about buying this title in bulk quantities, or for special sales opportunities (which may include electronic versions; custom cover designs; and content particular to your business, training goals, marketing focus, or branding interests), please contact our corporate sales department at corpsales@pearsoned.com or (800) 382-3419.

For government sales inquiries, please contact governmentsales@pearsoned.com.

For questions about sales outside the U.S., please contact international@pearsoned.com.

Company and product names mentioned herein are the trademarks or registered trademarks of their respective owners.

Printed in the United States of America

First Printing June 2015

ISBN-10: 0-13-421250-9
ISBN-13: 978-0-13-421250-0

Pearson Education LTD.
Pearson Education Australia PTY, Limited
Pearson Education Singapore, Pte. Ltd.
Pearson Education Asia, Ltd.
Pearson Education Canada, Ltd.
Pearson Educación de Mexico, S.A. de C.V.
Pearson Education—Japan
Pearson Education Malaysia, Pte. Ltd.

Library of Congress Control Number: 2015936710

Contents

About the Author

Max Cates received a bachelor of science from Missouri State University and a master of arts from the University of Missouri School of Journalism. He began his professional career with United Telecommunications (America's third-largest telecommunications company at the time) as Advertising Coordinator. After three years, he joined AT&T and served for 10 years in progressively responsible corporate leadership positions in advertising, corporate communications, and marketing management.

Cates's next leadership position was with Associated Electric Cooperative, a $2 billion electric power utility. After two promotions there, he became the youngest Division Director in its history, reporting to the CEO. His responsibilities included leading marketing, advertising, and corporate communications, as well as directing consumer sales strategy. During his tenure at Associated, he also completed Executive Development at the Wharton School of Business, University of Pennsylvania.

After 11 years with Associated and a number of national awards, Cates returned to AT&T, serving in sales and sales management positions, progressing from Internet Sales Manager to Telemarketing Sales Manager, to Area Sales Manager. Following an award-winning career with AT&T, which included the prestigious CEO Club Award, Cates joined Access Media, where he managed the sales force. He also served as a sales management professor at Webster University.

Introduction

T hink back over your sales career and count the number of really good managers you've had. You know, the ones who brought out the best in you. The ones who made your sales job exciting, challenging, and rewarding. The ones you could trust. Have you gotten past five fingers yet? Probably not. The Big Irony of sales is this: The ones who are most likely to become sales managers—salespeople—are usually the ones least prepared for the job. Couple that phenomenon with a lack of management training, and you have sales-fails waiting to happen. Ill prepared and under pressure to deliver results, many managers seek shortcuts, giving in to management fads and cookie-cutter approaches to sales management. Many fall prey to metrics addiction, which takes them further away from the basics. We sometimes forget that selling is a uniquely personal process composed of one person relating to another in a way that produces a sale.

Sales management's primary job is really pretty simple. It's not reaching sales goals. And it's not improving sales productivity or increasing company profitability. It is sales rep development, pure and simple. Everything else—goal attainment, sales productivity, and profitability—follows reps who are well prepared. Doing so requires the sales manager to embrace the complexities of human behavior from the rep's viewpoint and the customer's. There are simply no shortcuts. There's no app for that. But we keep looking, and often we keep getting further and further away from our salespeople and our customers.

It's a sad truth that a huge number of sales managers are either ineffective at best or, at worst, outright counterproductive. The impact of unproductive sales managers is huge, especially considering that more than 10% of the American workforce is in sales. We're talking billions of dollars of inefficiency.

Having spent half of my career in sales, and the other half in nonsales leadership roles (primarily in marketing and corporate communications for Fortune 500 companies on the "buyer" side of sales transactions), I've seen various management styles and personas. And my personal observation is that the biggest problem in sales management is an emphasis on "sales" rather than "management." The result is an inordinately large number of self-absorbed and domineering sales managers who seem to reserve their people skills for customers, not their sales reps. I've seen many, many good sales managers, but the bad ones are so bad that they really stand out in your memory.

Unfortunately, old-school sales management is still alive and well in corporate America in companies big and small. Many organizations—in spite of being technologically advanced and strategically sophisticated—are still embracing sales management tactics from the 1950s. And even though it has evolved from the boiler room boss to the coach mentality, the same manager-centric approach remains, which circumvents the power of sales team synergy.

The problem is not necessarily poor management, it's a lack of leadership. The interesting thing is that, paradoxically, it's easier to be a good leader than a poor manager. In the long run, it actually takes much less time and effort to effectively lead people than to ineffectively manage them. That's because good leaders are able to get the most out of their people, creating a team cohesiveness that drives sales with efficiency and effectiveness. They operate with maximal focus and minimal wasted effort.

This book shows how leaders create high-performance sales teams using team building, sales rep involvement, empowerment, and continuous improvement. All of these processes are key components of Total Quality Management (TQM), which is described in subsequent chapters. TQM has played a significant role in my 36 years of sales and marketing experience, primarily with AT&T, but also including United Telecommunications and two smaller firms. I've seen it applied successfully in sales teams of both large and small organizations. And I can tell you it's not just another sales management fad, but has stood the test of time.

The biggest challenge in sales management is not commissions, sales funnels, pricing, or prospecting strategies. The single-biggest problem is getting your people to sell at maximal capacity. I found the solution to be TQM.

Strip away the management jargon and *Seven Steps* is simply a book about getting better, about looking for ways to cultivate the joy of selling and improving sales performance. It's about the differences between leading and misleading, inspiring versus intimidating, and invigorating rather than deflating. It's a story of two kinds of leadership: Aha vs. Gotcha. One that creates a rich selling environment by leading reps to self-revealing "eureka" moments, the other that inhibits selling and personal growth by the constant scrutiny of a Gotcha manager.

All corporations have their share of effective sales managers—the ones who are comfortable enough with themselves to manage from a base of self-confidence, integrity, and empathy. And there are the weaker ones—the narcissists, the control freaks, the get-it-done-at-all-costs managers. It's the yin and yang you find in any group of professionals—accounting, engineering, human resources, or advertising, for example. In sales, however, everything is magnified because employee performance, or sales results, is measured every day. Commissioned salespeople don't have the luxury of their pay based on annual performance assessments. And the pressure to sell is unrelenting because sales is the cash flow of most organizations. It's a high-stakes game full of what T. S. Eliot called "decisions and revisions which a minute will reverse." You can bet on two things: Sales is a continuously changing landscape due to competitive pressures, marketplace changes, and product enhancements, and someone is watching the sales numbers every hour of every day to make sure that everyone is producing. This mercurial, pressure-packed environment has a way of twisting and derailing the best-laid plans. It has turned many an ordinary manager into a terrible manager. On the other hand, it has served as a furnace to forge a mediocre manager into a real leader.

The aim of *Seven Steps* is to provide direction and encouragement for those who want to be more than managers, those who aspire to be leaders.

Working in both large and medium-sized firms, I have observed and experienced a wide variety of styles ranging from traditional command/control to employee empowerment programs. I have been part of successful sales groups with established leaders who built their success on sales rep involvement, insisting on excellence and considering their salespeople as partners in success. These leaders realized that sales success begins by treating their sales reps with respect, as professionals who play a vital role in developing plans and procedures. Year in, year out, many of these leaders produce exceptional sales results because their people feel they have a stake in the business, that they are cared for and listened to.

I've seen underperforming sales groups absolutely electrified by a nondescript, low-key leader whose claim to fame was simply asking for sales reps' opinions, thereby building a high-performance team with mutual trust and loyalty. The exceptional leaders I've known have proven one thing: Personality has little to do with success. You don't have to be witty, gregarious, engaging, or charismatic. You *do* need integrity, a modicum of selflessness, and the ability to ask for input and act on your team's suggestions. And above all, you need to be able to simply connect to your people, to understand them and their needs.

Miracles do happen in sales groups, and complete turnarounds are possible. I've witnessed it time and time again. It starts with leaders who take care of and involve their people. These are the leaders you remember, the people you imitate. These are the ones who, years later, you recall and ask yourself, "Now, what would they have done in this situation?"

On the other hand, as a salesperson, I've also experienced being on the wrong side of an autocratic management system, an "I'm the boss" place characterized by overcontrol, micromanagement, and daily punitive measures. I know how it feels to be among the disenfranchised masses of salespeople who had no input or inkling of what was going to happen next. The pay and benefits were great but there was a price that came with the big money. You find your loyalty flagging, your enthusiasm dimming as the autocracy creates in you traces of distrust, frustration, and even recalcitrance.

Being at the bottom of this food chain is unsettling, like being a marionette controlled by tactics such as daily (even hourly) reports, late-afternoon "briefing" sessions, job threats, and other punitive measures—all sapping the strength, vitality, energy, and passion from the sales force. The tougher things get—missed objectives, worsening economy, and increasing competition—the tighter the reins are drawn, with more reports required and more threats. Even more surprising, management is so busy directing sales reps that they are failing to harness the knowledge and experience of the sales force to shape sales programs.

Experiencing a myriad of management styles as a manager and as a sales rep, I have found that sales managers create a sales team whether or not they know it. There are two extreme versions of sales teams. One type is the team that comes together on its own, independent of its manager. This team is characterized by dysfunctional, uncooperative sales reps, whose only cohesiveness is a contempt of and resistance to management. In many cases, the manager doesn't know what is going on behind the scenes, oblivious to the apathy or anger festering among the sales reps. The other extreme team that I experienced is one shaped by the manager as a partnership, emphasizing collaboration and success sharing among team members. Even in this case, I witnessed bickering and backbiting, but the difference was that the manager was aware of the problems and could address them in a constructive way.

In reality, most sales teams fall between the two extremes, led by managers with varying degrees of influence. When the influence is too weak, there are times when sales reps are better without a manager. Having known manufacturers reps and commission-only sales reps—who operate with minimal or no supervision—I've come to the conclusion that it's better to have no manager at all than to have a weak manager. That's because ineffective, overcontrolling managers get in the way by creating roadblocks, as well as superfluous rules and reports. Salespeople will sell their product—with or without a manager—because that's what they do for a living. The sales manager determines how *well* they sell and how much time and focus they spend on selling.

Many argue that the times are ripe for self-managed sales teams, that salespeople are more effective with minimal supervision and maximal empowerment. This concept, explored in Chapter 5, "Fifth Step: Sales Empowerment, Beginning with Ownership," is open to debate. But one thing is for sure, elements of the self-managed team process can be used in any organization to any degree. It takes sales leaders who are willing to reevaluate how they do things in order to reach their goals.

The successful leaders I've known are the ones with a firm foundation of values and beliefs who constantly seek better ways to do things. They are secure enough to experiment, adapt, and keep moving forward. For those leaders committed to self-improvement, fortunately, there are hundreds of books and blogs on sales management to provide a continuous stream of new concepts. In addition, but not as obvious, are hundreds of research projects on sales management being done each year at well-known universities. I've cited a number of studies to provide a sampling of the huge amount of data being generated about sales management that can be another valuable source of advice for sales leaders.

Also included are real-life case studies from a variety of industries that highlight how the basic principles are put to use by actual sales managers.

As you progress through this book, keep in mind, it is not a panacea. It is not a textbook either; you won't find chapter summaries or questions to answer. You won't find a packaged, formulized answer to successful sales management. There is no such thing. We all pick and choose from the management tools, tactics, and strategies available to us, incorporating a piece here, a piece there that fits our personality and skill set. Command/control tactics are a viable part of any management tool set, the important point being that they are only a piece of the puzzle. Today's sales manager faces too many complexities and pressures to rely on one simple, formulized managerial style.

The seven steps are laid out in sequential order beginning with self-management. After all, how can you manage people without first being able to manage yourself? Successful leaders have a high degree of self-awareness, self-control, self-determination, and self-development. If you're waiting for your company to develop you, you've already missed the train.

After considering your own development, the next step is hiring the right people to achieve your goals. With the right people onboard, the next five steps begin: team building, servant leadership, job ownership and empowerment, performance measurement, and continuous improvement.

Seven Steps is like a grocery aisle of ideas, some you'll put in your grocery cart, some you'll ignore, and some you might keep in mind until the time is right. Irrespective of your shopping disposition, I hope you find some good ideas to take home and use.

—Max Cates

1

First Step: Manage Yourself

H ere you are in the middle. Whoever said it's lonely at the top never sat in a sales manager's chair. It's a maddening, lonely process—trying to activate your people and satisfy the boss. The objectives, the people, the paperwork, the procedures.... The challenges are legendary, your control over them limited.

In the past decade, huge shifts in corporate America have exposed sales managers to a dizzying rate of change. Customers have become more demanding and price sensitive due to the proliferation of online competitive information. If they don't like your price, they'll find a better deal online. Combine global competitive pressures and shaky economic conditions, and you have companies cutting costs at unprecedented levels. On top of cutbacks, you have baby boomers phasing out of the work world and being replaced by millennials who present a new set of managerial challenges. This volatile mix of economic, technological, and sociological issues presents a host of perplexities for sales managers:

- Rep-per-manager ratios are steadily increasing every year, consistently expanding managers' scope of supervision while multiplying their workload.

- Training and administrative support for sales managers are decreasing because of increasing budget constraints.

- Pressures on managers to produce sales results are rising exponentially.

- New management techniques are required for the new generation of salespeople coming into the workplace.

It is the paradox of our times: At a point when sales managers are being asked to do more and more, they have less and less to work with. No wonder many studies of sales personnel are showing decreasing trust for sales managers' ability to effectively lead sales teams.

Chances are you were a good sales rep, or you wouldn't have been elevated to this exalted managerial position. But nobody cares. No matter how long you've been on the job, the expectations are the same: All your people want to know is that you're going to take care of them. All your boss wants to know is that you're going to deliver good numbers. The fact that you were a good sales rep might even be working against you. In fact, it is estimated that 85% of sales superstars fail as sales managers.

Here are a few reasons why salespeople don't succeed as managers:

- **Loss of Freedom**—A good sales rep has the freedom to set a daily schedule, come and go, be in the office when necessary, and his sole responsibility is making sales. When he morphs from a sales rep to a manager, freedom is replaced with responsibility—the manager takes on the burdens of sales reps and bosses. A manager is shackled by paperwork, team objectives, deadlines, and company directives. Reps who yearned to be the boss, to set the agenda and make the rules, quickly discover that they have significantly less autonomy than they did as a salesperson.

- **Inability to teach**—Frequently, we assume that sales reps know how to sell, and therefore they can teach it when they become managers. Not necessarily. The biggest part of teaching is not knowing the topic but knowing how to get your "students" to learn. Much of sales is intuitive behavior—reading people, timing, body language—that is difficult to teach. The bottom line is that salespeople are doers, not teachers. It takes a huge amount of self-discipline, energy, and patience to analyze one's steps to success and convey them effectively to subordinates.

- **Deferred gratification**—A sales rep works hard to make a sale and sees the outcome immediately. The sales manager sees outcomes over weeks, maybe months. Management takes a huge amount of patience, a virtue in short supply among salespeople.

- **Unrealistic expectations**—You were successful as a rep so you expect the same from your people. As a sales rep, you had an "I can do it" approach to challenges. You did, in fact, do it, and achieved success. Your success gave you expectations for your performance as a salesperson that consistently led to success. Unfortunately, the set of conditions that made you successful as a salesperson do not exist in sales management. You can't expect your people to be like you or as successful as you. If your expectations don't change, disappointment quickly sets in.

- **Tendency to do it yourself**—As a sales rep, if you don't do it, it doesn't get done. Sometimes, this thinking leads managers to micromanage, even to the point of selling for their reps. The result is chaos. For the manager, it means less time managing. For the sales reps, it means frustration and fewer opportunities to become effective salespeople. In sales management you simply can't do it yourself. You have to do virtually everything through your people, and that can be frustrating.

- **Failing to change your viewing lens from microscopic to panoramic, from pixels to landscapes**—The nature of sales requires concentrating on one customer at a time to make the sale. The nature of sales management requires a panoramic view of the sales team, the customer base, the market, and dozens of other components.

- **Independent nature of salespeople versus managers' dependence on salespeople to reach goals**—As a sales manager, you're no longer the gunslinger who's six-shootin' his way to success. You're more like a four-star general in the war room coordinating troop movements. Your success is dependent on your people.

- **Propensity to "sell" instead of facilitate**—There is a tendency for new managers to come onboard with a dozen preconceived concepts and begin selling them to their new "customers"—their sales team and their bosses. Essentially, they are continuing the sales process that made them successful. Unfortunately, the conditions and dynamics of managing a sales team are totally different. Now, it's more important to become a facilitator instead of a salesperson—that is, to utilize the energy and talent at your disposal. The manager is no longer the lone wolf who has to come up with the Big Idea and sell it, but rather the person who extracts Big Ideas from the sales team and helps them sell it. This requires a change in mind-set from the knee-jerk reaction of continuously selling to one of coordinating.

The good news is this simple fact: Your people want to be led. They want to believe in you. They want to be part of a winning team. They want to follow your example. Many want to give their full commitment to a boss and company they respect and trust. Remember when you were a rep, the enthusiasm and hope you felt in getting a new manager? And remember, in many cases, how quickly the honeymoon ended? Hope is hardwired into salespeople's psyche. The manager's job is to turn their innate hope into enthusiasm and commitment.

The goal of this book is to help you develop a successful sales team by using Total Quality Management (TQM) practices that have been proven effective over the years. The techniques include such things as continuous improvement, rep/manager collaboration, empowerment, team building, and shared learning. TQM is a powerful way to transform teams and individuals into champions, but it takes a strong leader to start the process.

The first step is addressing the one thing you can most influence: yourself. You wouldn't think of starting a sales campaign without goals, objectives, procedures, ground rules, and training. The same applies to self-management. Manage yourself so that you can manage your people and therefore manage your success and your career. Self-management entails an honest inventory of your strengths and weaknesses. More importantly, it requires the discipline to build on strengths and improve weaknesses. Strong leaders have a high degree of self-awareness; they know their strengths and what complementary strengths they need from others. They avoid being surrounded by people like themselves. Similarly, strong leaders are self-developers who seek information, training, and feedback on ways to be a better leader. They don't wait for a company-sponsored training program but proactively seek self-improvement.

As Dr. Wayne Dyer said in *Excuses Begone,* "Never underestimate your power to change yourself. Never overestimate your ability to change others." As sales managers, we all are faced with continuous change to the way we do things—change prompted by the marketplace, technology, and social trends. This is the easy stuff. We tweak commissions and bonuses, we revise sales pitches, we create product discounts. These are all *reactive* changes. Making *proactive* changes, elective changes to ourselves, is tough and arduous. Proactivity involves freedom of choice, willpower, and self-discipline. It is hard work but it's necessary. But no matter how difficult self-change is to you as a manager, it is the first—and easiest—step in the continuous-improvement process. The next step, changing others, will require twice the effort of self-change, so be sure to guard your expectations.

Case Study #1: Self-management in the Software Business

Jane had been sales manager at an educational software company for five years. She managed a team of eight sales reps who targeted high-school administrators in a three-state area in the Midwest.

Her first two years were marked by annual sales increases of 4% the first year and 2% the second. Then the recession hit and sales tumbled to a 1% increase the third year compared to a 6% goal, 1% the fourth year with a 5% objective, and –1% the fifth year on a 4% goal. As her boss pointed out, an aggregate 1% sales increase over the past three years was unacceptable. "Look, Jane," he had said. "I know you work long hours and I know you're addressing the problem, but another year of declining sales, and I can't guarantee you'll have a job. We need to get this thing turned around."

Following the first year's sales decline, Jane wasn't sure what had to be done, but she did know she had to do something to let her boss know she was working toward a solution. She carefully went over the numbers and created a metrics system that pinpointed weak spots in sales. That year the primary component of the sales decline was decreased new business and stagnant increased sales to existing business. She sponsored new business training seminars for the reps and began "New Business Mondays" to focus reps' attention on acquiring new business on a consistent basis. Her efforts did not slow the sales decline but at least she had addressed the problem. She made sure her boss knew the extent of her efforts.

Following the second year of sales declines, with increasing trepidation, Jane developed an enhanced Sales Funnel. The new reporting system was devised to keep her alerted to what her reps were doing day by day, even hour by hour. If they weren't selling, she wanted to know why. She reviewed the sales funnel results with her reps twice a week, reviewing their signed contracts and questioning them on their lack of sales. Essentially, she was losing confidence in her reps. It was a recession, but the reps' job was to sell through it, no excuses. After all, she thought, she was doing her job in setting up new metrics and reporting systems. Now it was time the reps did their job.

It didn't work. Following another year of sales declines, Jane was running out of solutions. She made a full-court press to get the reps energized. She told her boss it was time to get rid of the low producers and get the producers to produce. New standards were established to place reps on suspension for failure to meet benchmarks. Too many suspensions and the rep was terminated. She also instituted "Catch Up Fridays" for reps whose results were below objective—a full day in the office to focus on reps' particular weak points. If they had not set adequate appointments for the previous week, they were required to spend a whole day to work on appointment setting. The same held true for failure to meet other metrics such as new-business generation and number of closes.

She told her boss, "The reps just aren't selling. We're going to see more turnover but we'll also see the weak people gone, and the ones left are going to know we won't put up with low production." Despite the increased measurements and disciplinary actions, the numbers continued to drop and Jane's frustration grew.

The turnaround came one day when Jane overheard two of her salespeople talking about seeking new jobs. The pay and benefits were fine, they said, but they were tired of the pressure-packed environment and Jane's micromanaging. They were spending more time reporting their numbers than selling. For many, the sales week had been reduced to three days, with two days replaced by "New Business Mondays" and "Catch Up Fridays." Above all, one told the other, they weren't respected or trusted as professionals.

To her face, neither rep had ever mentioned having a problem. In fact, both were always pleasant and compliant with Jane's work rules. Jane's initial reaction was anger and a sense of betrayal. In fact, it took a week to get over the anger and think logically about the reps' points. After some soul-searching honesty, Jane realized she had become the kind of demanding boss she had always hated. She had failed, first to make objectives, and then, making things even worse, she had exacerbated the problem by alienating her sales force. She faced the harsh reality that she was about to lose her job. Ironically, she had recently read a newspaper article about drug addicts who had to "bottom out" to get better. This, she thought, was her bottoming out. Nobody was going to bail her out but herself.

Her first step in climbing out of the quagmire was fact finding. Jane decided to sit down individually with the two reps and probe. After all, she thought, nothing else seemed to be working, so why not ask them why they were so unhappy? Her first sit-down was with Josh, a third-year salesman who was a top-seller in the group. Jane, trying to avoid the fact that she was eavesdropping, started the conversation with, "I understand you're looking for a new job, and I was wondering if you're displeased with the company or anything else."

"No," Josh responded. "I'm always on the lookout for more money."

"So you're just looking for a better job, no problems here?"

"No, there aren't any problems," Josh responded. Jane knew he wasn't being honest; after all, she had heard him being openly critical of the sales environment. It dawned on her that he was afraid of reprisal from her, so she changed her approach.

"I'm glad to hear that," she said. "But I did want to ask for your advice. You know we haven't made objective in three years now, and I'm trying to figure out why. What do you think? Any ideas?"

"Well, I know there are some reps who might be a little demoralized. Of course, I'm fine with everything but some are feeling that there's just too much pressure and paperwork, and not enough time to sell...."

By asking for input, Jane got Josh to open up in a way that was safe from retaliation. Following the discussion, Jane decided to talk individually with each rep. It was painful but enlightening. The reps reiterated, politely, not only that morale was at an all-time low, but that there were so many rules, sales reviews, and meetings that the reps had little time or focus for selling. For some reps, it had become solely a metrics game.

Everyone's focus was more on trying to keep their job than on making sales.

After getting over the initial shock, Jane did more self-assessment. She realized that when sales began faltering, she might have overreacted and started pushing too hard, which alienated the reps. It was time to change—not the sales team, but Jane had to change. She had become a tyrant, having lost sight of her people's needs in the pursuit of numbers. The result was a continuing cycle of poor sales and, now, the prospect of successful reps abandoning a sinking ship. In an effort to right the ship, first, she sat down with each rep to get his or her input on ways to improve the sales climate.

Next, she did something she hadn't done since she was a new manager: She began reading articles, books, and blogs, as well as attending sales management seminars and webinars. It was time to study how other managers were succeeding in a down economy. All in all, this is not an overnight success story—it took months to undo the damage—but her efforts were respected and appreciated by the reps. The reps were impressed that Jane had the discipline to assess herself, the strength to admit her failures, and the tenacity to make amends to be successful. The reps knew that, in reality, she didn't really *have* to do anything at all. She was the boss. She could have labeled the two reps as malcontents, let them go, and hired people who would fit in better. Instead, she took the hard way and improved herself as well as the sales organization. She gained their trust.

Self-Management Question Number One: Are You a Trusted Leader?

The business world has changed dramatically in the past 20 years due to technology, global marketing, and social/demographic trends. At the same time, the leadership paradigm has been turned upside down and inside out, from vertical and personality-driven to horizontal and trust-driven. The charismatic, hard-charging leaders of the past are being replaced with team players who have ample collaboration and negotiating skills.

A recent *Forbes* magazine article, "Why Trust Is the New Core of Leadership," states, "Leaders can no longer trust in power; instead they rely on the power of trust." In addition, the article says:

- They [leaders] themselves will be skilled at trusting, because trusting and trustworthiness enhance each other.

- They will be good at collaboration and the tools of influence.

- They will operate from a clear set of values and principles, because opportunistic or selfish motives are clearly seen and rejected.

- They are likely to be more intrinsically than extrinsically motivated and more likely to use intrinsic motivations with others.

The article touches on the most important single element of your management job, which is *establishing trust*. Do your people trust you? No matter how competent and talented you are, your people won't follow you if they don't trust you. The three components of trust are care, integrity, and competence.

Care Is a Vital Part of Trust

Do you care about your people? They know whether you do or don't. You simply can't fake it. If most of your efforts are tied to your own best interests, your devotees will be scarce. On the other hand, if you exhibit a modicum of selflessness, if you are willing to occasionally fall on your sword for your people, you'll have loyal followers. Do you care about what they care about? Reps' main interests are (in this order) security, respect, and pay. Are you aligned with your salespeople in these areas? Do your decisions take into account the interests of your people as well as yourself and the organization? Even more importantly, are you aware of your people's interests?

Successful leaders fight for their employees. When it comes to pay, promotions, and working conditions, a leader is the sales rep's champion—defending his reps even when it's not popular with colleagues or bosses. Every time a sales leader goes to bat for a subordinate, that sends a resounding message to the team. Oddly enough, even when it means clashing with the boss, the boss will most likely respect your intentions and your principles.

Research shows that employees do want a personal touch from their manager. They want you to know them as people and know about their lives. But they do not want you to be their friend or confidant. It's likely they don't rely on you for emotional support. They rely on co-workers and friends for that.

The litmus test for caring is a single word: sacrifice. It's easy to hand out spiffs and gift cards to your people. Those types of gifts don't really require anything from you. The real gifts of caring are those that demand you take the time to go the extra mile, for example, to help a rep get a promotion. Or take a chance of failure to support an initiative from your sales team. Your people know you care when you have some skin in the game, when you're willing to take a risk for them, fight for them, and protect them. That requires getting a little bruised occasionally and perhaps irritating your colleagues or boss.

Sales leaders who really take care of their people are likely to be confident and self-assured. These are the leaders who know they are good enough to take risks, to take chances of offending people. They know they can recover from failure and overcome difficulties in the quest to support their people. And they know that the payoff—trust—is greater than the risk.

Integrity Provides the Foundation for Trust

Tell the truth. Always. In *The Little Book of Coaching*, Ken Blanchard and Don Shula said, "Champion coaches operate out of unquestionable integrity. They call it the way they see it. They do not have hidden agendas. They do not say one thing but mean another. They do not manipulate people. They are genuine and sincere."

From a practical perspective, irrespective of your moral or religious beliefs, honesty makes sense because few of us have a good enough memory to lie successfully, and your salespeople are pretty good at sensing untruths and manipulation. It's just too easy to get caught and the potential gain is never worth the damage to one's reputation.

Research at Bowling Green State University included a study of 193 salespeople from ten U.S. companies suggesting a strong, positive relationship between the integrity of a manager and sales force productivity/

job satisfaction. In effect, the study supports the concept that trusted managers create better relationships with their sales team, which leads to job satisfaction and ultimately better sales results. The element of trust was measured by such statements as "My manager would never try to gain an advantage by deceiving workers," "I have complete faith in the integrity of my manager," and "I feel quite confident that my manager will always treat me fairly." Results showed that managers who were role models of integrity, ethics, and fairness created a trusting relationship with subordinates, "which subsequently results in greater job satisfaction and overall job performance by salespeople."

Competency Fortifies Trusting Relationships

Do you know everything your reps are required to know, such as pricing, product details, procedures, and paperwork? We all know managers who don't waste time on the "details" as if those were beneath their lofty station as manager. Actually, it's often a throwback to their sales days when it was more important to persuade customers than to inform them. These managers are the ones who expertly avoid and deflect questions on new products and pricing, for instance, referring reps to the appropriate Web site or binder. What they don't realize is that everyone—their boss and their subordinates—notices their lack of knowledge.

An ill-prepared manager is viewed as incompetent and rarely commands the credibility needed to be effective. Managers need to know everything reps are expected to know. And it helps to know even more. For example, are you keeping up with the latest trends in selling techniques and technology? Do you know your industry and your competitors' pricing and products? Here's a key competency question: Could you lead a training session on any of your sales team's major issues, including pricing, products, competition, and sales techniques?

Taking it one step further, are you going beyond basic competency and finding creative ways to apply your knowledge that your reps might not have considered? For example, look for ways to combine your product knowledge to develop creative sales applications for specific industries or types of customers. Use your acumen of competitors' market positioning to develop selling strategies for your people. For example, if your major competitor is emphasizing product affordability, you can differentiate your selling strategy with a focus on product quality and durability.

Be the go-to person for your reps and you become the go-to person for your boss—a surefire way to advance one's career. And, more importantly, it creates the foundation of trusting relationships.

What's the Most Important Trust Factor?

Very simply, it is *care*. That's the single most important factor in establishing trust. You can make mistakes in judgment. You can make factual errors. You can even have an integrity problem. But as long as your people know you care about their welfare, it's all okay. Your people don't expect you to be perfect all the time. They know you will occasionally be forgetful, inattentive, or preoccupied. They know you will take your eye off the ball at times. But knowing that your heart is in the right place—that you will protect and support them—makes the biggest screwups bearable.

On the other hand, if they see as you as self-absorbed and oblivious to their best interests, your team will continuously add your every mistake to their list of items that make you a bad manager. In fact, even the good things that you do will be marginalized and ignored by your people; they won't want you to be successful because you don't care about their success. Essentially, if your salespeople think you don't care about them, there's no amount of competency or integrity that matters.

All in all, the element of trust allows your team to be innovative and aggressively seek new ways of doing things and tackling problems. It allows your team to reach peak performance by being "in the zone." Athletes describe it as moments when they play their best, free of distractions and self-consciousness while feeling confident and in control. Effective sales leaders enable peak performance through support and encouragement, letting team members know that the manager "has their back." The reps know that management isn't lying in wait for a "gotcha" moment. Without the distractions of fear or intimidation—but being held accountable—reps can relax and do their jobs productively.

David Novak, CEO of Yum Brands, which operates KFC, Taco Bell, and Pizza Hut, saw profits nearly double in three years. In *Fortune* magazine, he said, "What really made the difference was the idea that if we trusted each other, we could work together to make something happen that was bigger than our individual capabilities."

Self-Management, the Rest of the Story

Self-management requires self-analysis. Chances are you're not getting much real feedback from your subordinates and maybe not from your boss. If you are, that's great. But, as for many of us, a good deal of self-analysis is needed to complement what little feedback we get from others. Take time to do a self-inventory of some important issues that determine your ultimate success in sales management.

Following are 15 questions essential for effectively managing yourself.

1. Are You Advancing or Retreating?

Successful leaders and companies constantly adapt to succeed. It's an either/or situation: Either you're gaining ground or you're losing it. General George S. Patton, legendary leader who led key World War II campaigns, said, "I don't want any messages saying 'I am holding my position.' We are not holding a...thing. Our basic plan of operation is to advance and keep on advancing regardless of whether we have to go under, over, or through the enemy."

If you, as a sales manager, are holding your ground, staying the same, you can bet the train has already left you at the station. Sales managers are like sharks who breathe by continually moving forward. When sales managers stop forward movement, they don't simply stagnate, they retreat. That's the law of the sales jungle, the brutal truth of sales leadership.

The only thing predictable about sales management is continual change. Markets can change overnight. Customers' needs vary by the day. Competitors switch to new tactics faster than the eye can see. New threats and opportunities pop up like whack-a-moles. Technology, well, you know that story. The rate of change is daunting, even disorienting if you're not advancing and adjusting.

At the heart of a manager's growth are learning and self-development. This means seeking (and teaching) the latest in technology, sales techniques, market intelligence, and product applications. That's the easy part. The hard part is self-development, which requires self-awareness and fine-tuning your inner dynamics, such as patience, listening, and impulse control. The big challenge is that sales managers don't have a lot of help in developing their skills.

Only half of the top 25 business schools in America offer sales management courses, according to *U.S. News & World Report.* Many, if not a majority of, sales managers are former salespeople promoted into management with little training or organizational support. Researchers at Drexel University and the University of Florida studied 286 sales managers from a wide cross section of U.S. companies, stating that 57% had no training after being named sales manager.

For those of us who aren't natural born leaders (which is the vast majority of us), sales manager training has become a do-it-yourself program. Of course, it has always been like that since most training budgets have traditionally been aimed at the sales force itself, pretty much leaving managers to fend for themselves. In reality, the lack of company-sponsored training has had little impact on the success of top sales managers. That's because successful managers take the initiative to train themselves. Successful leaders have an insatiable appetite for learning. They continuously seek and gather information that makes them better leaders and gives their teams a competitive advantage. They realize that leaders are made, not born. You might have inherited traits such as intelligence or verbal ability, but two-thirds of leadership is learned. Regardless of genetics, many sales leaders have developed themselves into people of power and influence through continuous learning.

2. Are You Stuck in a Rut?

Some say that leadership is a matter of perpetually redeveloping or reinventing oneself. "Unlike past generations that could rely on a consistent set of core skills and a clear career path, today we all must constantly revisit our skills, reinvestigate our aspirations, and reconstitute our careers," said Samuel Bacharach, author of *Get Them on Your Side.* "This is often difficult because we're trapped in routine, avoid risk and simply like being comfortable. But we must reinvent ourselves because of the turbulence around us. Technological disruptions, shifting organizational structures and unpredictable markets demand that we pivot and take unexpected directions. The very core knowledge around us, the very organizations in which we work, the very markets that demand our attention, are changing at such a rapid pace that skills, insights and observations that were true at one point are no longer true or at best, are no longer accurate."

The Mills Study, conducted by the University of California at Berkeley, tracked subjects over 50 years of age, showing that it's never too late to reinvent oneself. "Even at 60 years old, people can resolve to make themselves more the people they would like to become," said study director Ravenna Helson in a *Psychology Today* article. The trick for sales managers is to start earlier, and to take the time to become your ideal self. Too many times, we're just too busy to make progress in self-development. We get caught up in the daily demand of sales management and fail to take the time to make ourselves better managers. In fact, high achievers are more likely to neglect their long-term goals and personal improvement because they are focused on solving today's problems.

Reinventing oneself, or becoming the manager you want to be, is a three-step process. First is an honest self-assessment of your strengths, weaknesses, and passions. You need to know the areas in which you need improvement. Observe successful managers around you. What do they have that you need? Consider taking a self-assessment survey; they're affordable and plentiful online. Listen to others' assessments of you, even if they're saying things you don't like to hear about yourself. A good self-assessment helps you to target your educational efforts, setting priorities for training and especially aiming to strengthen weaknesses that might be holding back your long-term potential. For example, do you have a short-fuse temper that hampers your relationships with peers and subordinates? Are you impatient to the point of being abrupt and abrasive? Do you delegate effectively? Do you need more polish in speaking to large groups? Do you need a better understanding of financials and the economy? There is something hampering your progress. Find it and address it.

Second, determine long-term goals in terms of career path and personal characteristics. Career-wise, do you want to be a vice president in two years? Do you want the CEO job in five years? Do you hunger to run your own company? What do these people do to reach these positions? What are the core skills needed? How do these people walk and talk and conduct themselves? Envision yourself in that position—what kind of person do you need to be to get and hold the job? Picture your ideal self, and then develop a program to become that person. In setting your goals, keep this in mind: Numerous studies suggest that people who are intrinsically motivated—working toward things they find personally fulfilling—are more satisfied with their lives than those who are extrinsically motivated, driven by money and status. Intrinsic motivation in sales management is loving the job and the people more than the pay and perks. The most successful sales managers are those who are fulfilled by developing their people and making a contribution to the organization's success. It's no coincidence that higher levels of intrinsic motivation lead to higher levels of extrinsic reward. On the other hand, if your goal setting is extrinsically motivated, chances are you might reach your ideal self but not be happy with what you find.

Third, just do it. Educate yourself to become who you want to be. Be a student of people management. Read books. Go to seminars. Attend webinars. Subscribe to newsletters and professional blogs. If you're not growing and learning, you're slipping behind. And that's a great disservice to your people and your organization. If, today, you are managing the same way you managed two years ago, you're stagnating. No matter how good your results are, it's delusional to think you can't get better. Continuous learning is the key to improving your skills and your results. Company-sponsored management training can be effective, but don't wait to be trained. Learn on your own, take the initiative to know the latest trends and practices of people management.

In addition, be a student of the sales profession and stay abreast of the latest technological and strategic developments in selling. Researchers and consultants offer a continuous stream of information on ways to improve your team's sales effectiveness. Much of it is free, with online convenience. Join sales groups on LinkedIn or other sales Web sites and blogs to get daily updates at no cost. For a small cost, you can subscribe to online newsletters and magazines that offer valuable sales tips and techniques.

Take it a step further—keep in tune with your industry trends. Subscribe to trade magazines and industry blogs. Be it telecommunications or office products or insurance, everything you know about your business can be translated to sales. The intelligence gained from industry trends helps your sales team adapt to product applications, pricing, and competition.

In addition, constantly monitor yourself and ask why you react in certain ways to situations. Take an online personality assessment to help evaluate your personality type and aptitudes. Self-knowledge will help you relate to your team and help you refine your interpersonal skills. At the same time, evaluate your goals and make sure you're making progress to that ideal self that you envision becoming. It will take reinventing yourself more than once, but that's something leaders do on a regular basis—that is to constantly evaluate themselves and their objectives to become the best they can be.

3. Are You Really Using Your Brain?

You could say that our brains want us to be better sales managers. The brain is wired to accommodate self-improvement and adaptive behavior. With the advent of MRI and other advanced research technology, researchers have found a fascinating function of the brain: Our thoughts can change the structure and function of the brain. The phenomenon is called neuroplasticity. According to Alvaro Fernandez, co-author of *The SharpBrains Guide to Brain Fitness,* neuroplasticity is "the brain's lifelong capacity to change and rewire itself in response to the stimulation of learning and experience. This includes both the lifelong ability to create new neurons—neurogenesis—and to create new connections between neurons—synaptogenesis.... A consequence of the brain's plasticity is that the brain may change with every experience, thought and emotion, from which it follows that you yourself have the potential power to change your brain with everything that you think, do and feel. So brain fitness and optimization are about much more than crossword puzzles and blueberries; they are about cultivating a new mindset and mastering a new toolkit that allows us to appreciate and take full advantage of our brain's incredible properties."

Contrary to scientific thought of just a few decades ago, the brain is not fixed and unchanging. It is amazingly flexible and can be shaped by positive thinking. We are capable of becoming our ideal selves. We can reinvent ourselves, adapt to change and bounce back from failure. Using the brain's powerful potential, managers can become stronger leaders by building skills and habits ranging from impulse control to mental toughness. It takes specific techniques such as visualization and positive self-talk, but more important is the awareness of our brain's powerful potential.

Neuroplasticity is like having four-wheel drive. The simple fact that you know you have it gives you confidence. When you know how to activate and use it, four-wheel drive will take you places others can't go. As Buddha once said, "We are what we think. All that we are arises with our thoughts. With our thoughts, we make the world."

4. Speaking of Adaptability, Are You an Adaptive Leader?

Many good sales managers have learned to maintain momentum by using adaptive leadership. The U.S. Army War College has an acronym for battle situations that applies to everyday sales activities: VUCA, which stands for volatile, uncertain, complex, and ambiguous. Similar to military leaders, adaptive sales leaders learn to live with unpredictability, anticipate changes, take risks, make decisions, learn from events, and adjust plans accordingly.

According to leadership researcher and author Warren Bennis, "The critical quality of a leader...is adaptive capacity. Adaptive capacity allows leaders to respond quickly and intelligently to constant change. It is the ability to identify and seize opportunities. It allows leaders to act and then evaluate results instead of attempting to collect and analyze all the data before acting."

The starting point is a foundation of core values that drive their actions and reactions. Such guiding beliefs as honesty, achievement, competitiveness, fairness, and compassion serve as a compass that guides their actions. Three skills—mostly learned on the job—create successful adaptive leaders:

Vigilance means constantly being alert to opportunities and threats. The adaptive sales leader hungers for market intelligence, craves technology advancements, and seeks new sales techniques, as well as product innovation and uses. This goes beyond simple alertness. It includes seeking, learning, and applying information in a way to give the sales team a competitive advantage. The adaptive leader has a network of intelligence sources—including blogs, magazines, colleagues, customers, competitors, and subordinates—that constantly provide usable information. This allows the sales leader to recognize changes in the market and identify ways to capitalize on them.

Agility refers to the predisposition of the sales manager to consider a variety of options in problem solving, to move quickly from unsuccessful alternatives toward viable solutions. This skill promotes innovative responses to challenges rather than considering only a few options and stubbornly trying to make them work. Vigilance feeds agility by providing a huge database that the manager can draw from, providing a seemingly inexhaustible source of potential options. The adaptive leader is able to design a plan and then make midcourse corrections when needed.

Synthesis is the ability to bring together a variety of people, tasks, resources, and data to achieve objectives. It's the capacity to recognize the challenge and assimilate available resources quickly and potently. From a people perspective, it's the knack of knowing the right people to involve and understanding how to best motivate them. It means knowing that you, as the sales manager, cannot overcome challenges by yourself but your sales team can. This essentially is a penchant for executing the plan in a way that empowers and inspires the people around you while optimally using available resources. Like a professional athlete, the sales manager quickly processes hundreds of details, using field position and teammates' skills to marginalize the opponent and make the play.

5. Are You Aware Enough to Be Self-Aware?

Self-awareness is vital to successful leadership for many reasons. (The sad irony is that if you're not a self-aware person, you don't know you lack self-awareness.) Self-awareness means that you know your strengths and weaknesses, motives, values, and personality traits. It allows you to deal with people honestly and provides self-regulation that enhances your credibility and rapport with others.

A study, "When It Comes to Business Leadership, Nice Guys Finish First," conducted by Cornell University and Green Peak Partners, indicates that self-awareness is a key component of management success. "Interestingly, a high self-awareness score was the strongest predictor of executive success," states the study. "This is not altogether surprising as executives who are aware of their weaknesses are often better able to hire subordinates who perform well in categories in which the leader lacks acumen. These leaders are also more able to entertain the idea that someone on their team might have an idea that is even better than their own."

In addition, self-awareness allows leaders to understand how they come across to others and how they are perceived. This helps them self-regulate characteristics—such as forcefulness, authority, and decisiveness—to promote effective communications with subordinates and avoid alienation. Self-awareness is a vital part of self-control. After all, how can you control negative impulses like anger and impatience if you can't recognize them? This self-recognition requires you to examine your moods and emotions. If you're able to recognize, for example, that you feel angry after a spat with your spouse, you can address the anger and control it so as not to let it spill into the workplace.

6. Are You Mentally Tough Enough?

Sales management can be an unforgiving, even brutal profession. It requires more than a little mental toughness. Management researchers have found that success in many professions has less to do with intelligence and skill than grit and persistence—also known as mental toughness. Perseverance might be the key indicator of leadership success, according to recent research in which an incoming class of cadets at West Point was studied to determine why some dropped out and others succeeded. Researchers found that the ones who survived the rigorous training were simply grittier. Their persistence was more important than IQ, athleticism, or other skills in determining their staying power. Successful leaders work through adversity and confront challenge. They just don't quit.

What is mental toughness? Very simply, it is the ability to activate certain emotional and cognitive skills to excel under pressure. Ironically, many of the attributes that we associate with mental toughness are actually just the opposite. A mentally tough manager is not a fist-banging, uncompromisingly stern taskmaster barking orders to underlings. In fact, this kind of leader shows more signs of mental weakness and insecurity than a truly mentally tough manager. Many times, we find fear masquerading as toughness.

Here are the key factors of mental toughness:

- **Self-control**—In the middle of a crisis, the genuinely tough manager controls emotions such as anger, fear, and impatience to remain composed while maintaining rapport with superiors and subordinates. There's no striking out or striking back in anger, only a resolve to solve the problem at hand. This enables the manager to function effectively, even when superiors are overly critical or subordinates are obviously inept.

- **Confidence**—Tough leaders maintain a poised, positive attitude despite adversity. They have the ability to avoid choking under pressure. This is the self-knowledge that triumph is possible, even probable, despite the circumstances. Confidence is functional optimism—the belief that things are going to work out if one concentrates on the goal and not the obstacles.

- **Focus**—Being able to deal with distractions without disrupting progress is another trait of mentally tough leaders. In addition to maintaining a laser focus on the issue at hand, it involves addressing important priorities first, while deferring other issues. Concentration plus prioritization equals focus.

- **Persistence**—Top sales leaders continue to pursue goals even when the going gets tough and problems seem insurmountable. This means having the tenacity to endure discomfort and hardship to pursue the objective. At the heart of persistence is the patience that their efforts will lead to accomplishing the mission.

- **Resilience**—Mental toughness means bouncing back from failures, setbacks, and disappointments. It's being able to smile in the face of adversity. Resilient people expect setbacks and know that they will get knocked to their knees, but they use adversity as a springboard to better prepare them for success. They learn from hardships. In fact, they are energized by difficulties. Rather than being embittered by defeat, they become stronger and smarter.

- **Flexibility**—The last component of mental toughness is having the ability to create innovative solutions by using a variety of ideas, concepts, and feedback from others. As opposed to rigidly clinging to traditional thinking, this includes solving problems by using novel, nontraditional approaches that might involve paradigm shifts to conventional thought.

Mental toughness is not something you are born with. It is not a personality trait, but rather a learned response that develops over time. Like a muscle, it has to be strengthened to remain powerful. Hundreds of sales coaches and consultants offer training programs in mental toughness. They might differ greatly, but many address a few core competencies. One is visualization, sometimes called guided mental imagery.

The goal of visualization, which originated in sports psychology, is to program your subconscious mind to achieve peak performance through mental rehearsal. For example, say you're running a major sales kickoff. Everyone will be there—your sales reps, your boss, all company executives, and support staff. Using visualization techniques, you create a movie in your head. You visualize the sights, smells, sounds, and feelings as you effectively speak to the group. You hear your voice as powerful, crisp, and clear. You feel your thoughts flow effortlessly, being received enthusiastically by your audience. You see people concentrating on your words and taking notes. You visualize your PowerPoint presentation and how well it supplements your speech with colorful subtopics. You take questions from the group and answer them quickly and precisely, no matter how difficult. You envision roadblocks such as objections, and overcome them without hesitation. At the end, you hear the audience applaud and see your people beaming with pride at your masterful oration.

Essentially, you have done what many professional athletes do. They play the game in their heads, creating mental pathways that assist in peak performance. They envision every touchdown or home run before they even touch the field. In addition, they imagine encountering possible setbacks and overcoming them. They do it daily and use positive images, sounds, and sensations. They even create their own mental highlights film focusing on their outstanding victories of the past. In this sense, many feel that visualization contributes to optimal athletic performance. The ostensible result for sales managers is more relaxed, confident, and focused job performance.

Positive self-talk is another way to build mental toughness. Proponents say that this technique improves self-confidence and goal-oriented thinking. The first step is to limit negative thinking. We all are nagged by varying degrees of negative mental chatter such as "I can't handle this" or "This can't be done." By being aware of these self-limiting thoughts, you can change them to "Why can't I?" and then to "I can." The trick to it is to monitor your self-defeating thoughts and eliminate them before they affect your performance, changing them into positive actionable thoughts. In other words, change problem-based thinking ("Why me? Why now?") to solution-based thinking ("Here's how we solve this"). Positive self-talk helps neutralize the fear arising from setbacks. For example, instead of retreating in dread at the loss of a major account, the effective sales leader is telling himself, "This is my time to shine, the chance to turn catastrophe into victory."

Positive affirmations are also a key part of this process. Repeating phrases such as "I am a high-performing sales manager" programs the subconscious to reach that heightened state of functioning. You can apply positive affirmations to a particular objective such as "I am going to lead my team to reach 100 sales units this week" or a longer-term goal such as "As a distinguished sales manager, I plan to be the next Regional Vice President." In addition, positive affirmations can be used for short-term setbacks or crises. These are such affirmations as "I've handled worse situations than this and will manage through it successfully."

Another technique to strengthen mental toughness is to challenge your-self, to practice anxiety control. We all feel anxiety in stressful situations, but controlling anxiety increases the likelihood of success. It helps to occasionally step outside your comfort zone, to experience anxiety and thereby learn to control it. For example, if speaking in front of groups frightens you, make an effort to put yourself in that situation. Try speaking out in small groups and move incrementally to larger groups. Learn to master the discomfort, small steps at a time. These situations teach us relaxation and stress management techniques that not only build self-confidence but also prepare us for unexpected crises. By doing something you don't want to, you are building willpower, or willing yourself to perform even when you really think you can't. Any way you can increase self-control strengthens mental toughness and, hopefully, improves impulse control, patience, and resilience. Challenging yourself to new and different situations also builds critical thinking and adaptive skills that can be used in crises on the job.

Sharpening mental toughness can be achieved through a variety of procedures including meditation and relaxation techniques. It's not easy to sort through all the methods to find the ones that work for us, but the important thing is to stay open to options and practice a variety of things until you find the ones that work. The ultimate goal for a sales manager is to be mentally and emotionally prepared for the daily difficulties and challenges presented by a host of external sources, including salespeople, customers, bosses, and competitors. You'll never be able to anticipate the type or volume of problems, but you can control how you react to them. Your reaction will determine your ultimate success.

7. Do You Have Bad-Boss Characteristics?

According to a *USA Today* article, Robert Hogan, a well-known business psychologist, noted that 75% of working adults said the worst and most stressful aspect of their job was their boss. Findings from two studies by Badbossology.com showed that 48% of employees surveyed would fire their boss and 71% of those looking for a new job attribute their job search to a bad boss. With all the daily challenges a sales rep faces (competition, problem customers, pressure to achieve objectives), the last thing she needs is additional stress from an overbearing boss.

We all have a few bad-boss traits but too many of them might mean you have the "bad boss" label (and might not even know it). Refer to the following items and ask yourself honestly whether you need to improve in certain areas. Better yet, ask peers, subordinates, and others to give you a realistic picture of yourself.

- **Poor communication skills with your team**—You communicate too infrequently, inaccurately, or manipulatively to keep your team well informed. You expect your people to read your mind, and you get frustrated when they can't.

- **Inflexibility**—You treat every person and situation similarly without regard to individual differences. This also includes clinging stubbornly to positions even when reasonable options are available.

- **Lack of follow-through**—You have a tendency to let projects get sidetracked because you did not continue to monitor progress.

- **Inaction**—You wait for situations to change rather than taking charge and changing the situation to control the outcomes. Inaction is closely akin to indecisiveness.

- **Not invested in your team members**—You have no interest in your people's careers, income, and well-being. This also includes the inability to see how your career goals are dependent on your sales team's welfare.

- **Uncaring**—You don't know your people, their interests, personalities, goals, and motivation. Your decisions are based on your personal career ambitions, not those of your subordinates.

- **Not accountable**—You blame others for failures and problems.

- **Intimidation**—You condition your people to be afraid of you. Your subordinates follow directions out of fear, not loyalty.

- **Resistant to change**—You don't seek feedback to improve yourself. You are slow to adapt to changes in technology and market conditions.

- **Egotistical**—You're a know-it-all and you don't need training, instruction, or advice. You rarely admit being wrong, and only then when you have to.

- **Lack of impulse control**—You have a proclivity to talk over others, display anger quickly, or make inappropriate comments. In stressful situations, you tend to be impatient and strike out at others.

- **Ingratiating behavior**—You "suck up" to superiors to ingratiate yourself to them. Your attitude toward your subordinates is the opposite, except when superiors are in the room.

- **Maintaining dominance**—You hire ordinary people who won't outshine you in the eyes of your superiors. You discourage employee initiatives that might surpass your ability. Likewise, you also discourage your people from stepping outside their job duties with statements like "I'll take care of managing. You take care of selling."

- **Referring to past errors**—You like to keep people in their place by reminding them of their past mistakes and failures.

- **Playing favorites**—You give preferential treatment to your favorite reps, and fail to apply rules fairly and equitably among your sales team.

- **Duplicity**—You say one thing to one person, then something totally different to another; for example, you might tell an underperforming rep that you're trying to save his job and then tell someone else that the rep is worthless and needs to be fired.

We've all had our share of bosses who have some or all of the bad-boss characteristics. And, in all cases of ineffective leaders, there's this irony: It takes a lot more time and energy to be a bad boss than to be a successful leader. That's because the traditional bad boss spends an inordinate amount of time devising rules and regulations to control his horde of unruly reps. In addition, it takes a lot of effort to monitor and enforce the edicts. Notwithstanding the great deal of creativity that goes into devising these instruments of torture for the reps, the end result is poor results. That's because reps hate to be controlled. Herein lies the paradox of control: The more control exerted, the less control achieved by the boss. When you tighten the reins, you increase the chance of losing your grip. Salespeople will rebel, developing their own underground resistance against tyrannical managers.

At the heart of "bad-bossology" is an element of cynicism and pessimism. Bad bosses, in general, doubt the ability of their charges to be responsible. Their lack of trust creates a need to micromanage.

Much of this is learned. Bad bosses frequently learn to manage from their own bad bosses. On the other hand, many times the elements of bad-bossology arise from personal insecurities—that is, these bosses have to believe in others' ineptitude to shore up their own value. Many feel obsessed to prove that they're better than their subordinates. If not, they might think, why would the sales manager be needed?

All-star sales leaders have learned to overcome personal insecurities. They have "unlearned" counterproductive lessons from the past. And they have discovered the power of working with, rather than lording over, their salespeople.

8. Are You a Sales Narcissist?

There's a difference between bad bosses and narcissists. Not all bad bosses are narcissists. Some are insecure, others obsessive-compulsive, and some are just plain incompetent. On the other hand, *all* narcissists are bad bosses.

Are your management efforts doomed by narcissistic tendencies? True narcissism is a clinically diagnosed form of psychosis, but many of us in sales have shades of it in varying degrees. The sales profession attracts those with narcissistic traits because sales is a manipulative process that rewards those who are independent, self-sufficient, and persuasive, and who love to be the center of attention. What true narcissist isn't lured by the prospect of being The Boss, The Teacher, The Coach, the one who's now ready to captivate the sales team with his or her many talents?

The truth is the narcissist has little hope for success in sales management. Sales management requires collaboration, coordination, the ability to thrive in the shadow of others, and a penchant for giving others credit. No matter how difficult it is to admit, the sales manager is dispensable. The process goes on, whether or not the sales manager is there. This is simply not an environment for the narcissist.

Charles H. Green, founder of Trusted Advisor Associates, further describes the narcissistic manager: "The narcissist...is wounded and insecure. He seeks praise and/or followers to reassure and shore up his shaky self-regard. But he also tends to use these people and even hold them in some self-contempt because, not really believing in his goodness or rightness, he believes he has manipulated and even fooled others into becoming his devotees and sycophants. He tends to shore up his own self-regard by devaluing others. He also is...sensitive to—and some times explosively reactive to—criticism."

Those with narcissistic tendencies are eager to talk about themselves, but not so eager to hear about you. They tend to focus conversations on their accomplishments and idealize their lives. Some are highly skilled and intelligent enough to mask their self-absorption, knowing that it can build resentment from others. In fact, you can find many who are generous and giving—as long as it doesn't impose a hardship on them. There's always an ulterior motive for their "good acts." There has to be public adulation or a business advantage from which to benefit. The key word to distinguish a narcissist from others is "sacrifice." Will they help you even if they have to make a sacrifice? It's very doubtful a narcissist will.

When it comes to protecting their career, narcissists will throw subordinates under the bus. They will lie, cheat, and steal to protect themselves, especially if they think they can get away with it. And even though they refuse to play by the rules, they are likely to establish a litany of rules to control their subordinates. By the way, there are many narcissists who don't try to hide their proclivities. In fact, many will openly tell you, "This is all about me." They revel in being viewed as a maverick, a kind of accomplished corporate outlaw who can get things done by operating on the periphery of boundaries and rules.

Similarly, other professions attract narcissistic types: attorneys, doctors, dentists, pilots, and others. The common denominators are that all these are skill-driven positions that place the incumbent front and center, in control of the process. This is the perfect arena for the narcissist. For example, even though a surgeon has a support staff, if the surgeon is not there, nothing gets done. The support staff is just that, support only. The surgeon—like a salesperson—makes it all happen, driving the process nearly completely. He or she is in the driver's seat with others along for the ride and requires little assistance or support. If necessary, these skill-driven professionals could do it all alone. Therefore, there is a sense of control because the support people ascribe and abdicate total authority to the principal, be it the salesperson, attorney, or surgeon. Support staff certainly can't do the job and probably wouldn't want to. The professional is the one receiving the adulation, adoration, and credit for the process. Narcissistic salespeople have ample social graces and charm but are usually loners at heart, sometimes lacking in empathy and rarely team players.

The self-centeredness of most narcissists is readily apparent to almost everyone but themselves. Essentially, a narcissist uses charm and the appearance of caring for others as a mask for manipulating them for the narcissist's benefit.

Following is a checklist of narcissistic characteristics outlined by Sue Barrett of the Barrett Sales Blog:

- Self-absorption and attention seeking
- Deception and rule breaking
- Arrogance and superiority
- Sense of entitlement and aggression
- Deflection of blame and exploitation
- Lack of empathy or remorse
- Lack of insight and self-awareness

You'll also find sales narcissists to be micromanaging managers who intimidate subordinates and have few long-term or deep relationships.

Although we all show some of these characteristics from time to time, if you have five or more on a consistent basis, you might have narcissistic tendencies. It's not something you overcome instantly, but by being aware of the traits, you can address them in a way that makes you a stronger leader.

In fact, many sales leaders have "adaptive narcissism," which is characterized by extroversion, drive, self-assurance, risk taking, persuasiveness, and initiative. They have learned to avoid the dysfunctional narcissistic qualities of intimidation, deception, arrogance, deflection, and lack of empathy. Effective leaders are bound to have some narcissistic traits. The leaders who are able to purge the dysfunctional characteristics are the ones who succeed.

9. Have You Put Your Ego on Hold?

Whether you're a narcissist or not, one of the largest obstacles for sales managers is the failure to check their egos at the door.

"I believe the biggest addiction problem in the workplace today is the human ego," said Ken Blanchard in the article "I'm OK, You're Not— It's All About EGO." He states, "When people operate from their ego, their behavior tends to be based on fear rather than trust. When people behave out of fear, they have a high need to control others and their environment and they have a win-lose orientation towards everything. Even when discussing the weather they want to make sure you know that *they* know more about weather than you do.... I became fascinated by people's perceptions of bad bosses, so I started asking people around the country to describe the worst boss they ever worked for. The primary description I heard was that of a high ego-driven person. The worst managers were described as poor listeners who were reluctant to share credit and always wanted to be in the limelight. While a lot of people would think people with a big ego had high self-esteem, I found the opposite to be true: Individuals who operate from their ego are usually covering up 'not okay' feelings about themselves."

As a salesperson, ego gratification is consistent and immediate. You make a sale, you get the praise individually and immediately. The sales manager who expects the same is doomed to failure. If you're in it for adulation and a quick ego fix, you'll continually be disappointed. Good sales managers become invisible at times, letting their people take the plaudits. The best managers get ego gratification from seeing their team succeed. Signs of an overactive ego include these:

- Acting as if you're better/smarter than everyone else
- Seeking praise and taking credit for achievements
- Winning arguments rather than seeking truth; having to be right all the time
- Boasting of accomplishments

- Denigrating the achievements of others

- Exaggerating one's role in projects

- Displaying arrogance, an inability to listen to others' advice

The reality is that you might really be a better salesperson than your people. It's likely that you were promoted to be a manager because you had superior sales and organizational skills. The key is to use your knowledge and skills to support and teach your people. When you come off as superior and arrogant, you will lose support and credibility.

10. Can You Empathize?

Empathy is understanding another person's feelings from his or her perspective. It's having the ability to disassociate one's personal perspective and walk in another's shoes. It's different from sympathy, which is only feeling sorry for someone. Rather it means going deeper to try to identify with a person's feelings while understanding the person's point of view. This is a monumental selling tool, and even more importantly, a vital managing technique. Empathy strengthens your decision making because it allows you to identify roadblocks and unintended consequences. It helps you develop loyalty from your people because they feel understood and respected. It heightens your level of credibility by helping you make decisions that are fair and equitable and that are backed by personal selflessness. Following are three ways to develop your power of empathy:

1. **Imagine**—Put yourself in the place of your subordinate, no matter how difficult the discussion might be. If you were that person in that situation, how would you feel? What would your needs and motivations be? What outcomes would you want?

2. **Defer**—Momentarily set aside your personal beliefs and agendas to fully understand the other person. Even if it's a stretch. For example, say you have a rep who refuses to sell a particular product. You don't and can't understand it—you've never experienced anything like this in 20 years of managing. The key is to defer judgment (and outrage). Probe to see what's behind the rep's thinking, assuming there's a good reason. You might find a legitimate ethical, moral, or business rationale behind the rep's

behavior. The secret is this: Don't jump to conclusions until you know the whole story.

3. **Identify**—Remember situations, feelings, and thoughts that you've had in the past that can create a link to your subordinate. Summon feelings of frustration, fear, anger, or elation to help you identify. Try to put those feelings into words, for example, "If I were in your shoes, I'd be mad too." A simple statement like that not only builds rapport but actually helps you really identify with the person.

11. Do You Have EQ? Are You Teaching It?

If you have empathy, self-awareness, and ego control, you have some of the major components of EQ—emotional quotient or emotional intelligence. EQ—which can be learned to some extent—is a natural remedy for bad-boss characteristics and sales narcissism.

Recent management studies have shown that EQ is even more important than IQ in management success. According to Travis Bradberry, co-author of *Emotional Intelligence 2.0,* EQ helped explain a peculiar research finding from the 1990s: Businesspeople with average IQs outperformed those with the highest IQs 70% of the time. Although IQ, for many years, had been the primary identifier of business success, EQ has been found to be a more potent characteristic of high managerial performance. Bradberry found 90% of top performers to be high in EQ but found only 20% of bottom performers to be high in EQ. Furthermore, those with high EQs earn an average of $29,000 more per year than those with low EQs.

EQ is composed of internal skills (the ways we manage ourselves) and external skills (how we interact with others).

Internal EQ Skills

Managing ourselves begins with self-awareness, previously described as the ability to understand one's strengths, weaknesses, motivations, and behavior. It allows us to recognize when our behavior is appropriate to the situation and how we affect others. People who are self-aware know when to talk and when to listen. They have an inner filter that helps them say the right thing at the right time or, more importantly, prevents them from saying the wrong thing. This inner gyroscope keeps them aligned with people and in sync with situations. This self-monitoring allows a manager to recognize whether he or she is, for example, coming on too strong and intimidating a subordinate. In this way, it helps the sales manager adapt behavior to effectively reach the sales rep in a nonthreatening way.

Self-regulation is the next phase of EQ internal skills. This is simply the ability to manage emotions. Sales management can be an emotionally charged activity, especially considering the mercurial nature of salespeople. Clearly, it's important to control our anger, disappointment, and frustration in order to maintain effective communications with our people. By omitting counterproductive emotions—and staying cool, calm, and collected—we're able to focus on mutually agreeable problem solving while maintaining good working relations.

Self-initiative is the third part of internal skills. Sales managers with high EQs usually have above-average levels of initiative. They are motivated internally without outside incentives. Their inner drive enables them to set high goals and develop strategies to achieve them.

External EQ Skills

Empathy, as outlined earlier, is the first element of EQ. This allows the sales manager to understand and try to connect to others' opinions and emotions. By putting themselves in others' situations, managers are more able to develop their salespeople by listening and giving constructive feedback. In many cases, the high-EQ manager is able to link others' expressions to their own experience, which further helps the manager identify with subordinates and provide appropriate responses.

The second external EQ factor is social perception, an aptitude for reading facial expressions, body language, and verbal cues. It takes focused concentration, but it helps the sales manager adapt to others' needs and target communications effectively. For example, if a subordinate's facial expressions show confusion about a new pricing program, the manager is able to change coaching tactics, perhaps using examples or anecdotes to make it clearer. Moreover, high-EQ managers are able to not only recognize but help others express their feelings through such statements as "I think I understand how frustrated you feel about this new product. It just doesn't seem to offer the benefits our customers expect."

Assertiveness is another EQ factor that successful managers (and salespeople) exhibit on a regular basis. In essence, they are able to communicate authoritatively without being authoritarian. They can guide and direct subordinates without micromanaging. They resolve conflicts firmly but amiably, leaving everyone feeling respected. In addition, they are able to facilitate change aggressively without alienating the troops.

Developing Your EQ and Teaching It

Many of us in sales constantly battle self-defeating behavior such as lack of impulse control and self-absorption. That goes with the territory when your livelihood is based primarily on your singular efforts to persuade people to buy. It's you against the vagaries of market conditions, resistant customers, and demanding bosses. In fact, it's a miracle if you don't develop some narcissistic tendencies that will work against you in sales management. You might never erase counterproductive behavioral traits but you can ameliorate them by developing your EQ. Here are a few ways to build your EQ and, equally important, to teach it to your sales force:

- Think about what you're thinking. Make a mental note, even keep a journal of your thoughts and feelings—especially those you experience in tense situations. Develop an awareness of how you feel and why. This self-monitoring will help you control your actions when needed.

- Take a pregnant pause. When you experience strong emotions such as anger or fear, pause before you act. Think through your options and the possible consequences of what you say and do. In the same vein, if you have time, sleep on it—you'll be surprised by the number of solutions that present themselves when you let problems gestate overnight.

- Calm yourself. A pregnant pause will give you time to control your emotions, to soothe yourself through positive self-talk, deep breathing, or other techniques that work for you. Instead of shouting a response, you have the chance to collect yourself and react in a logical way that maintains relationships with those around you.

- Be accountable. Don't blame others, no matter how tempting it is, for your mistakes. Admit your mistakes and assume the consequences. This element of self-regulation will not only prevent guilt feelings in you but also develop respect from others.

- Recognize your values. Identify and adhere to your value and belief system. A clear understanding of your ethics will facilitate your responses and behavior when you face tough decisions.

- Walk a mile in others' shoes. Imagine yourself in others' situation. How would you feel? What would you think? Changing *your* perspective to *theirs* helps develop empathy and understanding.

- Be a body-language detective. To help you empathize with others, watch their body language and facial expressions, and pay attention to verbal cues that might telegraph how they are feeling and what they are thinking. Even if you misread these signals, at least you're benefiting from the exercise of getting outside yourself and making the attempt at interpreting others. When you can't read someone's gestures or expressions, don't hesitate to ask the person what she's thinking or feeling at the time.

- Affirm others' feelings. Try to identify with others' feelings with statements like "I would be angry about it too" or "I know how frustrating that is." Doing so will force you to develop your empathic skills. At the same time, it's a certain way to develop rapport with your people.

- Practice assertiveness. Exercise the art of taking positions and making directives in a way that asserts your authority without threatening others. Focus on "we" rather than "I" statements to assure your people that you're acting in the team's best interests. Show empathy through statements such as "I hear what you're saying..." or "I know how you feel..." or "You have a good point. My opinion is...." The key to assertiveness is to get your point across in an amiable, caring, and respectful manner. This works in developing your sales reps and it works in their relations with customers.

- Boost your motivation. This is a tough one. Most sales managers and salespeople are internally driven by a variety of innate and external forces. Often, either you're self-motivated or you're not. But there are ways to reexamine and enhance one's self-initiative. What made you get into sales or sales management? Remembering those reasons, and looking at the less attractive options of other careers, can reenergize you. Do you still look forward to waking up and doing your job? If so, count the reasons why. If not, identify the obstacles and summon your problem-solving resources to reactivate your motivation. Build your optimism by looking for the good in people and in situations (read about "learned optimism" in Chapter 3, "Third Step: Building a Winning Team"). There is good, even in bad situations. Looking for the positive not only hones your motivation, but also keeps the darkness of pessimism from creeping into your thoughts and actions.

For additional information on EQ, hundreds of consultants, self-assessments, and tutorials are available online. Some are free, some are affordably priced, and others are more expensive, depending on your requirements and scope of work.

12. Are You Intoxicated by Power?

Researchers have found that power can create or increase a number of bad behaviors in leaders, including impulsivity and lack of empathy. In experiments, people given power are likely to rely on stereotypes when judging others, which creates questionable decisions. Similarly, they are more likely to engage in a type of emotional, verbal, or even physical bullying.

Even more surprising, Berkeley psychologist Dacher Keltner has found a "wealth of evidence that having power makes people more likely to act like sociopaths." In an article titled "The Power of Kindness," Keltner states, "High-power individuals are more likely to interrupt others, speak out of turn, and fail to look at others who are speaking. They are also more likely to tease friends and colleagues in hostile, humiliating ways. Surveys of organizations find that most rude behaviors—shouting, profanities, bald critiques—emanate from the offices and cubicles of individuals in positions of power. My own research has found that people with power tend to behave like patients who have damaged their brain's orbitofrontal cortex (the region of the frontal lobe right above and behind the eye sockets), a condition that seems to cause overly impulsive and insensitive behavior.... This leaves us with a power paradox. Power is given to those individuals, groups, or nations who advance the interests of the greater good in socially intelligent fashion. Yet, having power renders many individuals as poorly attuned to others as your garden-variety frontal lobe patient. What people want from leaders—social intelligence—is what is damaged by the experience of power."

The irony of power is that the more you have, the less effective you become at using it constructively. Successful leaders are ones who use self-awareness to monitor their impact on colleagues and subordinates, to share power or at least to use it judiciously. When used effectively, a leader's power can electrify a sales team by including others in decision making and building the team's confidence and self-esteem. Uncontrolled, abusive power will alienate your team and devastate sales productivity.

13. Are You the Smartest Person in the Room?

If your answer is "yes," you need to take some time to reassess your management style and your hiring practices. Top managers surround themselves with people who are better than they are. Of course, we all consciously or subconsciously fear that we're going to be outshone by those with superior skills. It's common to have the fleeting thought, "This guy is good enough to have my job." If that thought crosses your mind, consider it a good omen, not a threat. In fact, some make it a habit to hire only people who are good enough to be the boss. Quality people raise the bar for the team, provide a role model, and help the manager achieve stretch goals. For comparison's sake, look at the obverse of hiring good people—that is, hiring sales reps not as good as you. It might give you a sense of emotional security, being at the top of your team, but it's likely you won't have anyone other than yourself to help push results. And that is a lonely feeling. The practice of hiring people you can dominate creates stagnant sales teams and lazy managers. On the other hand, remember that managers are assessed on how well they hire and develop their people. Hiring people smarter than you is one of the best ways to build your career and generate upward mobility.

14. Have You Found Your Style?

Divest yourself not only from how you were managed, but also from how your peers manage. We all are tempted to succumb to institutional pressure. That is, we often have the illusion that if a company has been successful for years managing a certain way, then it must be good. The truth is that even the best can get better, and market conditions change every year, thus creating a need to change management strategies. Use your strengths to manage in a way that's you. Read professional literature, explore innovations, constantly seek new ideas. By all means, don't try to fit yourself to a management style simply because your peers are managing that way. In addition, a lot of bosses will tell you how to manage based on how they manage. That is simply wrong. We all bring different personalities and expertise to the management arena, and need to use all our strengths to our advantage.

Case Study #2: Finding Your Style in Spite of the Pressure

Alan had managed an office products sales team for three years, showing moderate but steady year-to-year improvement. His nine-rep team focused on businesses primarily in the Houston metro area. The sales team showed strengths in up-selling and new business, and cross-selling and overall customer retention were slightly below average. The group's aggregate net increase was 2% the first year, followed by 3% and 4% in the second and third years; the objective for each year was 4%, which placed Alan within the midrange of other managers' results.

Alan was an amiable personality, considerate and courteous, who got along well with his reps. Though he hadn't had any formal management training, he managed the way he would want to be managed—in a polite and organized fashion. He gave his reps plenty of support and encouragement. And even though he didn't completely trust all his reps, he didn't have time to bird-dog their sales activity. His focus was an aggressively offensive strategy, continuously searching for new sales opportunities. He kept meetings to a minimum, which the reps had requested for the sake of more selling time. Essentially, Alan spent most of his time responding to reps' support needs and keeping up with technology applications for the reps' sales pitches.

Contrary to many of his colleagues, Alan avoided confrontation and gave his reps flexibility to sell. He used a well-organized sales funnel to carefully track reps' results, offering coaching when needed.

When his former boss retired, a new vice president was appointed; he had a reputation as a hard-charging, take-no-prisoners sales leader. His first advice to Alan was to conduct "Daily Accountability" meetings with the reps to review every contract, every customer contact, and each day's schedule to keep them honest. "Now, I'm not telling you how to do your job," he told Alan. "But you're not showing much year-to-year progress. The reps have to know you're on top of their work. They have to know that you're going to ask them about every sale and why it succeeded or didn't succeed. Try getting more hands-on. It's worked for me. I've been around for 16 years, and a lot of my former managers have moved up through the ranks this way."

This was a new approach, a more in-your-face tactic that Alan had seen others use but never really felt comfortable with. However, the key thing now was to establish himself with the new boss, especially since his results were steady but not spectacular. And this guy did not seem to be the kind of person to take "no" easily.

"Maybe he's right," Alan had thought. "After all, my numbers are okay but nothing to brag about. They're definitely never going to get me promoted to the vice president level. Maybe he's right. He's got the experience and success to know what he's talking about. And all I have is three years' experience with no formal training at all."

Alan began a series of one-on-one meetings with each rep every morning, every day. Though he started off each day with the best of intentions, after reviewing the 15th or so customer contract, his brain went numb and all he could think about was getting it over with. He wasn't cut out for this kind of detail, and the whole thing made him feel like an interrogator. The checking and double-checking was irritating and time-consuming. Even worse, he just didn't have the kind of personality to do it effectively. Even though he handled the sales rep meetings with tact and diplomacy, the continuous questions he asked his reps created a sense of distrust that disturbed Alan. Honestly, Alan saw the benefits in the daily sessions in that it gave him insight into the reps' sales styles. And it made them accountable on a daily basis for their sales. It even forced him to learn to be more assertive and handle confrontation better. He saw how it could work effectively for someone who was more brash and analytical. Unfortunately, that was not Alan's nature and he was floundering.

The sales team went along with the change in procedure, accepting it as part of having a new VP. In fact, they initially tried to see the humor in the new process, referring to the reviews as "trips to the woodshed" and asking Alan whether waterboarding was the next step. But, truth be told, many saw Alan as weak and acquiescent, being a "yes" man to the new boss. They didn't like taking time for the sales reviews, and they felt an element of skepticism from Alan where they had previously felt he trusted them. Now their every move was being watched, and they felt a slight sense of betrayal from Alan.

The sales team was beginning to grumble to each other, some openly to Alan. An additional problem was that sales were stagnating, not necessarily dropping but staying about the same. Sensing the discontent from his people and his personal discomfiture—in addition to flat sales results—Alan realized it was time to take a stand.

Going into the meeting with his boss, Alan was nervous and had no idea how the guy was going to react. "I just wanted to give you an update on sales and make a proposal," Alan began. "For the past couple of months, I've used your accountability approach. And I've got to say, I've learned a lot. But I also have to say, I just can't quite get used to it. I'm not that detail-oriented. And I'm afraid the way I'm implementing this just isn't having much of a bottom-line impact on sales. If it sounds alright with you, I'd like to change the strategy to incorporate parts of Daily Accountability in a way that gives us more time to sell and seek new market opportunities."

Alan then laid out a plan that incorporated components of Daily Accountability in a way in which Alan felt comfortable. In a nutshell, the final plan was to continue accountability meetings on a weekly, instead of daily, basis. Rather than going over every contract, Alan would address the major sales and review highlights of the reps' weekly schedule. This approach would give Alan more time to explore sales opportunities and provide support to the sales team.

They agreed to try this custom-tailored accountability plan. It did not result in exploding sales, but they did regain momentum, a steady improvement over time. More importantly, Alan regained his standing with the sales team, and gained respect from the boss for standing up for his beliefs. In essence, Alan had taken Daily Accountability and changed it in a way that met the needs of his boss while adjusting it to his personal style.

15. Do You Have a Black Bass Strategy?

Okay, you have your sales goals and measurement metrics set to go. Your salespeople are trained. Your commission structure is fair. Your CRM is impeccable and your sales funnel is flawless. Now, take another look at all the components and ask yourself: Does it all fit together under a targeted, unified strategy? Or do you have a tactical plan without a strategy?

Salespeople focus on tactics—the daily activities that drive them to goal attainment, which includes such things as overcoming objections, closing the sale, pipeline metrics, and sales cycles. It's only natural that these tactical considerations carry over with the salesperson who moves into a managerial position. It's much more common to see sales managers having a tactical focus rather than a strategic vision. Unfortunately, you cannot lead a sales team with tactics. Doing so leaves the manager with a patchwork of activities that are likely to be driven by trial and error and susceptible to flavor-of-the-day management fads. It takes a well-defined strategy to provide forward and steady momentum by employing an integrated game plan rather than a "let's see if this works" attitude.

The complexity of a strong sales strategy is keeping it simple. It's easy to get overwhelmed with strategic considerations such as pricing, product, and competitive strategies.

In fact, all you need is one sales strategy: *customer segmentation.* That's because a strong segmentation strategy subordinates and coordinates all other considerations, making them tactics under the segmentation umbrella. Segmentation provides the spadework and direction to determine everything from competitive positioning to product applications and discounts. The essence of a segmentation strategy is simply targeting the right customers.

Have you identified your high-potential customers, the ones who will yield the highest sales return? A finely honed sales strategy maximizes the efforts of your sales force by putting them in front of high-potential customers. At the same time, it helps them avoid low-yield customers who drain time and energy. In many cases, a small, unprofitable customer takes the same amount of time to handle as a large, lucrative customer. In addition, an effective strategy tells you where your new business opportunities exist—you can bet that your existing top-drawer customer segment is only the tip of the iceberg of similar prospects who are not yet your customers. For instance, say your most lucrative segment is pediatric physicians. The pediatric physicians you serve constitute about 10% of those in your market, which leaves 90% of a valuable segment to target, allowing you to use what you already know about them to enhance sales. The beauty of discovering these clusters of high-yield customers is that the commonality they share—such as buying habits and price sensitivity—allows you to better prepare for each one individually.

Your sales strategy should guide your team like a heat-seeking missile to a target-rich environment. Accurate customer segmentation makes everything else much easier. It's like fishing. Without knowing what you're fishing for, you take various baits and lures and troll aimlessly around the lake until you get a bite. The fisherman who knows it's time for black bass to be feeding knows what bait to use, where to find the bass, and how to catch them. He has a specific target, knows what motivates them, knows where and when to find them, and knows how to catch them. It's done with an economy of effort that maximizes the yield and doubles the return on investment. (See Chapter 6, "Sixth Step: Success Through Performance Measurement," for additional details on sales strategy and customer segmentation.)

Fourteen Aids to Self-Manage Successfully

Today's sales environment is tough and unforgiving. The confluence of technology, market demands, and financial pressures provides unheralded challenges to the sales manager. This is a time to do more than think outside the box; you have to discard boxlike thinking and change the paradigms of traditional sales management thinking. Here are 14 essentials to consider as part of your personal management paradigm shift.

1. Reverse Appraisals Make Smarter Leaders

Do reverse assessments regularly. Give your people the chance to review *your* performance. Give them an assessment form of your critical skills and performance, including communications, responsiveness, technical knowledge, organization skills, vision, and overall leadership effectiveness. Insure anonymity so that your people will respond honestly. Reverse appraisals will show you areas for improvement but also gives your people a strong message that you care about them and the quality of their supervision. Be prepared to be disappointed. The glowing assessments you expect might not appear. That's because behind every smiling face, there lies some resentment, frustration, or even hostility that might emerge in the reverse assessment. Naturally, the boss is always the first person to blame. So be prepared for unfair criticism while realizing that this process provides some real opportunities to improve your team if you take a tough-skinned, problem-solving approach.

Many managers benefit from 360-degree appraisals, which include feedback from reports, peers, and bosses. However, these are more complicated to implement and assess than simple reverse appraisals.

2. Manage Your Expectations

Stress is the gap between what you expect and what you get. To some extent, you can manage your stress by managing your expectations. Reps are not going to be as good as you. Otherwise, they would be the boss. Expect excellence and inspect results but don't think your people will be as good as you. Nevertheless, don't give up on trying to get them to that level. Be realistic in your expectations, assuming that improvement is always a difficult challenge and it takes time. You're not going to turn around your team or individuals overnight.

Examine your expectations. Are you comparing yourself to your people? Don't. It's human nature to think, "I could have closed that sale in two weeks. Why did he take a month?" or "I could have easily overcome that objection." This type of self-righteousness creates many problems in the workplace. First, it can create a subtle—and unfair—contempt of others and their abilities. This not only builds walls between you and your team, but also provides the manager with a dangerously handy "hook" on which to lay blame. After all, if the rep is just not good enough, what's the point in analyzing and developing the rep? When managers use themselves as a comparison point, it's simply taking the easy way out.

Second, it sets up the manager for constant disappointment and frustration. It's doubtful that anyone is going to live up to your litmus test—yourself. Right or wrong, many of us in sales have an overinflated view of our own abilities, and—competitive creatures that we are—it's hard to admit that someone is as good or better.

Third, it blinds us to our own inadequacies, which prevents us from growing into a better leader. Finding faults in others—through self-comparison—keeps us from examining our own failures or weaknesses in management. In essence, it makes us less accountable and more likely to point fingers.

To effectively manage your expectations, you have to enumerate them. That is, put your expectations in writing, quantify them where possible, and share them with your team. Discuss them, get team feedback, and ensure that everyone understands the rationale and specifics behind them. Your expectations will include sales objectives but might go well beyond the run-of-the-mill numerical scores we use on a daily basis. For example, if you expect your reps to make post-purchase contacts with customers, tell them how many and how frequently. If you expect new business leads to be worked promptly, provide a specific time requirement, such as 24 hours. Likewise, clearly communicate your criteria to ensure rep integrity, such as customer signature guidelines and pricing honesty. Your expectations might include a wide range of issues important to you, such as sales meeting attendance, professional behavior standards, and sales cycle recommendations. After those have been listed and discussed, you should require compliance with these clearly stated, mutually agreeable expectations of your sales team.

After that, expect the best and prepare for the worst.

Long term, we all want to inspire and motivate our people to achieve team success. In reality, we might inspire our people but not reach team objectives. Or we might reach objectives without really inspiring our people. It goes without saying, sales is a battlefield of best-laid plans, derailed missions, distractions, recalculations, and adjustments. As with sales, we have to shoot for the moon but prepare for a cancelled launch. It takes time. Don't expect too much too fast. If your people are meeting your daily expectations, you are getting closer and closer to your long-term expectations. By simply articulating your expectations, you are helping create the sales culture that will lead to success. In essence, you have created boundaries for your people that help them function effectively. No matter how much we talk about the independent nature of salespeople, they do need structure to be successful.

By the way, expectations work both ways. Ask your team to list expectations they have for you. Not only will that help you lead effectively and sharpen your empathy, but it also will let your people know you care about their opinions. That is a great way to build trust and communication.

3. Best Practices Help Stimulate Success

For self-management purposes, a well-organized Best Practices program will help expand your knowledge base and your sales management capabilities. Not only does it help drive successful sales techniques and processes, but it also keeps you and your team up to date on the latest sales and technology trends. The most effective best-practices program encourages participation from everyone on the sales team, from reps to managers to support staff. To emphasize its importance, include it as part of every job description that has anything to do with sales. The manager should always be on the outlook for best practices through close observation of and discussions with your salespeople. In addition, all team members should be encouraged to identify practices within and outside the company, and share them. Best Practices is everyone's job, not just the manager's. The manager should, however, facilitate the cataloging and coaching of best practices to make sure that everyone has access to the practices. Best Practices is a formal, orderly process. At the same time, it should be an informal, ongoing activity between salespeople sharing ideas and practices with each other. (See Chapter 3 for additional details on Best Practices.)

4. It Takes More Than Money to Motivate

Study after study indicates that today's workers are in it for more than money. Arthur Brooks, author of *Gross National Happiness,* says that higher income does little to raise people's happiness, after basic needs are met. Even more importantly, beyond the basics, satisfying work matters more than money. "Like nations, once individuals reach subsistence, they get little or no extra happiness as they get richer—even massively richer." Brooks says the real value of money is to mark our success and measure the value we are creating.

Yes, your people are interested, very interested, in making money. That's why we get up early every morning and rev our engines. But simply making money is an empty, meaningless pursuit. There's much more than money that motivates today's salespeople. They want to feel valued, respected, successful, and involved.

The new generation of salespeople—millennials—especially seem to be less money driven than their baby boomer predecessors.

5. Get Out of the Way and Let It Flow

Provide training and support, set high standards, and then get out of the way and let your people *sell.* That's what salespeople do best. Closely monitor results, provide daily tracking reports, and let your people know that you're staying close to the action. But give them room to be the salespeople they aspire to be. Flow is what you want (see Chapter 4, "Fourth Step: Becoming a Successful Servant Leader")—that is, helping your people get in "the zone." They won't get there with you standing in the way. Few salespeople wake up in the morning and say, "I'm going to do a really crappy job today and see whether I can decrease my commission." On the contrary, 99% of your people come to work hoping for—maybe even expecting—that big sale. They want to do well. They need the money. And they crave respect. Your job is to help them marshal their resources to get there, to remove roadblocks and speed them on their way.

6. Grab the Tool Kit; a Hammer Just Won't Do

Ineffective managers embrace the old saying "If a hammer is your only tool, then everything looks like a nail." You know them, the managers who give directives and then sit back, hammer in hand, waiting for their orders to be carried out. They measure their own magnanimity, not by how much grace they extend to their people but by how much punishment they withhold. They are likely to pat themselves on the back for telling a salesperson, "I'm not going to beat you down this time, but don't let it happen again." It's like the man who says he's a good husband because he doesn't beat his wife very often. Even worse is the sales boss who threatens and intimidates reps to achieve sales results. Subtly or overtly, they push their reps with a results-at-any-cost approach. Many times, they'll try to minimize the coercion, masking it behind humor such as the manager who jokes, "If you don't produce, I've got a shotgun, a shovel, and an alibi." In other words, there's no hesitation to kill careers and dash dreams in the pursuit of a quota.

The truth is that a sales unit is an intricate mechanism of nails, screws, nuts, bolts, and even circuit boards and memory chips. It takes a lot more than a hammer to fine-tune it.

Getting hammered occasionally as a salesperson—deservedly or not—goes with the territory. But managers don't always realize the impact of negativity on sales reps' job performance and health. When it goes too far, it's called workplace bullying. In fact, 20 states have introduced legislation since 2003 against bullying in the workplace. The Workplace Bullying Institute says that 35% of the U.S. workforce report being bullied at work. The Institute's definition of bullying includes "Verbal abuse, offensive conduct/behaviors (including non-verbal) which are threatening, humiliating or intimidating."

Here's one way to look at the issue: Do you treat your subordinates with the same respect and courtesy as your boss? Realistically, few of us do. But think about it. Your sales force is going to have more impact on your career than your boss. Your salespeople, not your boss, produce sales that get you promoted. Your boss might steer your career path, but your subordinates provide the horsepower to drive the process. If your people aren't receiving your best attention (patience, courtesy, and respect), you're probably not receiving their best. You can bet that if your lack of civility morphs into bullying—no matter how subtle and surreptitious it might be—it will work against you.

From a practical standpoint, intimidation simply doesn't work with salespeople. Of all professions in the world, salespeople are savants in handling intimidation. They face it every day from customers. A boss who tries to intimidate is more likely to *inflame* the sales force. And the only result is distraction from selling.

Unfortunately, the narcissism that drives intimidation also prevents managers from learning and growing into real leaders. As noted earlier, numerous studies have shown that leaders with narcissistic tendencies frequently are failures as managers. They gradually lose support from subordinates, which creates morale problems, which, in turn, create loss of support from superiors. Their sense of entitlement leads to breaking the rules and other integrity violations that can sidetrack their careers.

New managers frequently take this "I'm the boss and that's all that matters" approach. After all, they've excelled in their previous role as a salesperson and they are ready to teach and lead. What they don't always understand is that their people are not instantly ready to learn and follow. Getting people to follow your lead requires trust and credibility that could take months to establish. Showing up, touting your credentials, and giving orders just doesn't work. It doesn't take long for most young managers to learn this lesson, but some never learn. Some can't learn because they are not able to forgo their self-interest for the good of the group: Meet the I-Manager, the manager who has learned to spell "team" with an "I." This manager is largely Inconsequential because the primary management tool he or she has to work with is Intimidation. This kind of manager emphasizes not so much *what* is right but *who* is right. For the I-Manager, it's more important to win the debate than to do what's best for the company and its people.

Everywhere you go, you hear sales managers referring to their "teams." Teammates, team members, team leaders—the words have become common usage in the business world to the point where they have lost their meaning. Some of the most autocratic, dictatorial managers refer to their subordinates as a "team" when the only teamwork existing is the shared resentment they feel for their boss.

Max DePree, in *Leadership is an Art,* said, "Abandoning oneself to the strengths of others" is the leadership approach that has made Herman Miller Inc. a leader in the furniture industry. DePree, president of Herman Miller, explained that the company's leadership depends on employees' suggestions and input to improve productivity, and that every employee has the "right and duty to influence decision making.... Around here, employees act as if they own the place." This kind of teamwork has led the company to be repeat performers on *Fortune* magazine's list of "Ten Most Admired Companies."

7. Stop Selling, Start Managing

Studies have shown that many sales managers spend as much as 25% to 35% of their time selling (doing customer presentations and closing sales). Granted, some jobs—such as "hybrid sales managers"—are shaped for sales managers to also sell (especially in smaller organizations). But pure sales managers need to manage and not sell. It's the manager's job to make sure each salesperson is fully capable of selling alone. Don't get the reputation of being "The Closer." And don't be the person who goes out on every possible account loss. There's not enough time in the day. And, that's not your job. Your responsibility is to make sure that reps can handle every phase of selling as well as you can. Yes, it's important to ride with your salespeople to observe and train. In the training capacity, it's good for them to learn your techniques, to see you sell, but selling for them is doing a huge disservice to them and you.

If you are a "hybrid" manager, it's important to maintain focus on your reps, on their coaching and training. Look at it statistically. Your sales, as a manager, are probably less than 20% of total sales volume. Are you spending a proportionate amount of time, 80% that is, managing your people? As we all know, sales is a seductive passion. But as a manager, "hybrid" or not, we can't afford to be lured into selling more than managing. Even the best-selling sales manager can't come close to producing what the sales team can produce as a whole. You can catch fish for your sales team or you can teach them to fish, and multiply your efforts exponentially.

8. Don't Try to Sell a Salesperson

Remember, you are not a salesperson, you are a leader. We all are guilty, to some extent, of "selling" our ideas and directives to our people. Many times it is necessary. But if "selling" is your primary or exclusive technique, you're overlooking the power of your sales force's involvement and ideas. Look at it mathematically. A good sales conversion rate is 50%. Even if you're very good at selling your ideas to your people, at best you're going to have half of them committed and the other half either indifferent or opposed to your program. Your sales machine will only cough and sputter on half its rated horsepower. Granted, you'll never have 100% support from your reps, but engaging them in decision making rather than "selling" them to follow your decisions should raise your conversion rate to well over 50%.

9. Develop an Effective Sales Culture

What is a sales culture? You might not be able to describe it, but you can feel it. It's the general attitudes that sales reps have about the company, their place in it, their enthusiasm, and their beliefs and values related to selling. Do they speak well of the company and its management? Are they excited about selling? Do they believe in the product line? Are they seeking excellence in selling? Are they proud of their individual reputations as well as the company's?

A sales culture can be characterized as who we are, what we do, how we do it, and how we feel about doing it. For better or worse, a sales culture is, first, a reflection of the sales manager. Second, it should be a reflection of the vision and mission of the company.

Within six months, most sales forces will become a likeness of the sales manager. Don't underestimate your influence. But you need to carefully analyze what kind of sales force you are shaping. Are your salespeople picking up your best qualities, such as enthusiasm, integrity, product belief, and commitment to customers? Conversely, are they picking up any ineffective characteristics, such as tardiness, sloppy paperwork, failure to follow up, or indecisiveness? Look at your own weaknesses and you'll probably find them embedded in your sales force. Analyze, and then address your weaknesses and reinforce your strengths to make sure your salespeople are receiving the correct signals to build a productive sales environment.

More importantly, are you actively planning and shaping your sales culture? Other than the attitudes and values your reps observe in you, are you consciously developing your culture on a daily basis based on your company's vision and mission?

A productive sales culture is developed top-down. It's up to you, the sales manager, to shape your sales ecosystem. If you don't actively create it, your culture is likely to be dysfunctional and counterproductive, shaped by chance. In the absence of values and beliefs, reps shape their own culture. For example, if you have never clearly stated the need for integrity, your reps might know the difference between right and wrong but might take a "who cares?" attitude when it comes to deceptive sales practices. It's the manager's job to clearly state who cares and why. Managers have to establish operating philosophies in words and actions.

Imagine your ideal sales culture, tie it to the company's mission/vision, and articulate it. If you can't communicate it, it won't happen. Describe in writing the sales culture you want to develop. Following is a sample sales culture profile of a fictional restaurant supply sales force:

Who We Are

- We are the ten-person, professional sales force of Burns Restaurant Supply, Ohio's second-largest restaurant supply company. Our mission is to lead the company to become the number one company in our category with sales topping $10 million.

What We Do

- Specializing in full-service restaurants, we have the responsibility to effectively market a full line of restaurant equipment, supplies, utensils, and furniture to the state's 13,000 restaurants.

How We Do It

- Our first priority is to proactively protect and expand our sales to existing restaurants.

- We will aggressively seek new business.

- Every salesperson will actively build and maintain customer relations through regular one-on-one contact and through industry trade shows and meetings.

- We will diligently promote our reputation with customers for honesty, integrity, and fairness.

- Our sales team will work with each other collaboratively to share information and provide in-house support for each other.

- We will stay up to date on the latest industry developments as well as selling techniques through extensive training and learning from each other.

How We Feel About Ourselves

- We thrive on competition and work hard to find new sales opportunities that will lead us to the number one position in Ohio.

- We are technically competent to solve customer problems and overcome objections.

- We feel energized by an atmosphere that encourages aggressive selling and continual improvement.

- We are proud of the company's reputation for integrity.

- Each of us feels valued as an integral part of the company's success.

- We feel empowered with the flexibility to take reasonable risks and make decisions in the best interests of protecting and expanding sales.

- We feel accountable for our results and have control of our destiny.

- Sales reps and managers feel secure in their mutual esteem for and trust of each other.

Describing your ideal sales culture not only fixes it in your mind, but also helps your team envision it and move toward your goal. Developing a sales culture profile is different from sales objectives, mission statements, and vision statements. It enunciates your team's values and beliefs. More than statistical goals, your culture profile is the soul and conscience of your organization. It sets the standards from which you measure right and wrong, good and bad. It is, for example, the foundation from which you develop code-of-conduct specifics. It is the way you describe your sales organization to job applicants and other outsiders. And, finally, it provides the conceptual framework that serves as a behavioral lighthouse for your salespeople. In advertising lingo, it is your product personality.

Simply stating a value or belief provides clarity for your sales team. The opposite is also true. Be careful of what you omit. That's not to say that you need a laundry list of everything that might be important now or in the future. Include only the things vital to team success, never more than ten items. Put them in order of priority to sharpen your team's focus.

When developing the profile, envision the kind of people you want to be surrounded by. After all, your people are the embodiment of your sales culture. What are their principles and sales ideologies? List these characteristics and make them part of your profile and your hiring practices. They might include such traits as these:

- Aggressive and competitive
- Honest and fair
- Loyal and trustworthy
- Technically proficient
- Customer service oriented
- Unafraid to take risks
- Hardworking and resilient
- Engaging and polished

Next, compare your ideal sales characteristics with your company's mission and vision statement to ensure a good match. Look for disconnects. For example, if your company values employees over customers, obviously a customer service orientation is of secondary importance.

Of course, the obverse is true if your company takes a strong customer-first orientation.

Finally, share your profile with your sales team for their input and discussion. The sales team will help you refine and amplify your thoughts. In addition, it will increase the chances of their owning the outcomes since they participated in the process.

10. If You Want Followers, Lead by Example

To develop an effective sales culture, you have to lead by example. If your people are required to be in the office at 8 a.m. every day, be sure you are there every day at 8 a.m. If you ask for quick response time from your people, it's your responsibility to give them quick responses. Dr. John C. Maxwell, author and speaker, said, "If you want your team members to be dedicated, then you must show them your commitment. If they should be willing to put the team first, then you should be willing to make sacrifices. If you want them to care for each other, then you must demonstrate your love for them. There's no substitute for *showing* them what you expect from them." Think about the autocratic bosses you've had in the past—chances are the more despotic they are, the less of an example they set. They are usually the ones who come in late, who respond slowly to their subordinates. Wherever you see this sense of arrogant entitlement by managers (who think they deserve special treatment because they are the boss), you will see resentment and resistance from subordinates. It is not possible to passionately follow someone you don't believe in, someone who doesn't walk the talk.

11. Knowing Your Reps Builds Understanding

Take the time to know your people—what motivates them, how they respond to authority and peers, their strengths and aptitudes. It takes time, close observation, and dialogue to analyze a salesperson. Rocket science and brain surgery pale by comparison. It means you have to understand your people individually. Managing successful sales teams occurs one salesperson at a time. Put yourself in their place, analyze their psyche and motives. Forget what you've learned about personality types. Labeling people with arbitrary tags—such as introverts, extroverts, type A, and analyticals—without a professional's help is dangerous because it oversimplifies the complexities of human personality. Though these typologies can be useful for general understanding, especially in hiring—when you need a quick assessment of candidates over a short period—they are not a substitute for careful study of your people's unique psyches. General typologies can provide an easy, but misleading, explanation for people's actions and for their potential. Take this statement, for example: "He's an analytical; therefore, he won't be able to take the lead in this project." The truth is, in a day's time he will morph from an "analytical" to a "visionary" to an "initiator" depending on the situation. He has components of all the typologies that rotate from occasion to occasion. No one fits into any one "type"—we are all products of our genetics, our experience, and our environment. It's easy to describe people with bumper-sticker clichés and simplistic caricatures. However, not only can that be misleading, but it also can condition us to think of people in one-dimensional terms, overlooking the richness of people's sensibilities. We're truly a weird mix of all the typologies, and each of us defies easy analysis. It's hard enough to understand ourselves, much less subordinates with whom we might spend only a few hours a week. The trick is to make those hours count. Observe, really observe, what makes your people tick. Ask questions and take notes, but above all resist the convenience of fitting them into a "type."

Along the same lines, examine your top salespeople. What are they doing to be successful? Identify their best practices and replicate them for others. Novartis, the pharmaceutical company, developed an entire sales training program based on skills, style, and procedures of their top salespeople.

On the group level, take time to analyze your team's dynamics. Know the leaders and followers. The leaders, when cultivated carefully, can help support and reinforce your objectives, adding momentum and credibility to your efforts. How do you cultivate them? Have frequent, informal one-on-one meetings to ask them what they think about new ideas and existing programs. Let them know you depend on their input as a leader of the group and how much you appreciate their involvement. Conversely, take care not to neglect your group's followers. They are your foot soldiers, and need to feel part of the process. With proper attention and grooming, some followers will become group leaders.

12. Understand Your Customers' Needs

Most customers don't need to be sold. They need to be informed. They need solutions, not presentations. There are exceptions, but customers really don't want to be manipulated, controlled, cajoled, directed, or interrogated. They don't want their objections to be overcome—they simply want to be heard. They don't have time for lengthy presentations. They detest being the unwitting victim of a six-step sales process, and they object to being "closed" after the recommendation.

In many ways, the millions of dollars we spend to train salespeople work against effective selling. That's because we target our efforts at wooden stereotypes we call *"prospects"* and sometimes forget our real target, which is *human beings*. We spend so much time focusing on sales that we ignore the buyers and their many needs. As top salespeople have proven time and time again, product knowledge and the ability to listen trumps any amount of sales technique we can teach. Good salespeople understand that the way to stand out is be the one who doesn't play the sales games, the one who can sit down and have a normal conversation with customers, having their best interests in mind.

Customers humor us and our sales spiels. They play the game, sometimes just to get us out the door. But, in reality, what they want is a conversation with a knowledgeable person to help them make a buying decision. Customers' expectations are highlighted in a recent *Harvard Business Review* article titled "What B2B Customers Really Expect." A study of 200 customers from a cross-section of U.S. firms showed that the top attributes they preferred in sales reps were first "Subject matter and solution expertise" followed by "Understanding of customer's business and industry" and then "Professionalism" (flexibility, responsiveness, respectfulness, and integrity). In addition, 39% of the respondents expressed dissatisfaction with their reps' level of "Understanding of customer's business and industry."

The same study showed a huge contrast between what customers want and how salespeople are hired. These customers' vendors were asked what criteria they considered most important in hiring sales reps who would call on the customers. Ironically, they said "Professionalism" was the first attribute. "Subject matter and solution expertise" (the first-ranked trait preferred by customers) ranked third in hiring criteria.

The research suggests that we, as sales managers, have a tendency to emphasize sales skills over customer needs. Perhaps in all the hustle and bustle to achieve objectives, we overlook the most important part of the equation: the customer. And the customer wants honest information first and foremost. This indicates the need for strong product and technical training for reps in addition to consultative sales techniques in order to ask questions that identify customers' real problems and challenges rather than merely symptoms.

In addition to being informed, many customers expect (either consciously or subconsciously) a sales appointment to be a "buyer's moment"—a stress-free experience that they control and even enjoy. Put yourself in the buyer's shoes. Whether the customer is a business owner or midlevel manager, a sales appointment is one of the few times of the day when he's not being controlled or manipulated. It's a moment when he's not confronted by demanding employees, scrutinized by bosses, buffeted by competitors, and scathed by unrelenting financial pressures. By the time a customer meets with a salesperson, he's probably frazzled by the demands of the day. This, finally, is a moment when he is the supreme decision maker, one to be respected and revered. It's a time when he can talk about anything he wants to discuss—family, politics, the economy, religion—and be listened to and acknowledged. (Or, if short on time, he may elect to get directly to the point, make a decision and move on to the next meeting.) This could be the only time of the day that he controls, and a moment when someone (the salesperson) expresses any interest in him. The last thing a customer wants is to have a sales rep take control of the moment and press to a close. Managers who understand this dynamic help their reps take advantage of the "buyer's moment"—to facilitate buyers to buy instead of making it a unilateral selling endeavor. These managers ensure that their training regimen includes the "soft" skills of sales—such as listening and empathy—in addition to product and technical training.

13. Shhhh...Are You Listening?

As managers, we're proud of what we've accomplished and what we've learned. That means we're always eager to let others know what we know—sometimes too eager. Often, we're too busy telling salespeople what we want, and not listening to what they need in order to deliver what we want. If you listen, and ask the right questions, your sales reps will tell you how to reach goals and even throw in the details of how to get there.

Your salespeople want to be heard, and they won't be fooled as you nod your head and make eye contact while all the time formulating your next comment as they are talking. Listen, really listen. Put away your smartphone and pay attention to what your reps have to say. One of the best ways to show you're listening is to take notes. Don't offer a quick answer and don't interrupt. Just make sure they are done, and then summarize what they said and respond. You might get some valuable input, maybe not, but the important thing is that your reps will feel that you have listened. That alone is worth a lot because the information you receive will help you manage the team and will help your people feel as though they are an important part of the organization.

14. Make Yourself Promotable

We all know that the single best way to get promoted is to make your objectives. However, it's really a little more complicated than that. First, are you making your numbers the right way—on budget with low turnover? Do you have profitability metrics in place that measure your cost of sales including product discounts, sales commissions and bonuses, training, and costs associated with sales employee turnover? You can make your numbers day in and day out, but if the cost of reaching your objective is disproportionately high, the result is as bad as missing your numbers. That's a surefire way to derail one's promotability.

In addition, how do you distinguish yourself from the other sales managers who are also making their numbers? Bosses love the *No Excuse Management* style and hold its proponents in high regard for promotions. Simply put, the No Excuse manager assumes responsibility and accountability, focusing on solutions to problems rather than explanations, and taking the responsibility to seize opportunities as they emerge rather than waiting for directives to do so. These are the kind of managers who effectively execute their assigned responsibilities and all other responsibilities not specifically denied them. It's a bit risky and takes a lot of self-confidence. But remember, those who risk nothing do nothing. In the end, bosses admire and reward the No Excuse leader. Here are the major components of No Excuse Management:

> **Accountability**—Assume full responsibility for your duties. We, as sales managers, can't control the economy, the market, or the competition. But we can control our reaction to them. If we don't adjust according to the elements, there's no one to blame but ourselves, certainly not the reps. Finger-pointing is a quick way

to lose the respect of your boss. It also sends a signal that you're at the mercy of market conditions and lack the control needed to make positive change. Your boss wants a winner, a doer, a fixer—not a victim or a whiner.

Responsibility—Take on all responsibilities of your job description, and ask for more. Seek new opportunities, especially those that match your skill set, which might take pressure off your boss. For example, develop sales training for use by other managers or create an analytics program that goes beyond your scope of supervision. Volunteer for projects that other managers don't want to do or can't do.

Proactivity—Take the initiative to identify and address problems and opportunities without being told to do so. Proactive managers are willing to take risks because they are self-assured, having a certain intuitive feel when and how to act with no supervision. They have the ability to launch the boat quickly, making mid-course corrections as they go. They have a "speed to market" mentality that provides a distinct competitive advantage.

Knowledge—Bosses want go-to guys, people who know their market plan, rates, procedures, and paperwork. They want a manager who knows everything the reps should know, and more. They want managers who learn, on their own, everything from the latest management techniques to economic trends.

Flexibility—The best sales leaders are nimble, able to function effectively in ambiguous situations in which there are no instructions or precedents. These situations are tests of a manager's judgment and creativity under fire. Weak managers get stuck. They stubbornly insist on plowing through situations rather than having the flexibility to seek alternatives. The No Excuse manager realizes, first, that no one else is going to fix the problem, and therefore goes about a complete work-through that includes as many options and variations as needed.

Complimentary Skills—Promotable people think two levels above. What skills are lacking in your boss and your boss' boss? Help them where they are weak or time-deprived. If they are strong on people skills but weak with numbers, your strength in analytics will give you an advantage when the next job opens up. Look for ways to highlight your strengths up the line. For example, develop a new sales tracking program and share the analysis with your superiors. Let them know subtly that you have the skill set for that position when it opens.

2

Second Step: High-Performance Teams Begin with Hiring

Hiring good sales reps is one of the continuing mysteries of sales management. It could, in fact, very well be the single toughest part of sales management. Just when you think you've broken the code, a new hire brings in a set of problems that sends you back to the drawing board. When you think you've learned from your failures, you're surprised again and again. Unfortunately, it seems the unpleasant surprises far outweigh the pleasant ones. We've all hired sure-thing reps who flamed out in six months. Conversely, we've hired ones who barely made the cut, and watched them turn into superstars.

Some say a 50% first-year success rate is good. But that simply is not good enough. You are doing something wrong if your new hire success rate is less than 75%. That should be your minimal requirement, and you can do much better. Of course, much of it depends on your onboarding and development after you've hired the reps. However, a huge factor in your success rate is hiring the right person for the job. That doesn't mean hiring the best person for the job who is available at the time. After all, wouldn't it be better to hire no one at all—to have your existing reps pick up the slack by handling more accounts, for example, until the right rep comes along—than to hire a mediocre salesperson that you're stuck with? Think about it. Are you really committed to hiring the right person or are you simply trying to avoid hiring a failure? There's a huge difference between hiring right and hiring safe. Most of us have been in the situation in which your pool of candidates just isn't that strong so you hire the best available. And, many times, that rep turns out to be an average performer. The constant challenge of hiring is not selecting a bad rep—those are pretty easy to identify and screen. The struggle is to avoid hiring the mediocre rep. Unfortunately, the laws of probability are working in favor of your employing average reps if you don't have a game plan for hiring the right people.

A critical part of a successful hiring strategy is maintaining this underlying principle: *Do not trust your intuition,* no matter how experienced you are. Intuition is a feeling. And salespeople are genius at making you feel good. Their job is to make you like them. Many have a sixth sense for detecting what you're looking for and becoming that person for a few minutes, long enough to get the job. It's ironic, according to research, that the ones who project the most likability might be the weaker candidates.

Granted, there are those among us who have the knack for hiring good people. However, they are few and far between. And they're probably not sharing their secrets of hiring success. If you are one of the many who lack the knack, who haven't found the secret sauce, or who are devoid of savantlike hiring intuition, here are three things to improve your hiring decisions:

1. **Quantification**—Numbers don't lie. The best way to judge candidates is sales *results.* Ask candidates to provide reports and other documentation to substantiate sales achievement and job history.

2. **Analysis**—Establish tests and techniques to validate that the candidate has the skills, aptitudes, and personality traits for the job.

3. **Collaboration**—Make hiring a team process. Involve your sales reps, other managers, and support staff to get a comprehensive view of your candidate.

With these three principles at work, consider the hiring process a science, not an art. The premise of this chapter is that, unlike much of sales management, hiring is an analytical procedure based on facts, careful observation, and analysis.

First Goal: Hire Those You Know

Don't hire unknowns. Make that your goal. Even though it's a goal you might never attain, it will force you to focus on strong networking—to create a pool of candidates ready for your next hire. If you're running a lot of hiring ads, you are hiring unknowns. That means your success rate is going to be lower than that of managers who use networking skills to hire salespeople with whom they're familiar.

Of course, professional sales recruiters can supplement your personal networking by providing candidates and helping you assess them. On the other hand, their services can be expensive and it takes time to get them focused on your particular sales culture and needs. Some managers find it more effective and personalized to do the hiring themselves, not to mention cheaper. Others, especially managers who are time-starved, find sales recruiters to be very cost-effective.

The midway approach between do-it-yourself hiring and sales recruiters is having a good Human Resources department. If you have one, HR personnel can save you significant recruiting and screening time. The ideal scenario is a Human Resources person dedicated to the sales department. That allows her to learn your sales culture and unique needs. If handled effectively, a few minutes spent briefing Human Resources should save you hours of efforts. It still helps, however, to stay actively involved with the hiring process. For example, your networking can help proactively identify a lot of quality candidates that Human Resources could not.

Whether or not you use outside consultants, the process of hiring can be separated into two phases: recruitment and selection.

Recruitment: The First Step to Success

The better your recruitment, the easier your selection. Strong recruiting increases the quantity and quality of "best available reps," which, in turn, decreases the chances of hiring mediocre reps. The best time to recruit is well before you have a job opening, therefore allowing you to avoid the rush of hiring in a hurry. Make your recruiting proactive rather than reactive. Doing so means you'll have a list of candidates well before you have a job opening. Another advantage of proactive recruiting is the opportunity to choose from candidates who are happy with their current job as opposed to dissatisfied, malcontented candidates who could easily carry over their discontent into your group. Recruitment is the prospecting phase of hiring, identifying people who have the people and organizational skills to help your sales efforts. This is an organized, orderly, and full-time process involving daily contacts and networking.

Daily Contacts: Finding Diamonds in the Rough

Consider your life a talent search. You can find prospects everywhere, every day if you're alert. The best candidates are those with people skills who are underpaid, making only a fraction of what they could make in sales. Following are a few examples of prospects—including experienced and inexperienced sales candidates—who could be waiting to be discovered:

- Servers and hosts/hostesses at restaurants are traditional candidates for sales jobs since they usually make a living with their people skills.

- Clerks at retail and service businesses ranging from cleaners to tire companies to jewelry stores may possess learned and innate sales skills.

- Receptionists at your doctor, attorney, or dentist may have superior organizational and people skills.

- Telemarketers who call you at home may be a source of experienced sales reps for your firm.

- Door-to-door salespeople might be looking for higher pay and be receptive to your recruitment effort.

- Bank and credit union tellers could bring a combination of conscientiousness and people skills to your sales team.

- Salespeople who call on you at the office are always possible candidates because of their experience in your industry.

- Your customers might also provide recruitable prospects. Many know when their favorite reps are looking for a job. They might refer these favored salespeople to you with the hope of retaining the relationship with the rep even if it's through a different firm (your company).

- Home contractors in such businesses as lawn care, pest control, security systems, and flooring spend a big part of their day selling—developing skills that can be beneficial to you.

- Satisfied users of your product can be groomed and recruited as salespeople.

- Attendees at trade shows and industry conferences could be familiar with your product or industry and may be open to hiring.

- Sales people from your competition can also be hiring prospects, possibly bringing a wealth of knowledge to your sales force.

- In-house employees from your company—receptionists, secretaries, sales support people, and those from other departments—might also have an interest in and aptitude for sales.

- People looking for sales jobs online—or even those seeking information about your company for other reasons—can be recruited through your Web site, LinkedIn, social media, and other job sites.

Observing people on the job is more valuable than any amount of interviewing unknowns. These interactions even give you the chance to see how they react to stress and challenges. Do they show patience and persistence in difficult situations with you and other customers? Do they maintain rapport with co-workers as well as customers? Is their customer charm genuine or do they roll their eyes or berate customers behind their back? Do they go the extra mile or just offer what's expected? Your close observation—especially over time—will answer many of these questions. In addition, you can test them with small stressors such as asking difficult questions or making changes to such things as your payment method that require more effort on their part.

What to look for are people who excel *because* of difficulty, not *in spite* of it. They expect challenge and they problem-solve their way out of it in a composed and pleasant manner rather than with grudging compliance. They have the ability to remain goal-oriented, aligning themselves with the customer even in tense situations in which they refuse to take angry statements personally. The important thing is not their actual sales experience, but their interpersonal skills and persuasiveness. In fact, hiring inexperienced sales prospects means you have a blank slate with which to work, and you don't have to worry about "untraining" the bad habits of experienced sales people. To further elaborate on the list of sales prospects noted earlier in this chapter, here are six places to find quality, inexperienced candidates who might be attracted by the challenge, freedom and income of a sales job:

- Restaurants—Waiters have a constant challenge of dealing with hungry people. Many are natural salespeople by virtue of being experts in handling grumpy people with lowered blood sugar levels. Their tips depend on their people skills, much like in the sales profession. In addition, they have to react quickly to customers' requests and provide follow-up throughout the transaction.

- Hotels and tourist attractions—Employees in the hotel and tourism industries are usually screened for their ability to align with guests and make visitors feel welcome. Furthermore, many receive training that further hones their natural people skills and sharpens their responsiveness to customers' needs.

- Customer exchange/return desks—These representatives learn impulse control and empathy by working with dissatisfied customers. Granted, many are as animated as a concrete block, but there are diamonds in the rough who could be quality salespeople. The ones who remain enthusiastic, even at the end of the day, may have the mental toughness that could make them a top seller.

- Banking and investment centers—Money is always a sensitive issue with customers. Bank tellers, credit union employees, and others in the financial industry learn to think on their feet to maintain customer rapport. Many are trained to provide friendly service with a trustworthy demeanor—important characteristics for sales people.

- Medical offices—Dealing with sick or injured people and their relatives also requires the same types of traits that make salespeople successful. Receptionists, even answering-service employees and other support people for doctors and dentists, often develop people skills that help soothe patients and put them at ease. The ones who combine these interpersonal skills with drive and initiative might make good sales people.

- High-traffic purchase points—This includes people who handle long lines of customers at airlines, movie theaters, and motor vehicle registration offices, as well as fast food and discount stores. The good candidates are the ones who are underpaid and have mastered the art of dealing with discourteous customers. If they can handle the vagaries of sitting in one place and enthusiastically handle impatient people in rapid-fire order, they might appreciate the freedom and pay offered by your sales job.

Engaging these prospects in casual conversation will give you a further feel for their initiative, competitiveness, and conscientiousness (the most important characteristics of top salespeople). When you're sure you have a candidate, ask whether the person has considered a career in sales and mention the earnings potential and other advantages of sales jobs. The next time you have an opening, these people can be a valuable source of applicants.

Networking Can Yield Top Job Prospects

Just as you use networking to make sales, use it for recruiting too. You should proactively exchange information about job candidates on an ongoing basis to those in your network, and they are the first people you want to notify of a job opening. Make sure your business and social network includes the following people and groups:

- Business associates and peers are important because they know your business and are familiar as well with the type of sales person who would be a good fit for you.

- Your vendors and suppliers can alert you to qualified candidates who have experience in your industry and might be looking for a job.

- Friends and relatives probably know a little about your business but more about you and the type of candidates who can match your needs.

- Neighbors can help you expand your pool of candidates through their contacts outside your normal business connections.

- Church members are another source who can provide prospects with whom you would not otherwise be exposed on a routine basis.

- Educators, especially at local universities, can provide high-potential applicants who are current students or alumni.

- Members of service clubs such as Rotary and Lions clubs (many of whom are sales people and hiring managers) frequently help each other find job candidates.

- Members of professional groups such as sales and marketing associations or your local Ad Club are another source for identifying seasoned sales people.

- Those with whom you have online contact through social media—such as LinkedIn and Facebook—can help build relationships with hiring prospects in addition to posting job openings.

- Your employees are an excellent source of identifying and referring quality candidates with relevant experience.

- Other managers inside your company—both sales and non-sales personnel—can be equally effective in your recruiting efforts.

There are hundreds of other networking opportunities that can yield successful sales candidates. But one single thread runs through effective networking: You have to *cultivate* your network contacts. Not only do you have to stay in touch with them, even when you don't have a job opening, but you have to be sure to help them find good candidates. You have to forward prospects to others—even on an unsolicited basis—as well as receiving them.

The Science of Selection

After you have your candidates identified, the science of selection begins. The two overriding questions you need to answer are, first, "Can the candidate sell?" and, second, "Can he or she sell successfully for us?" Documented sales results will answer the first question, telling you whether the candidate has performed successfully in other sales jobs. The second question is the tough one, requiring you to predict how the applicant's past success will be transferred into your organization. Unless you're one of the fortunate few who have mastered the mysteries of hiring, you've probably suffered through baffling transformations in which you've seen sure-bet candidates turn into wimpy sales reps within a matter of months. Is it possible to really predict success from the résumés and a few hours of interviews? No. But there are ways to increase your odds:

1. **Develop a profile of your ideal candidate**—This first step serves as a foundation for all your selections. Create a profile of the skills, aptitudes, and personality traits necessary to be successful in your organization. Tailor the profile to your particular environment—avoid generalized profiles of ideal salespeople or even successful sales reps in your industry. Your profile has to specifically address the needs, requirements, and structure of your particular company. Do not develop the profile in a vacuum. Get your sales reps' input, as well as that of your administrative clerks and anyone who has daily contact with salespeople. Team input will add perspectives that the sales manager might overlook. Look at your superstars—what characteristics do they have that you want? Analyze their performance and ask them what traits you should be looking for. On the other hand, look at your low performers and make note of the things you should avoid. Create a profile of the attributes you're looking for in priority order, for example, ambition, tenacity, closing skills, new business acumen, initiative, organization skill, ability to fit within your firm. Put your profile down in writing and make it available to your team. Develop a checklist for use by everyone in the interview process. More importantly, develop interview techniques and questions that will expose the traits for which you're looking.

2. **Get your team involved from the start**—Get their input on candidates, interview questions, and selection criteria. Have your sales reps interview candidates. They can provide you with a lot of street smarts in hiring that can be invaluable. In addition, it gives them a sense of involvement that helps build morale and

trust. If they've been involved, they're more likely to welcome the new hire and offer support. After all, your reps were part of the selection process, and they should want to do everything possible to prove they were right in selecting this candidate. In addition, ask other managers or staff people you trust to interview candidates. Usually three interviewers per candidate is a good number, providing ample input without wearing out the interviewee. Ideally, the three would include you, a sales rep, and another sales manager.

3. **Develop a list of questions and interview techniques**—This list will be used to expose your desired qualities in candidates. Develop a script to ensure uniformity and comparability among candidates. Ask everyone the same interview questions and take notes. Don't trust your memory, especially if you're talking to three or more candidates. Also, list interview techniques and tactics to be employed by interviewers. For example, if you're looking for an applicant strong in fact-finding, instruct your interviewers to provide intentionally vague answers about the job's specifics. Then see how well the candidate performs at questioning the interviewer.

4. **Ask behavioral questions based on their past job performance**—For example, don't ask, "Are you good at closing the sale?" Instead, ask for an example that typifies how the applicant closed the sale. Ask for specific examples that exhibit actual behavior: What was your best sale and how did you make it? What was your biggest failure and how did you react to it? How did you deal with a difficult customer?

5. **Ask "control questions" to establish a candidate's honesty**—For example, assume you're looking for a strong closer. If you simply ask the candidate whether she is a strong closer, you can bet the answer will be yes. So ask a number of "control questions" that are factual in nature and that you know the answer to. Ask what jobs the candidate has held in the past three years or where she went to college and what she majored in. Make note of her eye movement and body language in answering these factual questions. Then ask whether she is a strong closer and see

whether the body language changes. If the applicant looks to the right when answering control questions, then looks to the left when asked about being a strong closer, she could be hiding an inability to close. Look for other changes in body language, such as hand gestures, shifting in her seat, or a change in voice volume that did not appear during the control questions.

6. **Quantify sales achievements**—Ask candidates for sales reports year-to-year, as well as W-2 forms and other sales metrics and ranking reports from their past and present jobs. Analysis of candidates' results from the past can make predicting success easier. And most salespeople will have numbers to share if you ask.

7. **Probe to predict future success**—Remember that past behavior predicts future success. We, as sales managers, sometimes overestimate our transformational power, thinking that "This candidate has average credentials but I can turn him into a winner." The fact is that past performance will be repeated in the future. It's important to probe to discover candidates' past sales success (hopefully supported by verifiable numbers) but also have candidates describe such things as how they prospect, manage their time, set appointments, and organize their daily activities. If they're not doing these things well now, they probably won't be doing them effectively later.

8. **Don't hesitate to throw in a few tricks**—For example, say, "I disagree with your statement." and see what the response is. Or provide objections to overcome, such as telling the candidate that he might not be a good match for your firm, and observe how he responds.

9. **Consider role-playing exercises for candidates**—Some firms have elaborate half-day role-playing programs in which applicants sell a product to a fictitious company. Some even have two or more employees posing as "clients" for the candidate to sell to. Key components of these sessions include the following:

   ■ An information packet on the mock company is provided to the candidate. This tests the candidate's reading comprehension, ability to recall information during the presentation, and skill at organizing the details into the sales pitch.

- Those from the hiring company playing the decision-maker role are provided scripts that include objections to overcome as well as questions referring to the information packet to test the candidate's recall. In addition, questions are asked that don't pertain to the packet, requiring the candidate to think on her feet.
- Challenging scenarios are provided during the role play, such as a second "decision maker" entering the room to test the candidate's ability to perform when presented with unexpected situations that require flexibility, resilience, and patience.
- Participants from the hiring company are given checklists to note applicants' strengths and weaknesses.

On the other hand, role playing can be a simple, impromptu 10-minute session. Despite its complexity, a role-playing exercise can help you assess the candidate's capabilities, skills, and aptitudes.

10. **Look for potential disconnects**—Someone selling in a 30-day sales cycle might have trouble adapting to a 180-day cycle. A commission-only rep might not adapt to a more structured and formal salary/commission environment. Also consider product complexity: A magazine ad salesperson might not be suited for selling high-tech network services. Or someone selling to corporate midmanagers might be less successful selling to CEOs. Perhaps these disconnects are just small speed bumps. At best, they will slow down your onboarding of the candidate. And time is money. At worst, they can derail a candidate's viability.

11. **Similarly, pay close attention to the applicant's present work environment**—You'll want to get a feel for the candidate's current organizational structure, amount of administrative assistance, training requirements, work hours, emphasis on new business, number of weekly meetings, quantity of paperwork, and work rules. If their present environment is too dissimilar from what yours offers, there could be adjustment problems.

12. **Ask the candidate how a previous boss would describe him or her**—Next, ask whether you can talk to the boss. You wouldn't

expect to be able to contact the present boss but previous ones should be accessible. Ask them two questions:

- "What characteristics make this salesperson successful?"
- "What do I need to provide to make the candidate effective?"

Answers to these questions will provide insights that help you match the applicant's abilities to your needs, as well as revealing a candidate's needs that you might or might not be able to meet.

In checking other references, make sure that they are really familiar with the candidate's job, and ask about the duties of the job, company expectations, and the candidate's level of goal attainment. In other words, make sure that the reference is well aware of the candidate's work procedures and performance. Avoid references from colleagues and "character references" because you already know what they are going to say.

13. **Check your network contacts informally**—Ask whether they know anything about the candidate. These casual discussions can be highly beneficial in fact-finding. Go to vendors, competitors, customers, and business acquaintances who might know the candidate in a working environment. You can also go to LinkedIn to find people the candidate has worked with in the past.

14. **Ask these four questions of each candidate:**
    - How do you deal with your worst customer?
    - How do you deal with your best customer?
    - What was your best sale?
    - What was your worst failure?

    Don't ask the candidate the obvious question, "What did you learn from your failure (or success)? Wait to see whether the candidate offers these insights. If so, that's a good sign that shows trainability and the ability to learn from good and bad situations.

15. **Check "fake good" answers**—This is a common occurrence in which candidates answer questions according to what they *think* you want to hear. However, sometimes, "fake good" questions are given to hide a deficiency. In personality tests, a test taker will

"fake good" by answering "no" to questions such as "Have you ever lied?" or "Have you ever stolen anything?" Most people have lied or stolen something at least once, so a "no" answer immediately raises a red flag. For example, a candidate who wants to hide a weakness, such as a lack of ability to prepare for sales calls, might give an extreme answer to the question "Have you ever gone into a sales call without preparing for it?" An extreme answer would be "no," which rings untrue because we have all, at one time or another, been ill-prepared for a call. As test designers do, work in a discrete follow-up question on the same topic, rephrasing it, such as "Please describe your best sale this week," and see how preparation is addressed in the answer.

Other "fake good" test questions include "Have you ever exaggerated the benefits of a product to make the sale?" to test integrity or "Have you ever expressed anger at a customer?" to test self-control. The honest answer to both of these questions is "yes." A "no" answer indicates "faking good."

16. **Disguise your questions to avoid "fake good" answers**—For example, if closing is a major characteristic that you're looking for in a candidate, ask a ranking question such as "Please rank the following four items of a sales call in order of your strengths, strongest to weakest: presentation, preparation, close, and follow-up." Or ask the candidate any of the "Describe your best..." questions to see how she addresses your particular characteristic. Don't tip off the candidate to your interests to avoid patronizing answers. If you're looking for great presentation skills, don't tip your hand. Otherwise, after the candidate knows what you're looking for, you can bet the answers are going to be contrived to meet your needs.

17. **Look for listening and new business skills**—Two major success indicators for sales jobs are people skills (the ability to relate to and persuade customers to buy) and ambition (the drive, energy, and self-discipline to get the job done). Two shortcuts to determine these qualities in candidates are, first, observing their *listening skills.* Do they listen carefully before speaking? If so, this indicates empathy, patience, and the ability to genuinely

connect with the customer. Second, to determine ambition, focus on candidates' attitude toward and accomplishments in acquiring *new business*. This is the one single barometer that signals tenacity and follow-through. And it should be easy to determine by asking candidates to provide the appropriate documentation for new business achievements.

18. **Observe the candidate's quality and quantity of questions asked**—Too many questions in general might indicate a lack of self-confidence. Too few questions might show a lack of real interest in the job, or it could mean that the candidate is more interested in talking about himself than really learning about the position.

    Excessive questions about pay, benefits, vacation, and other banal subjects might be a sign that the candidate's priorities are in the wrong place. (By the way, these candidates are usually the ones who spend more time figuring their commission and vacation days than they do selling.)

    Do the candidate's questions show that he has done some homework, and understands your organization? The preparation he spends on the interview is an indication of how he might prepare for customer presentations.

    Does the candidate ask questions that seek to understand you as a person, your goals and ambitions? If he tries to understand you personally, it's likely he'll have the inquisitiveness to effectively reach customers.

19. **On the other hand, make sure you ask probing secondary questions**—Usually a candidate's first answer to a question is the rehearsed answer. To get to the revealing truth, drill down with secondary questions such as these:

    - "That's interesting. Could you tell me more about that?"
    - "What did you do to accomplish that?"
    - "What were the most important things you did to make that happen?"
    - "That's impressive. How many obstacles did you have to overcome to achieve it?"

As you probe, look for details that substantiate the story. People provide details about things they really did. Generalities and vagueness indicate a fabricated or embellished story. Don't hesitate to ask for specific details or steps taken to accomplish an achievement.

20. **Seek people who love selling**—For real sales naturals, sales is something they have always done. It's more than a job. It's a lifestyle. It provides them independence, challenge, creativity, income, and satisfaction. They would do it even if it didn't pay well, because that's what they do. Overcoming rejection and failure, to them, is like brushing your teeth—it's something you do everyday because that's the way sales is. Questions that will disclose the real salesperson are questions like these:

   - How long have you been selling? (The ideal answer would be "Since I was a kid.")
   - How do you react to failure? (Look for answers like "It's just part of the job." Beware of answers that indicate the candidate is affected too much by failure.)
   - Have you ever moved to another job and taken a pay cut? (Look for answers that indicate the candidate's love for selling over pay, benefits, and status.)

Don'ts of Hiring

Don't make the candidate too relaxed. Be sure to set an amiable, friendly tone to give the candidate a good first impression. After all, you are selling yourself and your company to the candidate. But don't hesitate to include a few difficult moments to uncover possible red flags. Inject a few subtle stressors in the interview to see how the candidate reacts to difficult questions or challenging statements.

Don't be afraid to put the applicant on the spot. Ask her to sell you something—a pen, a paper clip, a smartphone. Give the applicant objections to overcome, make it difficult. This will give you a feel for her presentation style as well as her patience, resilience, and mental agility.

Don't educate the applicant—interview him. Instead of starting the interview with information about your job and company, begin by asking candidates questions about themselves. This technique will help you learn about candidates before they have enough details about your job opening to say what they think you want to hear. Also, as noted earlier, don't tell the candidate the particular qualities you're looking for, to further avoid "fake good" responses. Give them no more than the basic information of the job, such as pay, hours, territory, travel, and general responsibilities. Then subtly probe for the skills you need. Make sure everyone interviewing the candidate follows the same line of interviewing. Be sure not to talk about past successes and failures of the sales team or specific team dynamics. This kind of information helps the applicant shape his answers, sometimes bending the truth to meet your needs.

Don't try too hard to make the candidate like you. Your job is to uncover red flags and unearth weaknesses. Don't be Mr. Nice Guy. Seek the truth. You can do it in a friendly, nonthreatening way. Most candidates expect some challenges in job interviews. The trick is to handle it in a way that leaves enthusiasm and respect for the position in the candidate's mind.

Don't include more than three people in the interview process. This way, you'll avoid overcomplicating and possibly overwhelming the candidate. It's always better to get a second and, maybe, third opinion on candidates but be careful not to overdo it.

Don't assume that the candidate has natural people skills. Our ranks are full of salespeople who are boorish, insensitive, impatient, and unempathetic. In particular, probe and observe the candidate's listening skills. Good listeners are likely to have other requisite people skills, such as empathy and engagement; a poor listener is prone to be self-absorbed and confrontational.

Don't let yourself like the candidate too much. Remember, that's the salesperson's job—to be liked. He will lay on the charm with hopes of making a favorable impression. Make yourself immune to it, remembering that likability is important but only part of the mix. Be sure your candidate's magnetism is backed up by numbers. There are a lot of engaging salespeople with mediocre results.

Don't rush into hiring "ricochet" candidates. Beware of applicants who are displeased with their present job, as well as those who are out of work (or who might soon be out of work). Like a stray bullet, they're ricocheting from one job in a random search for another. If you hire them, it's likely they'll stay just as long as it takes to find the job they really want. To identify the viability of stop-gap applicants, ask them these probing questions early in the interview before they learn about your specific sales culture—this decreases the chance of "fake good" answers to your questions:

- What do you like or dislike about your present or previous employer? This question will tell you more about the candidate than the employer, and reveal how he or she might fit into your organization.

- What specifically attracts you to our company and this job? Look for answers showing that the applicant has taken the time to study your organization. Preparation is usually a sign of genuine interest.

- Do you consider this job an upgrade to your present or previous job? The expected answer will be "yes," but continue to probe to have the applicant compare pay, travel, and working conditions. Someone who is willing to take less pay or travel more might be desperate for a job, any job. If he doesn't really view the job as an upgrade, he probably won't be around very long.

- Where do you see yourself five years from now and how to you plan to get there? The answers to this question will indicate the potential match between the candidate's aspirations and your company's opportunities.

In addition, look for evidence of "job jumping" from one sales position to another, which could indicate performance or personality problems with the candidate. And, as always, require that the candidate provide quantification (sales reports and W-2s) that further indicates sales deficiencies that might cause the candidate to look for a new job.

Don't overcompensate for current deficiencies in your sales team by placing too much emphasis on one characteristic over others. For example, if your present team is weak in setting appointments, don't place too much emphasis on that characteristic and deemphasize other basic, and more important, sales traits. Otherwise, you can hire a great appointment setter who, for example, can't close sales.

Don't get hung up on open-ended versus closed-ended questions. Open-ended questions beginning with "how" and "why" will help the applicant form her response coherently. But don't hesitate to throw in closed-ended questions requiring only a "yes" or "no" answer. Then let the applicant fill in the blanks. This will give you insight into the candidate's initiative and comfort level with the question. Beware of one-word answers.

Don't hire another rep before you know why the previous one didn't work out for you. Be sure to have detailed exit interviews with departing sales reps that include good fact-finding questions. If sales reps were asked to leave, do you really know why they failed? Don't settle for simplistic answers like they didn't have strong selling skills or they were too disorganized. Look beyond the obvious and determine how you could have developed them to be successful. Better yet, ask them what the real problem was and whether it could have been averted. Probe to get to the root cause for someone lacking sales success. It could be you, it could be the company, it could be the product line or numerous other issues. But make it your job to know. This knowledge will tell you what characteristics to look for in candidates but also can tell you what internal issues need to be addressed to develop and keep salespeople. Likewise, and equally important, examine why a successful salesperson left for a better job. Did the rep go elsewhere for more money? Or was it better working conditions? Getting to honest answers can help you make changes to retain good people, and it can help you determine the qualities you're looking for in applicants.

Hire for Traits, Not Skills

Sometimes we get enamored with a candidate whose experience and skill set match our needs. He's the guy who has worked in the same industry, handling the same kind of accounts, selling a similar product. It's like harmonic convergence. The stars aligned when he walked in the door. He was hired and started selling immediately with little need for training. Two years later, he was an average rep with mediocre numbers and little potential to improve.

The problem is he was hired for his skills, not for his traits. Sales skills and industry knowledge can be trained. The important thing is to hire salespeople who have the right mix of personality traits and aptitudes that predict long-term success. In fact, an inexperienced candidate who's a good listener, articulate, honest, and dependable might perform better in the long run than a veteran with years of experience selling in your industry. Hire for potential, not experience.

Who's Your Best Candidate—Extrovert, Introvert, or Ambivert?

We all know the stereotype of a successful salesperson being an extroverted, gregarious, back-slapping type. However, the more management experience we have, the more we find this isn't the case. Many successful salespeople are more introverted than extroverted. In fact, your best new hire might not be an extrovert or an introvert. They might be an "ambivert," someone who is midway between, having the best of extroversion and introversion without all the extremes of either.

This personality type is discussed in a recent study of salespeople by Adam Grant, The Wharton School, University of Pennsylvania. In his study, Grant found ambiverts to outperform extroverts by 32% and introverts by 24%.

To fully understand ambiversion, first consider the key characteristics of extroversion and how they can impede sales:

> **Sociability**—Extroverts thrive on human interaction, an essential ingredient for sales transactions. However, they might spend so much effort relationship building that professional expertise and product acumen take a back seat. Customers tend to become friends rather than associates. This can create friction in myriad ways, for example, when customers don't have time for socializing with sales reps. Or when customers—those who are more analytically oriented—want to get right to the point and avoid the small talk. Many times extroverts' friendships with customers lead to friction because they might take things personally, such as a customer's reluctance to buy. Sociability is a good door opener but has to be regulated for optimal sales.

Talkativeness—Never at a loss for words, the extrovert is adept at maintaining a conversation; however, there is a tendency to talk and not listen, which can be a huge hurdle in sales. Customers want to know that their opinions count, and that the sales rep hears their needs.

Assertiveness—Extroverts feel comfortable expressing their positions, their wants, and their needs. This trait sometimes is interpreted by the customer as being too pushy or self-interested.

Excitability—Enthusiasm is a hallmark of the extrovert. Sometimes it's contagious; other times it undermines the credibility of the salesperson. This characteristic occasionally leads the extrovert to overstate the benefits of a product or make unwarranted claims of product effectiveness. In addition, it can raise a red flag that the extrovert is more interested in persuading the customer than in discovering the customer's concerns.

Attention seeking—Extroverts enjoy being the center of attention. This frequently causes problems with customers who might feel that the rep is showboating and not paying attention to their needs. Extroverts can dominate conversations and inadvertently ignore or neglect customers' opinions.

On the other hand, following are the main traits of introversion and ways in which they can be counterproductive in sales:

Self-focused—Introverts are more self-aware than sociable. They are not energized by social interaction. The best sales transactions require an ability to engage the customer, which is not the introvert's strong suit.

Reserved—Quiet and reserved around people they don't know, and in group settings, introverts are not always capable of making customers feel at ease. Sometimes this social awkwardness hurts their sales ability.

Private—Introverts frequently keep their thoughts and feelings to themselves. And even though the thoughts might be more meaningful and profound than those of their extroverted counterparts, the inability to express them gets in the way of building rapport quickly with customers.

Bored by small talk—Introverts find small talk tedious and are more likely to need deeper, meaningful conversation. This puts the real introvert at a distinct disadvantage since most sales begin and end with small talk.

By bridging the gap between extroverts and introverts, ambiverts use the following characteristics to energize their sales ability:

Engagement—This means having the ability to apply sociability prudently. That is, to build rapport in a way that works for the customer, laying on enough charm to be effective but recognizing the customer's time constraints and personality makeup.

Listening—The ambivert avoids the pitfalls of extroverts' talkativeness, by listening to the customer and asking questions to elicit customer comments.

Assertiveness—Ambiverts know when they are being pushy. They are adept at applying adequate pressure to close the sale, for example, but know when to back off.

Enthusiasm—Showing enough enthusiasm to interest but not overwhelm the customer, the ambivert maintains credibility by avoiding excessive product claims. Similarly, ambiverts regulate their enthusiasm to keep customers from feeling they are being manipulated or persuaded to buy something that might not be in their best interest.

Attention seeking—Though at ease in the limelight, the ambivert turns the attention on the customers, emphasizing their needs and requirements.

Essentially, the ambivert takes the extremes of the extrovert and regulates them to make the sale. In an employment interview, ambiverts will come off as more reserved, lacking the gregariousness of the extrovert. Their answers to your questions will be more thoughtful. They might sound less enthusiastic because they are not likely to use superlatives and make outlandish claims. All in all, they will appear to be less supercharged than extroverts and more realistic in their assessments. They might seem to be more "real" than many salespeople. They might express realistic concerns about the job or company that sound negative or lacking in confidence. The truth is that they are managing their enthusiasm to avoid overstatement or exaggeration. That doesn't mean they lack enthusiasm or confidence; it means they express it reasonably in a believable way. At the end of the day, the self-regulatory style of ambiverts can lead to credibility with customers that creates productive, long-term sales relationships.

During the job interview process, the extrovert is going to make you like him or her immediately. The ambivert will need time to grow on you. If you have to choose between the two, your intuition is going to lead you to the extrovert. Try to fight that intuitive response and look at all the data and the long-term sales potential. Your ambivert won't be as exciting or charming, but might be able to generate substantially higher sales productivity.

Personality Analysis: Leave It to the Pros

The most difficult part of candidate selection is personality analysis. Most of us don't even know ourselves, much less others. Not only do you have to consider hundreds of behavioral variations, but you also must take into account the environment in which the candidate will be functioning. Personality tests and consultants can simplify the process at costs ranging from inexpensive online tests to more costly custom-tailored programs provided by experts.

The Big Five as It Applies to Salespeople

It's best to leave it to the professionals, but there are a few things helpful to know about sales personalities as you progress through your selection process.

A number of studies have analyzed the psychological composition of successful salespeople. Many of the studies use the "Big Five" personality components, traditional measures used in professional behavioral circles. These five dimensions intertwine like a complex formula, each ingredient combining with the other in varying strengths to create the human personality. Each of the five is composed of subcomponents that determine the ultimate potency of the dimension. The Big Five and their defining elements follow:

1. **Extroversion versus Introversion**—This category broadly addresses the extent to which one seeks stimulation through the company of others. Extroverts are energized by associating with others, whereas introverts are not. Key elements include these:

   - Sociability, the level of gregariousness and engagement with people
   - Forcefulness, marked by assertiveness and a penchant to direct others
   - Energy, the ability to maintain a sustained level of activity
   - Adventurousness, a need to seek exciting, challenging situations
   - Enthusiasm, emanating positive emotions
   - Outgoingness, reaching out and extending oneself

2. **Agreeableness versus Antagonism**—The level to which a person agrees or rejects others' ideas and opinions. The two extremes of this dimension are friendly/compassionate as opposed to detached/analytical. The main components are these:

   - Trusting, lacking a suspicious nature
   - Altruism, unselfish concern for the welfare of others, empathetic
   - Compliance, being inclined to cooperate and collaborate
   - Modesty, being able to defer showmanship
   - Compassion, exuding sympathy and concern for people

3. **Conscientiousness versus Lack of Direction**—The hallmarks of this concept include being efficient and organized versus easygoing and careless; acting with planned rather than spontaneous behavior. These are the primary parts:

   - Competence, efficiently creating a desired effect with a minimum of energy
   - Organized, being able to place discrete elements in order
   - Dutifulness, acting carefully with cautious awareness
   - Achievement oriented, being competitive with the desire to reach goals and succeed
   - Self-discipline, self-control, and the power to regulate oneself

- Deliberation, thinking through situations as opposed to impulsivity

4. **Neuroticism versus Emotional Stability**—This is the tendency to experience unpleasant emotions easily. The polar extremes in this category are sensitive/nervous versus confident/secure. Components of neuroticism are the following:

   - Anxiety, negative feelings such as tension, stress, and nervousness
   - Anger, emotions that include hostility and irritability
   - Depression, influenced by discontentment and sadness
   - Self-consciousness, characterized by shyness and avoidance
   - Impulsiveness, feelings of uncontrolled moodiness and spontaneous behavior
   - Vulnerability, lacking confidence and self-assurance

5. **Openness versus Resistance to Experience**—People with a high degree of openness tend to be creative, inventive, and curious rather than consistent, cautious, and conservative. Six traits define this personality dimension:

   - Curiosity, seeking and embracing new ideas and concepts, having intelligence
   - Imaginative, having the ability to create innovative ideas and inventive solutions
   - Aesthetics, showing an interest in beauty as well as artistic and creative endeavors
   - Variety, the extent to which a person favors a variety of interests over a strict routine
   - Feelings, characterized by being open to emotion and being excitable
   - Values, a high level of openness usually including being receptive to diverse values, and concepts

Which Traits Make the Best Salespeople?

For the typical sales manager, personality analysis is like your car's dashboard. It's helpful to understand the symbols and gauges that signal engine problems, but leave the mechanical diagnosis to the professionals. First, there are numerous inexpensive (some free) personality tests online. Just enter "sales personality tests" in your search engine. You'll see hundreds of online tests you can obtain for your candidates. Similarly, you'll pull up hundreds of hiring consultants who offer testing, analysis, and hiring advice.

Hiring and testing consultants all have their own spin or brand, but many are based on the classic "Big Five" personality typology. Applying the Big Five to sales candidates is complicated, with hundreds of variables, but there are some generalizations that are useful for the untrained observer or interviewer. The key to considering these traits is to match them to your firm's sales environment and to your ideal candidate profile. Here are five of the major traits and how they contribute to sales effectiveness:

1. **Conscientiousness** ranks first as the key predictor of success. Salespeople ranking high in conscientiousness are reliable, responsible, and accountable. They function best when they control their accounts, and are likely to chafe at interference from management. They are likely to take command of the sales cycle. They take accountability for results. Conscientiousness has a number of subcomponents; following is their top-to-bottom ranking:

   - Competitiveness is imperative as an inner driver of sales motivation. On a scale of 10, many successful salespeople rank in the 6 to 10 range. Toward the top of the range, however, a manager should beware of those who are over-competitive, who believe in win-at-all-costs, and who might cross the boundaries of ethics and relationships to win.
   - Achievement orientation is invariably found at high levels in top performers. Fixated on goal attainment, they continuously measure their results in relation to objectives.
   - Competence and self-discipline also rank high because they enhance competitiveness and goal achievement.
   - Deliberation is vital because it helps moderate competitiveness and is a sign of impulse control. This component helps salespeople maintain customer rapport while moving toward the close.

- Organization and dutifulness rank lower. Both are important as basic processes to keep salespeople on track, but in higher ranges they can be a sign of rigidity and formality that can counter sales effectiveness.

2. **Agreeableness** is a characteristic that helps build rapport and trust with customers. Many customers view antagonistic traits (debating, arguing, and analytical tendencies) as being self-serving and contrary to the customer's needs. However, salespeople who are too agreeable or trusting probably are not able to effectively probe customers' objections and move assertively toward the close. In fact, a healthy amount of cynicism can lead the sales rep to uncover customer perceptions that more agreeable and trusting reps could not. Many studies show that more successful salespeople are more cynical than trusting.

   Perhaps the most important part of agreeableness to predict sales success is empathy. This trait helps sales reps react to verbal and nonverbal cues to adapt presentations to the customer. For example, the empathetic rep has the ability to read the customer who is getting impatient or irritated and adjust comments accordingly.

   Studies of another subset of agreeableness—modesty—might surprise you. Research has shown that a very high percentage of top salespeople are modest and humble. Contrary to our stereotype of the overbearing, ego-driven salesperson, the superstar is likely to be soft-spoken and collaborative rather than brash and flamboyant.

   A modicum of compliance is helpful in sales situations because it demonstrates respect for the customers, making them feel in charge of the transaction. The downside of compliance is the salesperson being persuaded to accept the customer's point of view, in effect being sold by the customer rather than selling to the customer.

   In rank order of success predictors, cynicism has an edge over those who are agreeable, trusting, and compliant.

3. **Extroversion** and its subcomponents are what we normally associate with sales success. Unfortunately, this perception is a myth. Those measuring high on extroversion frequently rank lower in actual sales performance. The reason, in general, is that they tend to talk too much and listen too little. True extroverts also are viewed as being pushy and manipulative. On a scale of 10, an extroversion ranking of 7 to 8 is optimal.

   Salespeople studied by Steve W. Martin showed lower levels of gregariousness to be associated with higher levels of performance. The top performers in the study were 30% less gregarious than lower-performing reps. More gregarious salespeople, according to Martin, might be too close to their customers and unable to establish influence over their decisions.

   The litmus test is that the sales candidate must be friendly and engaging enough to develop alignment with the customer—after all, it's important to be liked—but show enough empathy and selflessness to create a bond built by credibility. Extroversion is unequivocally necessary for successful salespeople, but it's most effective in moderate levels.

4. **Openness to experience** is a lesser indicator of sales success, research has indicated. In fact, many view it as a neutral criterion for hiring salespeople. The presence or absence of openness just doesn't have much of any effect on sales performance. However, there are subtraits of the openness category that are beneficial to selling: The "creative" subcomponent is usually thought to be the most useful sales trait in that it allows salespeople to develop new and innovative approaches to meeting customer demands and overcoming objections.

   Steve Martin's study showed that 82% of top performers exhibited extremely high levels of "curiosity," another component of openness. Active inquisitiveness enables sales reps to gain information on customers' business plans and procedures and thereby develop effective product applications. They are likely to probe and even ask difficult questions to close gaps in information.

"Variety" is another viable subset of openness since most reps are faced with various and sundry types of business, people, and situations on a daily—even hourly—basis. Top sales reps are likely to relish the variety of customer personalities and business environments. They might require a framework of rules and procedural guidelines from management, but they're energized by new and different situations they encounter daily.

5. **Neuroticism** finds its strength in its absence. Reps free of anger, anxiety, narcissism, depression, self-consciousness, impulsivity, and vulnerability are considered emotionally stable. Neuroticism is a self-selecting characteristic. In other words, people who have a predisposition toward depression, for example, are not naturally drawn to sales. And those who are depressed usually don't last too long.

Also pertaining to neuroticism, studies have shown that top sales performers have extremely low levels of self-consciousness (timidity and shyness). Essentially, they are not embarrassed to ask for the sale or to ask uncomfortable questions.

In addition, sales superstars also exhibit impulse control. They rarely blurt out the first thing that comes to mind. Their conversation is marked by "pregnant pauses" that allow them time for an appropriate response while encouraging others to offer additional information.

Though we all are neurotic in one way or another, those who show higher levels of emotional stability are likely to be more confident and resilient, traits that are needed to meet the many ups and downs of sales.

The Sixth Dimension

In the early 2000s, an additional dimension to the Big Five was developed. Honesty-humility, the sixth criterion, is part of a refined paradigm by Kibeom Lee and Michael C. Ashton. Research has shown that honesty-humility is a predictor of success in a variety of jobs, but little, if any, sales-specific research has been performed.

These are the subfactors of honesty-humility:

1. **Sincerity**—Being honest and unwilling to be manipulative toward others.

2. **Fairness**—Having integrity and treating others fairly and equitably.

3. **Greed Avoidance**—Showing little interest in wealth, status, money, or luxury.

4. **Modesty**—Seeing themselves as no better than anyone else as opposed to expecting special treatment from others.

The honesty-humility factor is important in sales because salespeople cannot sell to customers who don't trust them. Exaggerated product claims, overcharging, misrepresentations, and other breaches of ethics eventually will ruin a salesperson's career. Honesty and integrity allow a salesperson to establish credibility with customers that increases up-selling, cross-selling, and repeat sales year after year.

Harris Plotkin, of Plotkin & Associates, shows similar findings in research of top salespeople. According to Plotkin, "Experience shows that the best salespeople are honest, scoring high in 'character strength,' which is characterized as being honest, dependable, and straightforward in dealing with people."

In hiring your next candidate, consider the subcomponents of honesty-humility. Obviously, we all want reps with "sincerity" and "fairness." Customers respect—and buy from—reps who are authentic and have the character strength to sincerely discuss the pros and cons of products as they apply to the customer. These types of reps will give customers a fair assessment of product applications regardless of the impact on commissions or pay.

The relevance of the other two subcomponents—"modesty" and "greed avoidance"—are not as obvious, but are equally important. Even though we don't always think of salespeople as being modest, it is a key factor in sales success. In fact, Steve Martin's study found, "Contrary to conventional stereotypes that successful salespeople are pushy and egotistical, 91% of top salespeople had medium to high scores of modesty and humility."

In reality, hiring managers have to consider the other side of the coin: Sales requires a degree of showmanship and self-promotion—the antithesis of modesty. However, the two different traits can, and should, coexist in successful salespeople, with modesty serving as a moderator to showmanship. This balance of traits characterizes ambiverts, who might be your top sales candidates.

Another instance of balancing characteristics is "greed" versus the "greed avoidance" subcomponent of honesty-humility. Many sales compensation models are understandably based purely and simply on greed. After all, money is important to all of us in sales. In fact, many sales managers consider the amount of "money motivation" as a key hiring requirement. We know, however, from numerous studies that money is not a key concern of top salespeople. It is important but it's balanced by "intrinsic" factors such as a need for achievement and meaningful accomplishments. In fact, we all have seen how an overemphasis on money can lead reps to manipulate customers for financial gain. No matter how peculiar it sounds, the element of "greed avoidance" is certainly worth considering as a hiring criterion.

The key takeaway is that salespeople are going to have an expected measure of showmanship. And they might be a little greedy. But, at the same time, they still can rate high in honesty-humility, which is a leading criterion of sales excellence.

The Best Predictors of Sales Success in Rank Order

Conscientiousness is the strongest sales trait among the six personality dimensions, followed by these subclassifications:

- Competitiveness
- Self-discipline
- Assertiveness
- Empathy
- Honesty
- Extroversion in the moderate range (also typified as ambiversion)

Moderation is the key. Any or all of the key characteristics can become problematic if carried to excess. A sales rep can be too competitive and can offend customers as well as peers by pushing too hard. A rep can empathize too much with the customer and fail to overcome objections. An overly extroverted salesperson can simply overwhelm customers.

Look for moderating personality traits, that is, characteristics that can offset counterproductive traits. For example, candidates can be too empathetic—to the point where it might seem that they are being sold by the customer rather than selling to the customer. However, they might have enough assertiveness or achievement orientation to overcome an overabundance of empathy. An applicant with extreme extroversion can still be a top candidate if she has the moderating effect of empathy and listening skills. The same applies to someone with high levels of agreeableness who also shows assertiveness. Or the person who shows a bit of cynicism can be successful if she also is competitive and a good listener. Likewise, you might see signs of moderating traits such as honesty or compliance that can mediate "win-at-all-costs" competitiveness, openness that moderates the rigidity of ultraconscientiousness, and other combinations of traits that can equalize negative proclivities.

Every applicant you interview is going to have a complex mixture of personality components (hence the need for professional help in testing and assessing). In general, personality traits mix and intermingle to determine selling effectiveness. Balance is the key. A well-balanced candidate offers either a combination of moderate personality traits or a few extreme traits that are offset by others. Here's a simple way to look at it: Competitiveness and self-discipline are the fuel that drives high performers. Extroversion opens the door to customers while empathy and honesty keep it open.

A candidate with optimal levels of key personality traits should excel in most sales positions. However, there are exceptions. Hiring managers should carefully compare their organizational environment and particular sales requirements to the candidates' characteristics. For example, if your firm is in a fast-moving, high-tech business that requires salespeople to quickly learn and adapt to change, openness might be toward the top of your list. Or if you're selling private jets, your candidate would need to rank high in organization, having the ability to bring together a wide variety of technological, ergonomic, psychographic, and financial elements to make the sale.

Body Language Helps Identify Success Traits

Body language can help you identify the existence and extent of certain personality traits. One way to maximize your reading of body language is to remove the "comfort barrier" of your desk or table. Find a comfortable setting and sit directly in front of the candidate. This might take you and the candidate out of your comfort zone, but it allows you full view of the candidate's body language including feet and legs. In addition, it gives you a preview of how the candidate might handle an uncomfortable situation in a selling environment.

Here are a few nonverbal cues that signal certain personality characteristics:

1. **Honesty/Dishonesty**—This is the hardest of all traits to interpret from a brief hiring interview. Many people have learned to hide deception behind a steady gaze and consciously controlled physical gestures. Nevertheless, look for the following cues that could indicate an honesty issue:

   - When people are recalling information, they look to one side; when deceiving they will look to the opposite side. Upward eye movements, in general, might indicate dishonesty.
   - Steady eye contact might indicate honesty. Studies show that the optimal eye contact is about 70% of the time. But keep in mind that really good liars are masters of eye contact.
   - Touching the nose area, lips, or face indicates that you are hiding something.
   - Hand gestures above the shoulders might indicate exaggeration.
   - Rubbing one's hands can indicate stress brought on by deceitfulness. Hands stretched out and interlaced shows even greater stress.

- Dangling legs could indicate boredom, that the person might really not be interested in the job even though he says he is.
- Toes pointed away from you, the interviewer, indicates avoidance—a dislike for you or a need to get out the door.
- The misplaced smile can tell you plenty. For example, you tell a candidate that travel is part of the job. He smiles and says, "That's good!" His answer is probably an honest response. If he says, "That's good!" followed by a smile, that could be a dishonest answer.

2. **Assertiveness**—Typified by smooth and balanced nonverbal cues, assertiveness (not aggressiveness) can be identified by the following:

- Palms up as opposed to fists (which signals aggressiveness) or palms down (which shows submissiveness).
- Matching of facial features and gestures to words. Inexplicable or excessive smiling might indicate a lack of confidence/assertiveness. Similarly, excessive gesturing might be a red flag.
- Gestures are used sparingly to accentuate words rather than emphasize emotions.
- Hands and arms are held low with no barriers across the body. Hands are kept off the face. Arms raise occasionally to accentuate what's being said but return to a lower position, signaling openness.
- Legs and feet are relatively calm. No foot fidgeting or leg dangling occurs. Toes will point to you, the interviewer.
- Vocal volume rises and falls evenly, without sudden changes in loudness or quietness.
- Eye contact is steady; eyes don't dart about nervously, nor does the candidate stare or glance downward.
- "Steepling"—hands connecting with fingertips meeting to form a church steeple—indicates assertiveness and self-confidence.

3. **Competitiveness**—A gunslinger's body language typifies competitiveness:

- Sitting directly face-to-face, hands in front, shoulders squared, feet pointing forward, shoulders slightly forward. Many times, it's a friendly kind of "Let's get it going" attitude.
- Feet might fidget, which indicates impatience, which is a manifestation of time management.
- An accelerated, but not frenzied, pace of speaking. Many competitive people have a sense of urgency that makes their speaking and gesturing direct but controlled, lacking verbal or physical flourishes.
- Verbal one-upmanship is common among competitive types. They'll have a better story in response to yours. Instead of showing appreciation or asking questions, they will one-up your comments.

4. **Empathy**—This characteristic is hard to read through nonverbal cues, but the following three actions provide an indication:

- Mirroring—Empathetic people tend to mirror others' voice tone and body language.
- Facial expressions—You'll see a wide array of smiles, frowns, grimaces, and other expressions in reaction to another's comments (remember that empathy means you understand and feel others' opinions and emotions).
- Active listening—An empathetic person listens intently, which is symbolized by steady eye contact, nodding, repeating stated information, and asking pertinent questions.

5. **Self-discipline**—This characteristic is apparent through a number of behavioral, visual, and verbal cues:

- Punctuality—Self-disciplined people are on time. In the rare case of their being late, they will call to let you know.
- Appearance—They should appear well-groomed and neatly dressed, shoes shined, and their clothes having few wrinkles.

- Conversational style—Self-disciplined people practice impulse control, which means they might pause before they answer questions. This style helps them stay focused on the topic and maintain rapport.
- Sense of control—These types exhibit a controlled pace in speaking. They avoid big fluctuations in voice volume and inflection. Their gestures and inflection are synchronized to the words. Often, hands will rest calmly on the lap and raise only occasionally to emphasize a point. Other than an occasional change of position, the legs and feet are calm with toes pointed toward you.
- Preparation—They will come prepared. They will know your business and pertinent metrics. They will probably even know your industry and current trends. Their questions and answers will show that they have done their research.

6. **Agreeableness**—A few nonverbal signs indicate a person who is compliant, perhaps too passive to effectively close sales or fact-find. Here are a few ways to identify too much agreeableness:

- Excessive nodding indicates an overwillingness to agree, signaling a high level of acquiescence.
- A certain amount of mirroring is good in hiring interviews and in sales. Replicating a person's posture, gestures, and voice volume and pace can help establish rapport—too much of it signals an excessive degree of agreeableness or perhaps the inability to push for a sale.
- A "painted on" smile frequently indicates excessive agreeableness.
- Closed or confined body language might be a sign of being overly agreeable or submissive/defensive. This occurs when one takes up minimal space by slouching, feet and legs held closely together, an arm grasping the other arm or palms downward.
- Finishing another's sentences can be another sign of trying too hard to establish rapport.

7. **Openness**—You can usually tell how open a person is through simple nonverbal cues:

- Crossing your arms in front of the body says you're not open or approachable. (However, it can also mean you are concentrating on something.) Arms *and* legs crossed is definitely the opposite of openness.
- An open position is arms and hands held low with no barrier between interviewer and interviewee.
- Hands held behind one's back indicates stiffness and resistance to new ideas.
- Staring or not breaking eye contact indicates a lack of openness.

8. **Extroversion**—It's important to identify counterproductive levels of extroversion through these mannerisms:

- Hand-pumping or a handshake that's too hard. The two-handed "politician's handshake" is another sign of over-the-top extroversion.
- An interviewee reaching out first to give his arm full extension, which forces the interviewer to bend her elbow. This gives her less personal space while he has full expansiveness, denoting a subtle dominance over the interviewer.
- "Helicopter arms" or too many gestures around the shoulder area or above.
- Frontal hand gestures between the interviewee and the interviewer.
- Leaning forward toward the interviewer and other "expansive" body language, such as draping an arm around a nearby chair or males sitting with legs spread apart. Another sign is fingers spread apart when making gestures, which shows comfort and confidence, perhaps overconfidence.
- Voice volume and pace that's out of synch with the interviewer.
- Talking over another's comments, which is a sure sign of excessive extroversion.

Seven Tiebreakers

When we have two equal candidates, we all start looking for tiebreakers to help make the final decision. Invariably, our minds will naturally default to "Who do I like the most?" Fight that temptation. We would never admit it, but a salesperson's charisma alone can hold you in a Svengali-like state devoid of reason and logic, leading you to a poor decision. Following are seven logical tiebreakers—behavioral/personality components that will help you make a solid decision. None of these should be a major part of the hiring decision, but all are an important part of the mix.

1. **Hire those who are stress-tolerant**—Stress is pervasive in sales. It's counterproductive in that it can create distractions and anxieties that detract from sales efficacy. Stress also causes myriad health problems ranging from increased blood pressure to immune system maladies. Some salespeople are naturally impervious to stress. They are more likely to have fewer sick days, but even more importantly, they have the ability to stay focused and mentally robust.

   This isn't to say that reps subject to stress won't sell as well as others. On the contrary, their success rate can be as high as that of people who are stress-tolerant. However, they are likely to burn out faster and have a shorter sales career than stress-tolerant types. There is a time when stress takes its toll. The result might be increased absenteeism and/or decreasing sales ability.

   Stress-tolerant reps are "hardier" than others. They are likely to feel in control and have an appetite for challenge. They are optimistic, being able to cope with stress in proactive ways. Also, they use problem-solving coping techniques to manage stressful events. They emphasize the positive aspects of challenging events.

   Sensation seeking can also describe stress-tolerant people. They are easily bored and might prefer physical activities that provide risk such as mountain climbing, white-water rafting, or surfing. The downside is that these types are also prone to risky behaviors such as gambling, drinking, drug use, and sexual excess. In some cases, their sensation seeking is associated with criminal behavior.

As with all traits of successful salespeople, stress tolerance is best in moderation. You are looking for candidates who have this characteristic without the downside impacts. You want a candidate who channels stress tolerance into a healthy lifestyle. Too much is, indeed, a train wreck waiting to happen. Too little is a potential heart attack.

How do you identify stress-tolerant candidates? And how do you detect the appropriate amount?

First of all, your background check should uncover criminal activity as well as drug and alcohol abuse. If you perform drug tests before hiring, you'll have further validation. With the absence of inappropriate sensation seeking, here are the characteristics to look for:

- Optimism—The penchant for expecting good things to happen; seeing difficult situations as opportunities rather than threats.
- Challenge—A predisposition to enjoy challenging situations; the belief that change rather than stability is the normal course of life.
- Control—A sense of mastery to shape circumstances to achieve goals (the opposite of being helpless); believing and acting as though one's efforts can change situations.
- Commitment—The devotion to a task, job, and responsibilities; involving oneself rather than passively accepting circumstances.
- Self-esteem—A belief in the value of oneself characterized by such expressions as "I am competent" and "I am worthy."

Ask the candidate to describe a failed sales situation such as an account loss or an expected sale that fell apart. The stress-resistant candidate will take accountability rather than blame others. In telling the story, he or she will express active involvement in developing options to save the sale. This candidate is likely to explain the failure as a learning experience rather than a personal defeat. Also, the candidate you're looking for is not likely to express anger or resentment about the failure, but considers it simply part of the job.

2. **Emotional intelligence is an advantage**—It takes IQ and EQ to sell effectively. EQ (emotional intelligence) kicks in where sales training and rational thinking leave off. As noted in Chapter 1, "First Step: Manage Yourself," EQ is a vital trait for sales managers. It's equally important for salespeople. EQ is the ability not only to monitor and control one's emotions but also to read and respond to others' emotions. For example, we've all experienced unsuccessfully addressing a customer's objections. Going into the presentation, we knew the possible objections, and we had the answers ready. We flawlessly provided the proper response with perfect supporting data and a strong rationale to buy. However, the customer shrugged us off and remained obstinate. Perhaps the problem was that we were using only IQ (logic and cognition) rather than incorporating EQ to read and respond to the customer's emotions. A large body of research suggests that selling takes more than using skills, techniques, and "book learning." It takes street smarts, being able to read between the lines and respond to subtle customer cues.

Salespeople scoring high in EQ can identify with customers. They are able to focus on the customer's needs and problems. They are able to read customer's emotions by observing and interpreting facial expressions and body language. The process goes beyond simply recognizing customers' emotions. The high-EQ salesperson is able to link customers' feelings to the salesperson's own experiences. This helps salespeople adapt their message to customers in a way that is understandable, credible, and convincing. In addition, salespeople having EQ are able to help the customer express emotions effectively. On sensing a customer's irritation with a product feature, the high-EQ salesperson might say, "I can tell you're frustrated by its performance, and I don't blame you. I'd feel the same way. To help me solve the problem, can you tell me more about the ways it annoys you?"

Those with EQ have a sense of self-awareness. They are able to see how their actions and behavior are being received by customers, and adjust accordingly. They also have the ability of self-regulation to control their emotions. Instead of showing anger, frustration, and disappointment, they remain calm and stay focused on the sale. Moreover, these types are self-motivated, not relying on outside sources of motivation. These intrinsically motivated salespeople perform at high levels without the need for coaching, contests, or monetary rewards. They are internally driven people.

How do you identify EQ in candidates? They are usually curious, and likely to ask you questions about you as a manager and you as a person. In general conversation, they will show an understanding of their strengths and weaknesses (beware of candidates who don't voluntarily mention weaknesses).

Assertiveness is another critical part of EQ. They can negotiate with you (or a customer) while maintaining rapport. They have the verbal artistry, for example, to make a salary demand without sounding demanding. They can ask tough questions without offending. They assert opinions that could be contrary to your beliefs without alienating you.

They also show the ability to concentrate on the conversation without being distracted by sounds and visual stimuli. This talent helps them identify verbal and nonverbal tips to better understand you or the customer. Similarly, they are likely to keep their comments on track and avoid going off on tangents. To test their level of focus, arrange for distractions such as a ringing cellphone or people walking by, and observe the candidate's reaction. A candidate with concentration probably will not even recognize the distraction, much less turn her head or verbally pause.

Salespeople with EQ are intuitive. They rely on their instinct and show comfort making intuitive decisions. A simple question can demonstrate this quality: "Do you trust your intuition in making decisions or do you rely more on the facts?" Interviewees with EQ not only will say they are intuitive but are very aware of having this trait. Candidates who pause as if they never considered the question probably are not high on the EQ scale.

Candidates high in EQ will have a "real" conversation with you rather than playing the role of the job candidate. They will comfortably talk to you person to person, like a new neighbor who stopped by to chat. Instead of being poised and ready to pounce on the next question, they are likely to simply be exchanging information with you, telling you about themselves but wanting to know about you as well. Those low in EQ will be trying hard to impress you favorably, so hard that they will probably affect you negatively with their self-promotion and hyperbole. You can bet they will have the same effect on customers.

3. **Sports background is an edge**—Research indicates that people who have participated in high-school or college athletics might have an advantage over others. A few of the benefits gained by a sports background include these:

   - Knowing the value and dynamics of teamwork and being a team player

   - Learning resilience and resistance to setbacks

   - Being receptive to feedback and coaching

   - Having an ability to focus and to persist to win

   - Acquiring a sense of controlling one's destiny

   - Learning the value of practice, preparation, and self-discipline

   - Being able to assimilate data quickly and react accordingly

   - Knowing how to play by the rules of the game

   - Being familiar with the benefits of physical activity, nutrition, and diet

Not everyone with an athletic background is destined to be a super salesperson. Some learn only a few of the lessons of sports. However, the principles and required behavior in sports provide a match with sales that can serve as a possible predictor of success.

4. **Team players bring benefits**—Here's the thing about hiring team players: If you're serious about team building, hire people with team-player attributes. If you're not serious about team building, still hire people with team-player attributes. You see, many of

the things that make good team players make good salespeople. A word of caution: Instead of focusing on hiring a team player, hire a person with the attributes of one. Here's the difference. The defining characteristics of a team player do not necessarily include the key components of competitiveness and achievement orientation. Both are must-haves of top sellers. If you find a team player with these must-haves, you might have a real winner. But there's no assurance that a team player will have all the traits of the candidate you're looking for.

Team-player traits will help your candidate function successfully in a team environment. And there's a definite trend of companies, and sales groups, moving toward team orientations. The days of the lone-wolf salesperson are coming to an end. The new generation of salespeople—millennials—is likely to work better in a team atmosphere that provides affiliation, support, and sharing. They are accustomed to working in teams and intuitively see the value of cooperation.

Within the sales team, team players are able to collaborate and share information in a way that makes each a better salesperson. They tend to share information honestly and selflessly while communicating openly and amiably.

Outside the sales team, the team player is likely to reach out horizontally to other departments and nonsalespeople involved in delivering the product or service. Team players are likely to coordinate with technical and administrative people to prevent overpromising the customer. Working together, they avoid making customer commitments that can't be delivered on time or on budget. They are likely to bring in the foremen, the installers, the technicians, and others in charge of implementation after the sale. They are comfortable coordinating with a wide variety of personalities and skill sets. The result is post-purchase actions that match the terms of the sale. Not only does this make customers happy, but it also decreases in-house fighting and friction within the organization. In many cases, the attributes that make a good team player provide the salesperson with an aura of authority and believability.

How do you identify team players?

First of all, you're looking for the characteristics of openness, cooperation, flexibility, and dependability. These traits facilitate conflict management, a vital part of selling (and teamwork). Team players inherently have diplomacy and negotiating skills that they use on a daily basis with customers, and use in-house to avoid conflict and promote internal harmony within the sales team and among departments.

By the way, two characteristics that work against team playing are "dominant/controlling" behavior, a manifestation of excessive extroversion; and high levels of agreeableness, since teamwork requires assertiveness in the form of stating one's opinion.

During interviews, here are questions to ask to identify team players:

- "Is it possible to be an effective salesperson *and* a team player?" This is the seminal question that hopefully separates the team players from the lone wolves. Those who don't have the patience for teamwork will see it as an impediment. That doesn't mean they won't fit in, because all teams have their share of loners. In some cases, they can provide valuable reality checks for the team. However, lone wolves will be irritated at the time and energy spent in team efforts. Over time, some will adapt and benefit from teamwork, but a manager should be prepared for the worst-case scenario of a salesperson who always remains on the periphery. The obvious answer to this question is yes, followed by examples of working with other reps and post-purchase implementers within the salesperson's firm. Look for the words "we" and "us" rather than "I" and "my."
- "What's the value of teamwork in a sales environment?" Similar to the first question, this is aimed more at people with little team experience. It's a bigger-picture, open-ended question that requires a verbal essay. Especially look for answers pertaining to teamwork with other sales reps, which indicates the candidate's ability for open and candid communications. Be sure to probe and ask for examples.

- "What personality traits make you a good team player?" This is a more focused question requiring a measure of self-examination. The team player should be able to voluntarily offer examples without prodding. Look for and seek behavioral answers. In other words, you're looking for ways in which their actions have shown teamwork. In some cases, their behavior might match their self-proclaimed personality traits, such as the ability to get along with others. In other cases, their team behavior might occur *despite* personality traits that could inhibit teamwork, such as independent thinking, goal orientation, and competitiveness. The important thing to remember is that people can exhibit "lone wolf" characteristics but still have moderating traits that make them a team player.

- "Can you be a good team player and disagree with your sales manager?" This question is designed to elicit the assertiveness of a candidate. The best answer is something like, "Yes, in a diplomatic and constructive manner." Probe for real-life examples in which candidates have been able to assert themselves in a productive way.

- "Do you prefer working alone or as part of a team?" Answers to this question could be all over the board. Many salespeople can function effectively in both roles. Some might prefer working alone but can see the benefit in teamwork. Others will outright be opposed to teamwork. This question will usually separate the team players from the lone wolves.

- "Can you give an example of when being a team player worked against you?" Look for answers that might express animosity or lack of accountability. Some candidates could have a deep-seated opposition to teamwork that might show in answering this question. If they blame other team members for failure, chances are you have a problem. Many of us can answer yes to this question. If they answer no, you might have a "fake good" answer. The optimal answer is yes, followed by a nondefensive explanation and accountability for the problem.

The answers to these questions will depend to a great degree on the candidate's involvement with teams. Some might have experienced organized sales teams. Others, perhaps only casual one-time teams built around a specific task. Some might have experienced cross-functional teams or perhaps just self-initiated contact with nonsalespeople to implement the sale. Responses to the preceding questions obviously depend on the candidate's exposure to team dynamics. Nevertheless, the important thing is not looking for experience but looking for team aptitude. In all honesty, some who have worked in teams will find teamwork boring, frustrating, and confining. Others will find it liberating and empowering. Most will be in the middle, which might hold promise for them to be effective team players.

5. **Lone wolves can be "top candidates"**—Despite the fact that many loners don't fit well into modern sales teams, there are some who can be your best candidates. In some cases, a lone wolf deportment can be a tiebreaker. It's well known that salespeople love their freedom and independence, especially compared to their office-bound counterparts in other professions. It's not uncommon for an applicant to tell you they prefer working alone, making their own decisions. These self-avowed lone wolves can provide the best or the worst hires.

   With everything else being equal between two candidates, look for the lone wolf who has collaborative and cooperative characteristics. These candidates might provide the strengths of assertiveness, self-discipline, and competitiveness while offering the moderating traits of openness and cooperative skills. If you're moving toward a self-managed sales team, this is your kind of candidate. Even if you're beginning to give your sales team a little more empowerment and decision-making authority, these candidates can function effectively. Ironically, these lone wolves can make valuable team members because they might be able to work well with others. Chances are they are already working in a kind of team relationship with their customers. The uniqueness they offer a sales team is their independent thinking. They might have the ability to assert their ideas and positions diplomatically, without feeling a need to conform to group-think.

The lone wolf to avoid is the sales narcissist. This is the self-absorbed loner, interested primarily in making the sale and getting the commission. This candidate is likely to manipulate customers, peers, and superiors for selfish interests. Sales narcissists are comfortable breaking rules and developing their own code of conduct to suit their needs. These candidates can offer a short-term boost to your sales output, but in the long run are failures when customers and others realize their selfish motivation. Keep in mind that sales narcissists are smooth operators. They can be hard to spot in a job interview. If they have any inkling of what you are looking for, they will momentarily become that person to get the job.

The best way to identify them is to, first, closely conceal your requirements for the job. Then look for an abundance of "I" answers instead of "we" answers. Narcissists will embellish personal accomplishments and will take sole credit for achievements.

They like to talk about themselves but are loathe to talk much about others, and will probably have few questions to ask about you as a person. Narcissists are sensitive to criticism. Ask them a question impugning their skills or talents, such as "I see on your resume that you went three years without winning a sales award." Or "The longest you've stayed with any one company is two years." The response will be defensive in nature, blaming events or others rather than taking accountability. Some irritation might be visible as well in the voice and body language. Another tactic is to inquire about the applicant's long-term relationships with customers and former bosses. The narcissist is likely to have few long-standing relationships and probably won't have many customers or superiors with whom they have stayed in contact through the years. They also won't speak much about mentors because that would diminish their sense of self-grandiosity.

6. **A sense of humor is a plus**—A sense of humor is a plus for a job candidate because it can be a significant benefit to powerful sales transactions. When used appropriately, it can help maintain customer alignment and defuse tension. Humor helps overcome objections and close the sale. Humor can overcome deficiencies

in a rep's presentation and can even ameliorate customer irritation over billing or product problems.

On the other hand, when used inappropriately, humor can be a sledgehammer to relations. Some salespeople seem to be obsessed with being viewed as witty. They are likely to blurt out inappropriate humor irrespective of time, place, and people. They might generate laughs at the expense of others, and probably don't even realize it. If they're confronted about their inappropriate humor, it's certain their response will be something like "I was only joking. Come on, don't take things so seriously."

Essentially, regarding humor, there are three general types of people you will encounter from applicants: Those who are pretty much humorless, those who are inappropriately humorous, and those with a beneficial sense of humor. You don't have to probe to assess a sense of humor. It is as obvious as the candidate's hairstyle. Since it's pretty easy to identify a lack of humor, the biggest challenge is distinguishing between a productive sense of humor and an ineffective one. A sign of inappropriate humor is that which is biting and sarcastic and maligns others. Similarly, look for humor that aggrandizes the candidate while subtly putting down others. On the other hand, productive humor will show up as self-effacing humor, making fun of one's self or situation. Good humor can include puns or observations on the human condition that avoid criticizing people.

In addition, you can always ask the candidates how they have used humor to improve sales. Another tricky way to assess a sense of humor is looking for an appropriate time to ask the candidate, "Heard any good jokes lately?" It's an awkward question but it can be very enlightening. Those prone to bad humor will have a hard time resisting the temptation to blurt out their latest joke. It also can illuminate negative characteristics, such as impulsivity and lack of self-awareness.

7. **Would you want the candidate to be your boss?**—Another tiebreaker you can use is a concept employed by Mark Zuckerberg, founder of Facebook. He said, "I will only hire someone to work directly for me if I would work for that person."

Envision the candidate as your boss. Would he or she inspire you or intimidate you? Would you trust the candidate? Is the candidate sensitive to others' needs?

Obviously, this is not a top hiring criteria for salespeople because many, if not most, candidates have no interest or aptitude for managing. But as a tiebreaker, it can change your viewing perspective, which might give you new insights into the applicant. For example, let's say you're thinking, "I wouldn't work for this guy for a million dollars." The reasons might be that he's brash, loud, egotistical, or self-absorbed. Think about it. The qualities that make him a poor candidate for boss are the same traits that can hamper his sales ability.

If you had to hire your own boss, you'd look for many of the qualities that make a successful sales rep: fairness, initiative, conscientiousness, competitiveness, integrity, sincerity, cooperativeness, and selflessness. In the final analysis, these are the qualities that establish trust between the boss and subordinates, as well as reps and customers. After all, you're going to be turning this applicant loose on your customers to represent you and your company. You need someone who's responsible and accountable, not someone who's out there only to make quick sales for fat commissions.

A by-product of the hire-your-boss strategy is that you'll hire people with the potential to become sales managers, giving you a bigger pool of viable candidates when manager jobs open.

Red Flags to Consider

Some candidates don't reveal themselves until it's too late—when they're on the payroll, and either failing to produce or creating distractions for the sales team and manager. Here are red-flag situations to contemplate:

Natural-born salespeople—You know them, the ones exuding charm, poise, and grace. The ones you instantly like. Occasionally, they will describe themselves as "born to sell." They will be your best performers or they will be your worst. The ones with drive and discipline—those who work hard, prepare, and learn new skills—can be your top performers. Then there are the others, the ones who slide by on social graces. They are likely to walk into appointments with little preparation, and just figure out a way to get the signature. They are also slow to learn new skills. In a word, they are lazy. They will do just enough to get by but not enough to excel. In many cases, you can identify them by analyzing their sales numbers—through their detailed sales reports—which are usually average. Another way is to probe for their ability to prepare for sales calls and their enthusiasm for learning. These two elements will separate the winners from the also-rans.

Perfectionists—Many sales candidates are self-described perfectionists. And that can be a sign of a quality rep: one with attention to detail and uncompromising standards. However, it might also signal a candidate who can overcomplicate customer transactions to the point of losing the sale. The perfectionist might try to add just one more detail—a cross-sale, for example—and see the whole transaction fall apart. Perfectionists—having an eye for detail—sometimes are overwhelmed by minutia and have difficulty meeting deadlines and completing tasks. Functional perfectionists, the ones who make good candidates, are the ones who can get 90% of the job done and then move on rather than spending excessive time fussing over the remaining 10% of details. The good ones have learned to take advantage of the best options available rather than procrastinating for the perfect option to appear. They also are the ones who avoid getting caught up in the details of a sale to the point where they lose the big picture of the customer's reaction. To identify those with over-the-top perfectionism, probe for their ability to meet deadlines (those who wait until the last minute might be excessively perfectionistic). Likewise with those who have uncompleted projects, whether hobby, home, educational, or job-related tasks. Finally, look for conversational cues: Perfectionists tend to go into more detail than needed to make sure you understand them.

Sales Narcissists—Chapter 1 noted that narcissists make poor managers. They also are ineffective salespeople. The sales field is populated with these self-absorbed types, and chances are you have encountered them frequently on the job. Many times, they show pretty good numbers at first, and then start a downward spiral after a year or so, when their selfish interests begin to alienate customers as well as colleagues. We all have elements of narcissism, but the true narcissist manipulates people and bends the rules to meet their personal goals. Most sales narcissists are very skilled in interview situations. They will look you in the eye and tell you what you want to hear with a contrived sense of sincerity, even humility. Identifying sales narcissists is tough. Look for sales report numbers that decline over time (2 to 5 years). Another good way, as mentioned earlier, is to make a statement critical of the candidate's credentials. For example, say, "I'm not sure you have the quality kind of experience we need to handle our customers." Most true narcissists hate to be maligned in any way, and might show defensiveness or irritation. Also, ask the candidate what his weaknesses are. The answer will be a strength that he masquerades as a weakness. For example, he might answer, "I tend to spend too much time with customers," or, "I sometimes overprepare for my sales calls." In addition, as mentioned in dealing with narcissistic lone wolves, you should look for a lot of "I" statements, a lack of genuine interest in you (the interviewer), and a tendency to blame the economy and others for failure to achieve objectives.

3

Third Step:
Building a Winning Team

Y ou've been there. A missed sales objective, and the boss from hell shows up. The search for the guilty begins. He threatens. The sales reps run for cover. A temporary fix is put in place. In time, however, everyone goes back to what they were doing before. Then, a couple of months later, an objective is missed again, and the process is repeated—only with a little different fix. It's a kind of corporate insanity, doing the same thing over and over and expecting different results. The real result is stagnant sales performance and alienated salespeople.

A recent study of sales employees in various professions—"The Global Mindset Survey" by consulting firm rogenSi—showed that salespeople are losing confidence in their leaders: "Salespeople have been the most negatively affected by current challenges...they have reduced knowledge about how to handle the challenges ahead, find little comfort from their colleagues' skills, and are reluctant to turn to their managers for support. These beliefs and behaviors will inevitably and progressively have a negative impact in their energy, confidence and resourcefulness, leading to decreased sales performance."

Obviously, we're in changing, challenging times. We are in an age when the autocratic sales manager just can't survive. A fast-moving marketplace demands collaboration of salespeople and sales management to reach peak performance through high-functioning team efforts rather than manager-centered thinking.

Teamwork Begins with Partnership

It's easier to describe teamwork than define it. You know you have teamwork when salespeople work with each other and with sales management as partners to improve sales by sharing and implementing innovative ideas in all phases of the sales process, including product improvements, sales techniques, sales campaign implementation, competitive strategies, pricing, and a multitude of other procedures and policies. For the purposes of this book, it doesn't necessarily mean a team of salespeople coming together to handle an account, but rather a team of sales reps working together with management to support and develop each other in their daily sales activities. In this context, teamwork is an incubator providing salespeople with peer encouragement and development to better do their job.

A Stanford University study recently showed that people who worked together on a difficult task persisted 48% to 64% longer than those working individually. Collaboration, as opposed to working solo, increased people's intrinsic motivation and made the challenging project more interesting.

More specifically, here are a few of the benefits of sales teamwork:

- **Improves sales team performance**—If two heads are better than one, the multiplier effect pertains as all your salespeople work together with the manager to improve each other's success. The result is better sales for the whole team. And, of course, better bottom-line results for you, the sales manager.

- **Enhances individual performance**—Salespeople in a team environment learn from each other about better ways to sell. In addition, a sales team adds an element of peer pressure and accountability that further amplifies sales potential.

- **Speeds innovation**—Salespeople working together can quickly identify problems and solve them by sharing information and creating solutions.

- **Improves retention**—People enjoy working within a supportive team in which they are part of decision making. In addition to allowing salespeople to play a meaningful role in the company's future, a team environment decreases stress since salespeople are working together rather than working against each other. That means the good ones are more likely to stay on the payroll.

- **Makes it easier on the manager**—It provides sales managers with more time to manage and takes away the pressure of making all the decisions and designing all the sales programs.

Filling the Wheelbarrow

You might have heard the story of the tightrope artist who, after a daring series of jumps and rolls on the wire, pushes a wheelbarrow across the length of high wire. He smiles and waves to the spellbound audience that's offering a standing ovation to the mastery of his art. When the applause subsides, he addresses the mesmerized audience, "As the grand finale, I will push the wheelbarrow one more time to the other side. Does anyone doubt that I can do it? If so, raise your hand." Not a hand was raised from the hundreds in the audience. "Good," he said. "Now, for the audience participation part of the program, may I ask for someone to ride in the wheelbarrow?" There are laughs but, not surprisingly, no one volunteers.

There's a big difference between sitting in the audience applauding and being an active participant. Likewise, it's a lot easier for sales reps to *say* they believe in you rather than actually *be* a committed follower, to get in the wheelbarrow. This wheelbarrow analogy gets to the heart of managerial success in one word: trust. Without it, you have an empty wheelbarrow. And it takes more than a spectacular stunt to fill your wheelbarrow; it takes time and careful cultivation of your people.

Despite how much we've read about high-performance teams and inspirational leaders, our real-life experience in sales is probably closer to the "boss from hell" experience. His wheelbarrow was empty. No trust. No real followers. Most of his people found it easier to fake allegiance and then sabotage him behind his back. Chances are you've been in an environment where the joy and excitement of selling has been replaced with a singular focus on results. It's a place where there are more disgruntled salespeople and frustrated sales managers than high-performing teams and inspiring leaders.

The real question is this: What creates high-performance sales teams? What makes people excited about coming to work every day? What makes them sell?

There are no simple answers. But there are two fundamental building blocks for developing high-performance sales teams:

1. **A shared vision.** Your people have to know where you're going and how you're going to get there, and trust that it's going to be a worthwhile trip. It has to be meaningful, more than just making money. It has to have the gravity of changing the company or changing the world. The most important word, however, is "shared." As a leader, sharing in the creation and execution of the vision makes it powerful. Granted, it's a lot easier to give your people a vision and ask them to follow than to make the effort to ask for their participation; however, the more they're involved, the more committed they are to the vision. Your people might surprise you with the ideas they generate that you had never even considered.

2. **A sense of ownership.** People who feel like a contributing partner, an owner of the business, will make things work for you. Giving your salespeople a voice in the business and encouraging their involvement in creating policy and procedures can create buy-in, a kind of sweat equity that drives success (see Chapter 5, "Fifth Step: Sales Empowerment, Beginning with Ownership," for more on ownership).

Of course, creating these building blocks takes time and effort, but after you're there, you'll have unleashed a collective power that's greater than the sum of its parts. The ultimate goal is having your people create, believe in, and support a vision, making it their own. In a sales environment, the challenge is in getting your salespeople to work together to increase individual and overall sales results.

In *Leading Teams*, authors John Zenger, Ed Musselwhite, Kathleen Hurson, and Craig Perrin discuss "stuck" or stagnant organizations: "Most stuck organizations are also management centered. In other words, managers see themselves as the central players in the organization and assume they need to control almost everything.... In contrast, successfully changing organizations use employee involvement to build and benefit from the knowledge, skills and commitment of non-managers."

There's a certain pride and protectiveness that comes with involvement and ownership. Do you want renters or owners in your sales group? Mercenaries or warriors? Do you want team players who can help you and each other attain results, or would you rather settle for a fragmented group of salespeople operating only with their own best interests in mind?

In traditional, command/control sales hierarchies, managing people is relatively simple: The sales manager provides the commands and uses control mechanisms to facilitate the commands. The control methods are *pay* (commissions, bonuses, etc.) and *punishment* (reprimands, demotions, termination). Remember Pavlov's dog, taught to salivate at the sound of a bell? It's pretty much operant conditioning—rewarding desired behavior and punishing undesirable behavior. No matter how manipulative it sounds, pay-or-punish is fundamental to any sales group; it's how we reward high performers and weed out underachievers. However, it is not the *only* way to motivate a sales team. Studies have shown that employees increasingly are looking for more than a paycheck. They are searching for meaningful work, recognition of their abilities, and control of their work life. This is where the principles of Total Quality Management (TQM) can augment command/control methods. TQM gets employees involved in decision making and gives them a sense of ownership in and commitment to the company. In addition, it allows managers to tap into the combined energy, knowledge, and experience of their people to improve everyone's sales.

This notion of team and teamwork became the buzzwords in the 1980s as Japanese manufacturing prowess reached America. Originating in Japan after World War II, TQM was facilitated by Edward Deming, an American consultant. The original effort was called Kaizen and incorporated the idea of continuous improvement through employee participation at all levels. TQM was an underlying force that led Japan to world dominance in the automobile and electronics markets. In America, its popularity has waxed and waned over the years until, in some organizations, only the words remain. In other cases, the Kaizen concept has taken a foothold and led to significant successes, especially in manufacturing industries. However, the basic principles of TQM have a huge potential to shape high-performing sales teams.

Make no mistake, there simply are no quick fixes or panaceas for sales management. Managing salespeople is a tough, thankless business. You're stuck between impossible objectives and difficult people to deal with. To further complicate things, your customers are better informed and more demanding than ever because of quick access to product information on the Internet.

With increasing corporate downsizing and budget cutting, there is less and less training to help sales managers deal with the challenges of managing in the mercurial world of sales reps. Unlike salaried employees, salespeople are unique in the workforce, their commissions created by initiative, aggressiveness, competitiveness, and persistence. The result is a high percentage of self-absorbed mavericks—the antithesis of team players.

Let's be honest. Sales management is difficult because of the wide range of personalities you have to manage. Sales is a melting pot for natural-born salespeople, lifetime professionals, washouts, has-beens, never-weres and C students who couldn't find a job in their major. If variety is the spice of life, it also creates sparks. Look at it this way: A typical sales department is composed of salespeople with teaching degrees, history degrees, business, science, math, no degrees at all.... Now, look at the accounting department, the engineering department, human resources—all are composed of people with similar education and experience. This homogeneity at least gives a manager a common starting point of shared education, practices, standards, and beliefs. The sales manager has no such luxury, having to deal with huge disparities in personal and professional values and experience.

A recent *Huffington Post* article underscored the challenge of managing salespeople. It highlighted the results of a study by psychologist Kevin Dutton, which showed that the sales profession contained the fourth-highest percentage of psychopaths among all professions. The top three were CEO, lawyer, and media (TV/radio), with surgeon ranking fifth. The research defines psychopaths as having "shallow emotions...stress tolerance, lacking empathy, coldheartedness, lacking guilt, egocentricity, superficial character, manipulativeness, irresponsibility, impulsivity...." Ironically, the things that salespeople need the most of might be the things that they inherently lack.

Combining these self-defeating tendencies with varied personalities and backgrounds makes the sales profession a combustible mixture of human dynamics. As with nuclear power, if you can harness it you've created a high-octane selling machine. Unharnessed, it's a volatile formula for sales implosion. The beauty of this challenge is the powerful potential just waiting to be unlocked. In salespeople there's an energy, a toughness, a resilience, optimism, and fierce loyalty waiting to be channeled. These are tough people who live and thrive despite rejection every hour of the workday. They are like the cheetahs of the business world— magnificent hunters who frequently lose their prey to lions and larger competitors but keep coming back with relentless ferocity to capture their next prey.

A research team from four universities (Colorado State University, University of Louisville, University of Jacksonville, and Indiana University), in a study called "New Directions in Sales Leadership Research," put it simply: "The job of leading sales teams into a new world that values team-building dimensions such as (group) cohesiveness, helping behavior, courtesy, peacekeeping, and conflict management will require that sales managers adopt new skill sets.... The notion of putting team goals ahead of self-interests requires that trust in both the senior leaders and field sales managers be developed over time." The researchers' findings indicate that sales productivity can be improved by developing a management model in which managers and salespeople are treated as equals, in which supportive leadership leads to empowering and inspiring the sales force. This model opposes the more traditional strategy of command/control leaders who focus on issuing directives and monitoring compliance of those directives.

Reaching a balance between team goals and selfish interests is the key. It requires managers and the sales force to share ideas and power in a way that helps each individual benefit from the system. Teamwork does not replace individual competitiveness, which has been and always will be the force that sharpens our abilities; rather, it enhances our skill set and makes the entire organization more successful. Jack Welch, former

CEO of General Electric, called it the "boundary-less" organization in which information, decision making, and power are shared at all levels of the company by managers and nonmanagers.

Of the hundreds of sales management studies at well-known universities across the nation, many have focused on—and shown the effectiveness of—the following TQM management principles in team building:

Cohesiveness and Collaboration—Having sales managers work with the sales force as a team unit (as opposed to a boss-subordinate relationship) developing mutual trust, respect, and learning to reach sales objectives.

Empowerment—Allowing salespeople to participate in decision making and provide input into sales plans, strategies, and tactics.

Consideration—Providing an atmosphere in which sales managers are supportive, friendly, considerate, respectful, and communicative with their subordinates.

Learning—Creating an environment where the learning and sharing of skills, techniques, and market intelligence is emphasized as an ongoing, critical component of the sales culture (in addition to traditional sales training).

Trust—Establishing the integrity, honesty, and reliability of the sales manager (which is the single most important dynamic between salespeople and their managers).

Continuous Improvement—Making the commitment to get better. No matter how good you are, there's always room for improvement.

Starting this team-building process requires that the basics already be in place: effective training, resources to support sales, and a compensation package that is matched to your sales objectives. If the basic building blocks aren't in place, you'll have a hard time with team building or developing any kind of effective sales programs.

Teamwork Becomes More Important with Millennials

The days of the "my way or the highway" manager are gone. Sales has become way too complex. Any market in the world is just a click away. This is truly a global sales arena, no matter what your product is. And we have a new cast of characters in the sales force called millennials.

Millennials (age 18 to 35) compose 36% of the workforce in America. By 2020 they will be half of the workforce, replacing aging baby boomers as the largest demographic segment in the workplace. They are technologically savvy and well educated. More importantly—and differently from baby boomers—they require more than money to motivate them. They want to feel a part of something important. They desire meaning and impact in their work, and are adept at excelling in a team environment—especially when there are challenges to address. They require feedback and are motivated by encouragement and regular input from managers.

From a sales management perspective, perhaps the greatest challenge of managing millennials is that they have lost faith in their leaders. According to the previously mentioned study "The Global Mindset Survey" by rogenSi management consulting firm, "Younger employees (age 25-35), more than any other age cohort, have lost faith in their leaders and in their organization as a whole, believing there is not enough skill, strategy, teamwork or leadership to successfully manage the challenges ahead. They are more stressed, more doubtful and more distracted than their colleagues. This is cause for concern...because if these future leaders remain disengaged this will no doubt have a damaging effect on their performance now and in the years to come."

Following are a few ways to keep millennials interested:

- Give them challenging sales goals and provide regular reports and coaching to keep them on track.

- Provide autonomy to reach the goals and make sure they are receiving positive feedback for successes and constructive critiques in case of failure (millennials do not seem to react well to criticism without instruction).

- Make sure they know how the sales function contributes to the overall success of the company and, as important, how your vision fits into the company's success, as well as how the salesperson's efforts fit into your vision.

- Sales incentives and spiffs are good, but don't forget a simple "thank you." A sincere "attaboy" goes a long way with millennials.

- Provide a career path and guidance on how to advance, since many millennials are hungry and interested in promotion opportunities.

- Similarly, provide opportunities for training and self-improvement in order for them to advance their careers. Pay for sales seminars, webinars, and training downloads for the ones who are interested.

- Provide an opportunity to collaborate with peers and superiors. Millennials gravitate toward teamwork and cooperation in the workplace.

When it comes to team building, the keywords for new-age sales managers are flexibility and adaptability. "The illiterate of the 21st century," noted futurist Alvin Toffler, "will not be those who cannot read and write, but those who cannot learn, unlearn and relearn." We have to adapt. We can't expect our salespeople to adapt to us. Historically, managers who work with—and work for—their people in a team scenario have been able to surmount the challenges of change.

Teamwork in a manufacturing environment is one thing; but in a sales group? Is that some weird oxymoron? How can you have a real team composed of competitive, self-absorbed, self-motivated salespeople? And why would you want to? It sounds like trying to herd cats. Granted, it's no walk in the park, but after you get the momentum built, you'll be surprised how collaborative a sales force can be. The beginning stages of TQM are the toughest. Early on, no one is going to tell you how much they like the process. In fact, they will fight it at first through silence and indifference. After all, why would a top seller share his ideas to help others compete against him?

The truth is you are building a team whether or not you're a team builder. Employees come together and form bonds—with or without you as their leader. If it's without you, you have problems. Indifference, resistance, and even a form of sales sabotage occur when your people aren't working with you. The real problem is that you'll never really know. As the ultimate pleasers, your sales folks will react to you with a nod and smile, and then do whatever they want to behind your back.

The Unseen Team Will Make You or Break You

Every hour of the day, your salespeople are talking, texting, and tweeting among themselves. They are communicating personal and professional information, much of it inane but a great deal of it shaping the team's sales effectiveness and determining your ultimate success. They are usually communicating who, what, why, and how:

Who—Sales reps love to talk about other sales reps and managers. Unfortunately, much of the talk creates one-dimensional caricatures, especially of managers, that undermine their managerial credibility. The rule is that the more they dislike you, the more they talk about you—to the point of distraction. As resentment builds, trash talk increases. You'd be surprised at how much selling time is wasted with rants about the boss. If a manager has a perception for being a cost-cutter, for example, you'll find your team starting verbal feeding frenzies with comments like "There she goes again, saving pennies but wasting dollars." In contrast, the manager might be totally clueless to these behind-the-scenes tirades. That's because it's a lot easier for reps to be agreeable in front of the manager, and then go into the attack mode behind the manager's back. The biggest problem with these behind-the-scenes rants against managers is that they erode trust while creating managerial roadblocks of which the manager is unaware.

What—A steady stream of chatter on company policy and procedure can marginalize programs or procedures even before they are in effect. When announcing a new program—for example, a reconfigured commission plan—you can bet that your salespeople are going to have plenty to discuss among themselves. Chances are, these conversations won't have the benefit of your input. In effect, opinion leaders among your reps will have more power shaping the issue than you.

Why—Sales teams will, rightly or wrongly, determine their own version of the reasons for managerial decisions. Many times, they try to fill in the blanks when they fail to understand the management's rationale, creating unfounded rumors. Other times, they simply don't believe what they've heard and create sinister scenarios that might include such imagined threats as looming layoffs and pay cuts.

How—Reps help reps much more than managers help reps. They assist each other in everything from applying technology to sales techniques to paperwork. In doing so, they create their own methods and short-cuts, some efficient and some counterproductive. This is the area where you see reps sharing details on how to "game" the system or how to circumvent the rules for their own benefit. In extreme cases, this is where sales saboteurs develop ways to undermine hated managers.

All this communication influences your reps' attitudes, motivation, beliefs, and values. And it is done unbeknownst to you. This is the Unseen Team at work. Not the team that you encounter in meetings, this team operates behind the scenes with its own code of silence. Whether you know it or not, you have shaped this team. And it is either working for you or working against you. There is no in-between. If a team is neutral—not really for or against you—it is apathetic, and apathy is as counterproductive as animosity.

Effective team building takes the mystery away from the Unseen Team. The need for secrecy and a code of silence is replaced by honest and open communications between management and sales reps.

You can't be with every salesperson, every hour of the day. The big question is what are they doing when you're not there? Unfortunately, you're not there 90% of the time. You'll never know everything going on behind your back, but you'll know a lot more after implementing a successful team-building process. And, more importantly, you'll be able to positively influence the activities and effects of the Unseen Team.

The leader who actively builds and shapes a sales team through TQM processes is an integral part of the sales team, not just a boss barking orders. The continuous exchange of information and ideas with reps keeps the team builder on top of market conditions and rep performance. This means the team builder is in the know and able to make quick corrections to sales plans, enabling him to stay on target. On the other hand, the boss who is busy giving directives and waiting for results is out there, all alone, struggling to figure out what works.

Researchers at the University of Texas–Arlington and Northeastern University reviewed studies on sales leadership, noting that "supportive leadership" directly improved sales reps' self-efficacy (self-confidence), motivation, and effort. According to the study, supportive leaders create an environment "where employees feel free to present ideas, develop innovative solutions, and experience a family-like feeling. When employees think that they are treated as equals, they develop the perception that their suggestions are truly listened to by the supervisor and that they have the confidence and support of the supervisor to accomplish job tasks." The study says that unsupportive managers often blame poor results on salespeople, which decreases motivation and lowers salespeople's self-confidence. "Results actually show that lack of support might be the underlying force behind such low motivation and self-efficacy."

Effective team building is a discipline, an art that takes time, patience, and energy. Mary Barra, CEO of General Motors, said in a recent *Fortune* magazine article, "I believe in the power of teamwork, and I think you will have superior results if you are aligned and win the hearts and minds of your employees if they understand where the company is going." A team is a group that is interdependent and supportive, with a common goal. Taking it one step further, a high-performance team transcends ordinary teamwork and creates a shared vision, passion, and energy that empowers its members to achieve extraordinary individual and group results.

High-performance teams are everywhere. Look at lions hunting prey. They work together—communicating with each other to chase, encircle, and snare water buffalo twice their size. Or consider armed forces special operations units working together to outmaneuver a larger enemy force. If you're a fan of Arthurian legend, the Knights of the Round Table embraced equality and partnership, and there was no head of the table. The common thread is that no *one* is better than *all* of us.

The beauty of it is that after you build team momentum, it's a powerful force that energizes your salespeople and delivers results with an economy of effort from managers. This process also empowers managers to spend more time on things that directly boost the bottom line.

Put simply, productive team building takes the pressure off the manager—from developing salespeople to meeting objectives—and spreads responsibility among team members instead of the manager doing all the heavy lifting.

We, as managers, need all the help we can get. The Conference Board's 2013 Annual Job Satisfaction Survey showed that only 47% of respondents were satisfied with their jobs. This job dissatisfaction has steadily decreased since the first survey in 1987, which indicated 60% were satisfied. A recent Gallup study, "State of the American Workplace Report," said only 30% of employees surveyed were "engaged and inspired" at work, and the remaining 70% were either unexcited or actively disengaged, roaming the halls spreading discontent. That's pretty unnerving to think that 70% of your salespeople are either apathetic or discontented. What's your satisfaction rating?

What Makes an Effective Team Leader?

Effective leaders engage their subordinates as competent professionals. Showing a genuine respect for their skills, talents, and experience, they set up a constructive dialogue with the sales team.

Lou Holtz, legendary football coach, said, "There are only two types of leaders: those who believe in themselves and lift others up and those with a poor self-image who pull everybody down. If you're in a leadership role, don't worry about being popular—worry about raising the self-image and productivity of the people around you."

Supremely self-assured, real leaders don't have to beat their people into submission. They don't bully, they inspire. They don't manipulate, they empower. They recognize the individual and collective power of their salespeople and let them know it.

Such leaders set the stage for ownership, knowing that it's human nature to take care of things you own. Getting salespeople's input is the first step in getting their buy-in. The next step—the revolutionary part—is helping each other succeed. That is the dynamic of salespeople *helping* each other rather than only *competing* against each other. This is the toughest part of the process. But it invariably starts at the top and filters down. As one sales leader put it, "We're all competitors. That's part of being in sales. But when I win, I want to beat you at your best. We get to be the best by helping each other."

Commission is the bread and butter of salespeople: Break down the word and you have "co" and "mission" a mission shared by everyone on the team—salespeople and managers.

Kenneth Bartkus, Utah State University, studied the effects of group cohesiveness on the sales performance of a national sample of travel agents. Findings suggest that sales leaders play a vital role in helping reps work together: "Conscious and appropriate efforts to direct the cohesive group will likely result in a more satisfied and productive sales force."

The collaborative power of salespeople was further supported in a study of 489 insurance agents by researchers from the University of Minnesota, the University of Kentucky, and St. Cloud State University. Their findings: "Salespeople's job satisfaction tends to be enhanced to the extent that they develop relationships with their sales peers, are concerned about how sales peers evaluate their performance, and use their sales peers as important referents.... As important referents, sales peers can serve as role models, offer advice and support.... So, sales managers should encourage salespeople to seek out their sales peers for direction and guidance."

Competition among salespeople will always, and should always, exist. It energizes, it elevates sales efforts. The key is for the manager to regulate and shape the level of in-house competitiveness. Without the social lubricant of teamwork, too much competitiveness among your salespeople can be counterproductive. Researchers at Southern Methodist University and the University of Texas quoted a previous study finding "high levels of competition among members of the sales force to be dysfunctional."

From a sales-floor perspective, results of this dysfunctionality, in its worst form, include reps working against each other, as well as engaging in backstabbing, infighting, and jealousy. In many cases, this worst-case scenario is facilitated by managers who pit reps against each other, creating a stressful, win-at-all-costs environment. We all love competition, but it can go too far when it results in reps tearing each other down rather than building them up. In addition, it is a huge missed opportunity for sales managers. It eliminates the chance of cross-pollination by reps working together, which in turn creates a more harmonious and sales-focused climate.

In-house competition and the competitive nature of salespeople is just one of the many obstacles managers face in building high-performance teams. Other challenges include the following:

Overcoming inertia—It's a lot easier to maintain the status quo, to stay within one's comfort zone. Sales reps are usually wary of any program that will raise "the curve." If you're a top performer, you're probably wary of any program that will help others catch up with you. If you're a low performer, you might worry that it will be even more difficult to reach the office sales average where there's job security. This is where WIFM—"what's in it for me"—comes in. Everyone should clearly understand the benefits of high-performing teamwork ranging from higher compensation for reps, better working environment, less pressure on individual reps, improved job security, and upward mobility. All these benefits result from one simple fact: Teamwork makes individual salespeople better salespeople.

Institutional distrust—If your sales force has seen layoffs, cut-backs, and take-backs, chances are the reps don't totally trust the company. There's no way for a single manager to solve this problem. The best response is to build the highest level of trust in *you*—their leader—as strongly and quickly as possible. Subordinates trust trustworthy leaders, even in an environment of corporate cynicism.

Lack of upper management support—Reps will ask whether the company really supports empowerment and participatory management or whether this is just another management fad. There's not an easy answer to this concern, but the truth is this: If it works, and sales improve, you have as much support as you need at all levels of the organization. Even if your boss is skeptical about a nontraditional approach, he or she can't argue against improved sales results.

The independent nature of salespeople—Perhaps the biggest obstacle, as alluded to earlier, is sales reps' independent nature.

Most are used to working alone, solving problems by themselves, making solo sales and taking the sole credit. Getting them working together, supporting each other, and making each other successful is not as hard as you'd think, but there will be those who never get it. There's no easy solution to this problem other than persistence and your insistence that everyone must give it a chance. After all, you're not asking them to give up their independence. In many ways, this process will make them even more independent, especially if you're moving toward a self-managed sales team.

Resistance from power players—Within your existing sales force, you have "power players" who wield influence in the daily politics of your operations. Usually, these are veteran reps, or they might just be highly charismatic people with natural leadership qualities. Either way, they can be territorial and might resent team building that could erode their power base. Be sure you identify these thought leaders and include them in a way that protects their power base. Consult with them up front. Let them know that you know they are leaders. Acknowledge their influence. Ask them to help shape the team-building process.

Your ability to change—The final obstacle could be yourself. Are you ready to make changes in your role with your sales team? Can you sit back, loosen the reins, and give more power to your salespeople? This means frequently withholding your opinion so that others can express theirs. It means possibly slowing down the decision-making process so that everyone can provide feedback. You'll also have to occasionally give in to ideas you don't like and see how they work. Bottom line, you'll have to relinquish some control and let the team do things you might not necessarily agree with. Just as in sports, a real team player can't be the star all the time; sometimes you have be the backup and not the hero.

Five Ways to Set the Stage for Team Building

No matter how expansive your team-building efforts might be, there are five processes that will facilitate team building in the early stages:

1. **Build team confidence by taking the time to research the sales force, rep by rep**—Try this assessment on the group (even if you have to fudge a little): *You guys are good.* (In reality, maybe they're not that good but "fake it till you make it." People who think they're good are a lot better than those who don't. You have to start with something to build on.) Emphasize things that the sales team has done well. You might have to look hard for good metrics, but most people or teams do some things well—make it a point to build on those things. Numerous sales research studies and common sense tell us that self-confidence is vital to salespeople's effectiveness in all phases of every day sales ranging from selling product benefits to handling customer complaints. It can even make them work harder, according to a University of Pittsburgh study. A study of 114 industrial product salespeople indicated that "because salespeople's self-esteem has a strong effect on their belief that hard work will result in good performance, managers should try to improve the self-perceptions of individual salespersons.... Salespeople who think highly of themselves are more likely to be motivated to work hard."

   Some call it confidence priming. Here are a few ways to build team confidence:

   - Make a list of three things: strengths, achievements, and things you like most about the team (or person). Use this list as a reminder to encourage them with statements like, "I know you can reach this objective, look how well you did last quarter" or, "You're some of the best closers I've seen; all you need to do is get in front of more customers to close."
   - Build confidence by strengthening weaknesses. Set small, easily achieved objectives, and then build on them. For example, if acquiring new business is a team's weakness, establish an easy objective for setting appointments. After that objective is met, set gradually more challenging goals until you work your way up to a stretch objective of new business revenue. Make it an incremental process rather than a big objective that overwhelms the sales team.
   - Say the words. Look for examples in which you observe positive traits. And say the words: Tell your people they are

smart or persistent or resourceful or creative. Give them words they can use to develop positive self-talk. If you have the chance, brag on them—individually or as a team—in front of others. That's a powerful way to build self-esteem.

- Show a can-do attitude. As a leader, be a confident problem solver. It is contagious. Don't bemoan the challenges or bad-mouth those responsible for setbacks. Do not play the role of the victim. Be the victor. Showing a positive can-do attitude sets the tone for your people to respond similarly.
- Prepare. In everything your people do, make sure they are prepared. The will to win is not as important as the will to prepare to win. Salespeople have a tendency to "wing it," to rely on their persuasive skills to get them through situations. Adding preparation to the mix exponentially increases the chance of success. And success breeds success.

Oriental philosopher Lao Tzu once said, "Health is the greatest possession. Contentment is the greatest treasure. Confidence is the greatest friend."

2. **Set a JFK-moon-landing vision**—As soon as John F. Kennedy declared that we would put a man on the moon, everything happened to reach that objective. He enunciated the vision simply and inspirationally: "We choose to go to the moon. We choose to go to the moon in this decade and do the other things, not because they are easy but because they are hard, because that goal will serve to organize and measure the best of our energies and skills, because that challenge is one we are willing to accept, one we are unwilling to postpone, and one which we intend to win." Create a vision with your team, using their ideas and their words. Make it big. Following are a few ideas for ambitious visions:

- Achieving a "number one" ranking in your industry or among your company's sales offices.
- Capturing a precedent-setting market share such as 40% of total product sales in your territory.
- Attaining a prestigious award either within your corporation or in your industry.
- Reaching a sales milestone such as doubling last year's sales.

Make sure your vision is specific, is measurable, and has a time frame. Avoid nebulous visions such as "to increase customer loyalty and annual sales." You can turn those words into a workable vision by adding a measurement metric such as "to increase annual sales and repeat purchases by 50% next year." If you do use sales metrics, make sure they are "wow" numbers—that is, record-setting, milestone metrics that will be remembered in years to come.

Laying out a grand vision and a plan to get there creates a kind of magic. It's a self-fulfilling prophecy. Say out loud you're going to do something grand and watch things happen. Setting a realistic vision will energize and motivate your sales force, especially when they're part of the goal-setting process. In fact, most salespeople expect high goals. Of course, salespeople are always careful to grumble about challenging goals, but it's amazing how frequently we all discover new things about our abilities when we're challenged to go beyond the usual.

As a manager, be prepared for varied responses to ambitious visions. During the vision-setting process, invariably, there will be complainers, detractors, and resisters who would rather coast than accelerate. No matter how irritating they might be, listen to them—you might uncover legitimate institutional or procedural obstacles that require changes to current practices. But most important is the fact that you are listening, you are a partner in setting and achieving the goal.

Next, carefully develop a game plan, how you and your team are going to rise to the challenge. A little empathy followed by a solid game plan will go a long way in reaching your vision.

3. **Practice selflessness for success**—Really, really good leaders are so self-assured that they don't have to throw their weight around. They create a partnership and get their people working together to brainstorm and collectively solve problems. The good ones don't have to prove they are the boss, because everyone already knows it. The good ones support and lift up rather than tear down their people. This takes selflessness, and consideration of how

your actions impact your sales group in everything you do. On the flip side, after your sales reps see you as selfish, chances are they will never trust you, no matter what you do. We all have our own selfish goals; however, in sales management your ultimate success depends on your ability to develop a win-win atmosphere with your people. When you take care of them, they will take care of you. This is the Law of Reciprocity, or "positive reciprocity," which means simply that we must give first before we receive. In sales management, however, this law is never a one-to-one ratio, so don't expect immediate and equal reciprocity from your people. When the payback comes, you'll probably see more of a five-to-one ratio: You give five times what you receive. In fact, as cynics sometimes say, "No good deed goes unpunished." Occasionally, your noble acts will backfire on you, but in the long run, the Law of Reciprocity will win out. If you don't believe in this ultimate payoff, sales or sales management is definitely not a good career choice. By the way, negative reciprocity also exists in equal measure. You can usually expect your rudeness, thoughtlessness, and harmful acts to be returned to you in overt or subtle ways.

4. **Realize that the essence of sales leadership is the action following your words**—Be bold. Encourage your team to make sure that your words are being followed with actions. Urge your people to let you know if your actions and words are inconsistent. This takes the self-realization that the leader is not a salesperson. The bread and butter of many sales jobs is the spoken word because you have to say the right things at the right time considering that you might not get a second chance for the sale. *Words are everything in sales. Actions are everything in sales management.* As a sales manager, you still have to say the right things but your follow-up action is what everyone notices and remembers. Subordinates have an uncanny memory of words, and the actions following those words. They will keep a mental catalog of how the two relate. Are you doing the right things and doing things right or simply trying to talk your way through every situation? This is a guarantee: If your actions aren't consistent with what you say, there are no words that will get your team to follow you.

5. **Practice mutual accountability**—There's no better way to energize your team than to let them know that you are accountable *to* them. You should expect them to let you know if you're not meeting their needs, if you made a wrong call, or if you're not following through. Invite their critique of your performance. It takes a lot of self-confidence and discipline, but it sends a message of strength and unity that builds trust and credibility.

Many of us, as young sales managers, have struggled through the "I'm the boss" stage of our careers. We had begun managing with a simple formula learned as a salesman: The sales rep's job was to make the sales manager happy, and the sales manager's job was to make his boss happy. This was going to be easy, we had thought. Because we had been an outstanding salesperson, we were going to show our reps how to be successful, to mold them to our own likeness. If the reps couldn't or wouldn't be successful, if they did not make us happy, we had the power to hire and fire. Full of ourselves and our newly found power, we stumbled through high turnover and confrontations with reps. Even the successes felt like failures because our reps were intimidated, alienated, and unsupportive.

The problem, as we might later discover, went back to the Law of Reciprocity. If we demanded accountability from our people without being accountable *to* them, we lost their loyalty. People would follow orders because we were the boss, but no one showed a lot of passion, loyalty, or trust. They were just following orders, going home at five o'clock, and trying their best to forget the job.

Downward accountability—the leader's loyalty to her subordinates—gives your people a sense of involvement and control, but more importantly, it positions you as a leader who is strong enough to handle the responsibility and sensitive enough to care about subordinates.

Case Study #3: Team Building, Corporate Style

A sales manager in a large telecommunications corporation with offices across the nation, Mike was transferred to a low-performing office. His job: to turn it around.

Now, Mike stood in front of his 14 reps to get things started. He had visualized this introduction for three weeks. Making it go the way he planned was not going to be easy. The group was underperforming and getting hammered by the competition. Understandably, morale was low. As a group, the team was drifting into a cycle of missed objectives followed by punitive measures used by the previous manager, such as twice-a-day "update" meetings or what the reps called "interrogation sessions" or "sales prevention conferences." The low performers were just trying to hang on to their jobs, and the high performers were attempting to stay confident and enthusiastic in the midst of a losing season. Many of the good ones were looking for other jobs.

Mike began, "I'm thrilled to be here and look forward to working with you all. Some of you I know and many I don't. The ones who know me know I'm not a hatchet man. And I'm not one of those fast-track guys on the way to the top who'll be here five minutes then promoted somewhere else.

"I'm not much of a joke teller but our situation here reminds me of one my favorite sports stories: a Dad who comes a little late to his eight-year-old son's baseball game. They're behind 15 to nothing. He goes over to his son and tells him to hang in there and not get discouraged no matter how far behind they are. The son smiles and says, 'Why would I be discouraged? We haven't even got to bat yet.'

"So I guess we can say it's our turn to bat now.

"Straight up, here's the deal. Your group numbers are at the bottom of the company and my job is to turn things around. The problem is that I'm not a miracle worker. I can't do anything by myself. But working together, I'm convinced that we can be the number one office in this company soon. That's because I know you can do it. I've read each of your personnel records and talked to others about each of you—your strengths and weaknesses. I gotta tell you, I am really confident in this team, individually and collectively. Pound for pound we're as good as any sales team in this organization.

"Being number one in the company means each one of you is going to have to be at the top of your game, in the top 10% of every sales index we have. Now don't get me wrong, I don't have any magic fairy dust to sprinkle and make us number one. It'll take some hard work. But I do know we can do it together, as a team. This means we're going to work together, support, and learn from each other and do a lot of brainstorming to solve problems. At our next meeting I'll get you the details.

"In a nutshell, my job is to make sure you have what you need to get us to the top. That means removing roadblocks for you, making sure you're making money, and shooting straight with you.

"Your job is easy—all I ask is that you make us number one. Pretty simple, huh?

"Okay, I know you're sitting there thinking, 'I've heard this idealistic crap before but it never lasts.' But don't just listen to my words, *watch* what I do on a daily basis. If I'm not living up to these words, tell me, remind me where I need to be.

"Let me say I'm a big believer in team building. Now, I know you all have pretty much operated independently here in the past. But I'd like to ask you to work with me to develop a team atmosphere. What's in it for you? First of all, it will make you better. And it will make you more money. In a nutshell, here's how it works: We work together to make each other better salespeople, which means we make higher commissions, get more bonuses, and have more job security because we're making this company successful. As an added benefit, we accomplish all this a lot easier than you could ever do by yourself.

"Let's start with the vision statement. I like to keep things simple, so it's one sentence, seven words: to be number one in the company. The key metric of our success is net sales increase. This vision is a discussion starter. I want your input, your questions and comments. It's important that the vision statement is ours, not mine. So I'd ask you to spend some time thinking about it and giving me your honest thoughts and suggestions. I'm sure your first thought is that it's absolutely impossible to achieve." He chuckled, allowing a moment of comic relief. "Yes, I realize that we're competing with 42 other sales teams in this company. And, yes, I realize that we are number 40 now. But write this down and date it today: We'll end up on top. Here's how we're going to do it."

The reps watched as Mike wrote four words on the easel: *Excellence, Teamwork, Learning,* and *Involvement.*

"Excellence is wanting to be the best and becoming the best we can be," he said earnestly. "It's continuous improvement and not settling for second best. Our job every day is to be the best we can be. That's what keeps the paychecks coming, and makes the company competitive and profitable. That is the reason we are here today. This means setting the bar high with stretch objectives. We'll work together setting the goals to keep standards high but reachable.

"Teamwork: Working with and respecting each other. Being account-able to each other. Listening. Trusting. Not waiting for a manager, but assisting each other. Sharing ideas to help each other succeed. No back-biting, infighting or name-calling allowed.

"Learning: Even the best can get better. Learning makes us all better. When you stop learning you stop progressing. We learn in all ways, from each other, from training, from customers, from competitors, and from reading.

"Involvement: I want your input in decision making. This is your team, your accounts, and I count on your street smarts to create and reality-test decisions that affect us all. As we know, life in this corporation is not a democracy; there are a lot of things in which we don't have a voice or a choice. But we can choose how we implement corporate directives. And there are still a lot of things we can decide. I'll be the facilitator, the referee, but this team will make decisions and solve problems together."

Then he handed out a Team Contract. "This is our contract, what we are accountable for." The contract read:

As a leader I am accountable for...

1. *Providing training and resources.*

2. *Removing roadblocks to ensure sales effectiveness.*

3. *Standing up for the sales force.*

4. *Honesty. I will not lie to you.*

5. *Respect. Every subordinate deserves respect and will not be criticized unfairly, ignored, or embarrassed.*

6. *Responsiveness. Questions, requests, paperwork will be responded to in a timely fashion.*

7. *Seeking your input on operations, procedures, and policies.*

8. *Establishing and sharing best practices that make us all better.*

As a salesperson you are accountable for...

1. *Meeting deadlines.*

2. *Reaching objectives.*

3. *Honesty and integrity.*

4. *Respecting and supporting your teammates, and sharing information with them.*

5. *Providing suggestions and being involved in all phases of our business to improve your and our effectiveness.*

"This is a rough draft," Mike said. "I'd like to get your input on it and refine the rough spots. But, in the meantime, these are the things that are important to me and I expect you to let me know if I violate any of these items," Mike said. "I'll do the same for you."

"Throughout this process, keep in mind that there is one reason we are here. That is to sell, and to exceed company objectives. If we don't, we don't have jobs. Simple as that. There are no guaranteed jobs in this corporation, and the pressure to perform increases each year as we get more and more competition. This is a tough business and getting tougher and less forgiving. The key is to get us all working together to make sure we're all here next year and the year after that."

Building Team Momentum

In the preceding case study, Mike built his team on a strong, existing structure of clearly defined sales objectives, policies and procedures, job responsibilities, time schedules, and meetings. Salespeople need structure. We all do. You need this kind of structure before establishing the team-building process.

The first thing Mike did was emphasize the "why" of team building. What's in it for sales reps? How will they benefit? He not only stated the financial and job security rewards, but also emphasized their role in the overall success of the company. He explained team building in a way that went beyond personal incentives to include how meaningful their impact would be on overall company success.

To get the ball rolling, he laid out a clear vision statement (to be number one) and asked for input and comments, encouraging the sales team to make it their own. In addition, he suggested a metric to measure the team's progress toward the vision. It was a "man on the moon" vision but it was concrete, achievable, and measurable.

Additionally, Mike established two major frameworks for team building: a behavioral framework and a values framework. First, he explained the behavioral principles behind this team-building effort: excellence, learning, teamwork, and rep involvement. These were the actions the team had to perform to be successful. These performance keys were the behaviors necessary for developing a smoothly functioning team. Second, Mike made the transition from actions to values. His "Team Contract" clarified critical team values—such as respect, integrity, and responsiveness.

By defining accountabilities, Mike emphasized important values as well as describing his commitments and sales reps' responsibilities. In doing so, he articulated roles and boundaries that provided additional clarity to the process.

The previously mentioned University of Pittsburgh study of 114 industrial salespeople states that salespeople's role clarity "has a strong impact on their specific self-esteem and job satisfaction. Managers therefore should periodically have discussions with salespeople to ensure that they understand what is expected from them and how they are expected to perform their jobs." Good leaders find a way to set boundaries and expectations without constraining the initiative of their people. Essentially, Mike outlined an atmosphere of mutual interdependence and accountability, displaying his leadership but underscoring his support. In fact, he clearly outlined roles and accountabilities in writing, leaving no room for misunderstanding but also emphasizing that he was open to reps' input.

Values Help Create a Successful Sales Culture

Mike laid the foundation for designing a high-performance sales culture. A clear statement of values is the first step. "In a nutshell, values exert influence over our attitudes and attitudes influence our behavior," states Charles D. Kerns, Ph.D., at Pepperdine University in the school's *Graziadio Business Review*. He notes in the report that there are three steps to establishing values in a work group:

1. First, leaders need to be clear about what values they hold.

2. Second, they must effectively communicate what values they hold.

3. Third, managerial leaders need to ensure that their actions are in alignment with their espoused values. This connection between what one says and what one does can be described as one's "Behavioral Integrity Quotient" or BIQ. Leaders need to have a high BIQ—act consistently with their espoused values—in order for others to trust them.

Emphasizing involvement and trust, Mike was filling his wheelbarrow with reps willing to make the journey on the tightrope of sales.

In *The Art of Supportive Leadership*, author J. Donald Walters states, "Genuine leadership is of only one type: supportive. It leads people. It doesn't drive them. It involves them. It doesn't coerce them.... Leadership implies running at the head of the pack, not driving it from behind. This is also true in military matters. Those who serve under a great general know well that he asks nothing of them that he would not first do himself."

Creating a Learning Environment

Of prime importance, Mike emphasized the creation of a learning environment, one that stresses continuous improvement, employee involvement, and innovation. This includes, but goes far beyond, traditional sales training. It seeks to create an environment in which ideas, opinions, sales techniques, and market intelligence are shared openly and received willingly among sales team members. In this environment, learning becomes an everyday, every-hour process involving sales reps, managers, clerical people, and everyone with a stake in sales. Part of everyone's job description, from reps to support personnel, should include "teacher" and "coach."

Learning as a part of sales productivity was examined by Southern Methodist University's Cox School of Business in research that included a study of medical supply salespeople during a three-month promotion of a $5,400 medical device. They found that salespeople with a "learning goal orientation" performed better than those with a "performance goal orientation." The difference being that those with a learning orientation were more concerned with developing their skills and ability, whereas those with a performance orientation were concerned with obtaining a positive evaluation of their performance. Those with a learning orientation embraced difficult goals because they provided a challenging opportunity that could lead to personal growth. Those with performance orientation avoided difficult goals because they provide a greater potential for failure—as goal difficulty increases, the probability of obtaining a positive evaluation through goal attainment decreases. The study suggested that managers can increase learning orientation among salespeople through "cooperation among colleagues, encouragement of experimentation and developmental appraisal systems" as opposed to more traditional systems "that encourage competition among sales personnel, punishment of mistakes and evaluative appraisal systems."

Best Practices Emphasized

Mike stressed the importance of always looking for best practices from his team or from the outside. Best practices are procedures that can range from casual sharing of information among team members to more formal and orderly procedures. Their key element is the spirit and intent on which they are established. The spirit has to be active participation by all team members with the intent of sharing information to make everyone succeed.

There are five main steps to implementing a best-practices program:

1. **Identify**—First, everyone has to be on the constant lookout for best practices. Many programs focus on in-company best practices. These can be sales techniques or processes that have proven successful by your sales reps, especially the practices of your top

sales people. In addition to your top performers, encourage and incent all your salespeople and support staff to share their success stories and process improvements. The continual churn of ideas will make your best practices successful. You know you have a good program when your salespeople are informally exchanging tips and techniques outside the best-practices program. (Nevertheless, try to capture these informal exchanges for inclusion in your program.) This is a difficult subject, however, for sales groups because reps are frequently reluctant to share their personal best practices for fear of competition from other reps. To overcome this reluctance, the manager has to insist and persist until idea sharing becomes a productive habit, a tide of sales success that raises all ships. Also, consider incentives such as gift cards or cash awards for the best practice of the month. This will build excitement for sharing practices and should stimulate involvement.

The second type of best practices are those outside the company. These can come from trade magazines such as *Selling Power*, general business publications such as the *Wall Street Journal* or *Forbes* magazine, and even scholarly journals such as the *Sales and Marketing Journal*. In addition, there are hundreds of sales bloggers who share best practices daily. And don't forget your colleagues outside the company, and even competitors, as a source for innovative practices. Keep in mind, though, that not all best practices are created equal. For example, a best practice from a megacorporation like IBM or Intel might not apply to your smaller sales organization; or a best practice in one industry might not work in another.

2. **Analyze**—To be pertinent, a best practice should pass three tests. First, has it been proven successful? Do you have analytics or strong anecdotal evidence that demonstrates its success? If no measurements exist, does the practice seem to fit your needs enough to warrant a market test? Second, is the practice replicable within your sales team? Can you reproduce it as is or do you need to adapt it to your needs? Finally, how do you measure the results of the practice? Do you have clearly defined objectives for the practice, and do you have metrics to demonstrate its success?

3. **Implement**—After due diligence, the standard is implemented for daily use in sales operations. The implementation stage includes the following:

- *Scoping*—It can be initiated incrementally as a market test. This would entail selecting a few reps or a targeted geographic or market area to test the practice first. This procedure enables you to test and refine the practice before utilizing it on a widespread basis. On the other hand, the practice can be rolled out on a full-scale basis to the whole sales team. A rollout makes sense when you are confident that the practice will yield positive results with minimal disruptive effects.

- *Training*—This phase includes training and promoting the practice to ensure proper utilization. The manager and team should share the responsibility of follow-up observation and coaching to make sure sales reps are using the practice optimally. Reps should be encouraged to share their personal experiences in using the new practice. This information should be disseminated regularly—through meetings, e-mails, texting—to keep the sales team abreast of suggested changes and refinements to the practice. This is a good time for the manager to ride along with reps to personally experience how the practice is being handled in real life. Implementing a best practice is a fluid process. It has to be adapted to your specific needs and personalities. You can't afford to have your people blindly following procedures. Encourage them to communicate best practices within the best practice. Then make sure they are shared with the team.

- *Measurement*—Establish metrics to measure the efficacy of the practice. Your measurements should give you a real-time look at progress toward your objectives, as well as a snapshot of profit/loss efficiency. Share the analytics continuously with the sales team to keep them apprised.

4. **Standardize**—When you have shaped and refined the practice, standardize it. Make it a part of your practices and policies. Make sure your sales team is applying it uniformly on a permanent

basis. Also ensure that your data systems are prepared to support the practice on an ongoing basis. Part of the standardization process is continuous monitoring of implementation and metrics to keep the practice updated to market conditions.

5. **Catalogue**—After a best practice has been identified as a bona fide operational improvement, it should be filed and cataloged for future reference. A good database will provide a record of refinements you make, as well as documenting the metrics. It also serves as a repository for practices that might have not been useful at the time but could be usable in the future. As managers change, a good cataloging system will ensure that best practices are not misplaced.

Keep in mind that a best practice wasn't always a best practice. It had to be created to solve a problem or improve a process. Sometimes your most successful best practices are created by your sales team. In the absence of known practices, your team should innovate its own ways to solve problems and then test, adapt, and standardize the solution. The best practice of all is innovation by your team.

Teamwork Expected

Mike emphasized that he expected teamwork. This was something dramatically new and foreign to his team. In the past, sales managers had stifled teamwork and encouraged individual competitiveness. They would often pit salespeople against each other with statements like "John is almost on objective this week; do you think you can beat him?" In addition, the salespeople themselves knew little about teamwork, rarely sharing their secrets of success. The prevailing thought among the reps was "Why give anyone else a competitive advantage that might put me in second place?"

Mike's insistence on teamwork established a value and belief system that was nonnegotiable. At the same time, however, his people were empowered to voice their opinions as they worked through this transformation.

There are times, in implementing any new system, when the leader simply has to lay down the law, and make nonnegotiable demands. In uncharted territory, Mike was doing the steering until the group got their bearings and could take over. His directive, for example, that team members respect each other and work together was a marching order needed to get the ball rolling and establish a value set that would lead to revamping the group culture.

Mike clearly encouraged the reps to be involved in all levels of decision making. Not only does this ensure better decisions, because all phases of the issue can be analyzed if more points of view are considered, but it also gives the reps a sense of ownership and that ever-so-important feeling of control over their destiny. No company is a democracy; there are times when we all simply follow orders. On the other hand, there are many times when employees can come up with innovative solutions that a single manager could not.

Finally, Set Ground Rules

Ground rules help establish the rules of engagement as you go about the team-building process. Getting good input and rep involvement usually requires team meetings. As you know, sales meetings can get chaotic. It's the nature of the personalities involved to be outspoken, assertive, expressive, self-interested, and territorial. In the early going, ground rules help to streamline the process and, more importantly, avoid tensions that derail team effectiveness. This is where the leader has to exert a little command/control authority to preserve the peace and facilitate group productivity.

Following are a few ground rules that might be effective in getting your sales team on the same page:

- Everyone participates.

- In meetings, no one talks over another.

- We support each other and we help each other succeed.

- Every comment is valuable and encouraged.

- There are no hidden agendas. We seek excellence, not personal gratification.

- All opinions are valued, but personal preferences sometimes have to be surrendered for the sake of decisions that are good for the team.

- The only bad question is the one not asked.

- Not all ideas can be used, but all ideas are welcomed and beneficial.

- Not everything is up for vote. (The leader's job is to build consensus when possible and be as fair as possible for everyone; however, the leader makes the ultimate decision because the leader has ultimate accountability.)

- We seek overwhelming agreement in team decisions when unanimity is not possible.

- Team members (regardless of their individual positions) are asked to support team decisions.

- All input is created equal—managers' and non-managers' opinions carry equal weight.

Ask your team for additional ground rules, and encourage them to help set a tone that keeps everyone working together and feeling good about the process. The last thing you want is a few outspoken people dominating the sessions, or people feeling intimidated or afraid to participate. For best results, managers have to ensure that their ideas are treated the same as everyone else's—team members should feel comfortable disagreeing with managers' input or discarding their suggestions as they would any other team member.

Customize your ground rules to fit your team climate, then write them on a large poster and make it visible in your team meeting area as a constant reminder of team values.

Forming, Storming, Norming, Performing

In 1965, psychologist Bruce Tuckman described the path that many groups traverse on the way to becoming high-performing teams. He described the process as "forming, storming, norming, and performing."

Forming is the initial stage, when the team roles and boundaries are defined, responsibilities are assigned, ground rules are established and purpose is articulated.

Storming is the next stage, when you find members going through team growing pains. Some will push boundaries, some will jockey for position, and others might challenge your authority. The additional workload might irritate or even overwhelm some. Interpersonal conflicts will inevitably arise as members offer opinions and challenge others. These friction points are normal and a necessary part of team growth. Strong leadership will prevent many conflicts through an insistence on collaboration and through clearly defined roles and procedures.

Norming comes as the team learns to work together despite their differences in work styles and perspective. As they become accustomed to the team-building environment, they learn to provide constructive feedback and ask each other for help. It takes time to learn team coping skills, but the eventual result is mutual respect for each other and you as the team leader.

Performing is the final step when the team begins achieving its goals with minimal conflict. At this stage, team processes have been refined to the point that the leader can delegate work and spend more time developing individual team members. In fact, a high-performing sales team will identify and solve problems as well as exploiting opportunities without a lot of managerial direction.

Your First Meeting

The first team meeting is surprising, rewarding, frustrating, and puzzling—all the stuff that makes sales management fun and maddening. Dozens of voices and ideas, in varying degrees of volume and wisdom, require sorting and prioritizing. Here are seven ways to streamline your first and subsequent meetings:

1. **Control the setting**—Pick a quiet place to meet with minimal distractions. Meeting rooms without windows help team members concentrate. Be sure that all smartphones, iPads, and other communications devices are turned off.

2. **Have two easels or presentation boards**—One should be for you to note team members' input. This is the focal point for jotting down all ideas relating to the main task at hand. The other is the "in-box" for ideas that arise which don't directly pertain to the issue but are worth future consideration. The in-box accomplishes two things. First, it allows the leader to keep the team on track by deferring off-topic issues for a later day. Second, it provides a repository of good ideas for the future. In the early going you'll get extensive entries in the in-box because salespeople have a tendency to digress from the topic at hand.

3. **Prominently display an enlarged copy of your ground rules**—Refer to it during the meeting to remind team members. Also distribute copies to the team at the beginning of the meeting.

4. **If you have a predetermined issue to address, prepare the best you can**—Study the issue in advance, and then write it at the top of the blank easel to provide focus for team members, for example, "How Do We Reach New Business Objectives?" This makes the issue visual and encourages focus.

5. **Ask for a volunteer to take minutes**—You will refer to the minutes later for task assignments, key issues, and other topics discussed. Another option is to use your original easel paper for later reference, but often it lacks the detail you have in minutes.

6. **Get a volunteer to lead the next meeting**—You, as the manager, should lead the first meeting. After that, reps should lead the meeting on a rotating basis.

7. **Conduct the meeting in four segments**—The segments you should use are itemize, prioritize, analyze, and mobilize.

   Itemize—The first step is to itemize everything on the minds of your team pertaining to a particular topic—in this case, for example, the topic is "How do we reach new business objectives?" This is the brainstorming part, when team members should feel free to verbalize their ideas—no matter how outlandish or fatuous. List them all on the board, giving equal credence to each. Encourage all team members to participate while discouraging any from dominating. To encourage quieter team members, you can ask for their input during the meeting; some teams' ground rules call for 100% participation, which is a little heavy-handed but it does make everyone prepare. A subtler approach is to allow input at any time following the meeting, which gives introverts time to voice their opinion through e-mails, texts, or chats with the manager. Sometimes you'll get additional information from team members by allowing anonymous responses outside the meeting, especially if you're dealing with sensitive issues. Your initial list might look like the following example:

How do we reach new business objectives?

- Developing a new business marketing kit to provide prospects
- Getting updated lists from city hall of business start-ups
- Improving order entry to speed new business paperwork
- Creating visuals specifically for new business
- Purchasing new business lists
- Improving new business training
- Offering discounts to new business
- Assigning reps to specialize in new business only

Prioritize—After you've heard and listed all the ideas, prioritizing the issues helps the team sort and focus on important things first. Using the new business example, let's say you have 15 items listed by your reps. As a team, vote on a prioritized list from 1 to 15. You will not have a unanimous consensus at this point or any point of the meeting, and you shouldn't. But, at the same time, all team members should feel that their input was valued and respected.

Analyze—The analysis phase begins now with the selection of the top issue to examine first. This takes some drilling down and might require research beyond the initial team meeting. Let's assume "Discounts for new business" is number one. Analyze the pros and cons and potential benefits of discounts. List them on the board. Discuss everything your team knows about such discounts, as well as the unknowns that require follow-up investigation. The analysis phase ensures that the team has looked at all phases of the issue and is comfortable with moving ahead.

Mobilize—The final step is to mobilize your resources and people to activate the team's decisions, to either implement or to explore the issue further. This is the time to assign sales team members and support staff to enact activities prescribed by the team. Develop a task list showing actions and those assigned to the task. It would look like this:

"New Business Discounts"

- Obtain research, articles on new business discounts—Karen
- Create a price elasticity study—Ashley
- Develop order entry refinements for new business sales—Bill
- Design a market trial for new discount program—Chris
- Establish metrics to measure results of the discount program—Kim
- Review competitors' discounts for new business—Josh

During this phase, it's important to keep the team apprised of progress and results. Encourage team members to interact among themselves, to help and inform each other. This interaction is vital to the team process. In fact, you should encourage team interaction as much as, or more than, communicating back to you.

Understanding Team Dynamics

A team's first few meetings are ideological free-for-alls, replete with conflict, inappropriate humor, arguing, hidden agendas, apathy, and verbosity. You can reduce the chaos by understanding team members' dynamics.

First of all, avoid the dynamic of "groupthink." This is the phenomenon that occurs when people defer their opinions to conform to group thinking. A certain amount of compromise is needed in groups, but it becomes counterproductive if it silences team members' opinions. Those who keep quiet to maintain team conformity are actually contributing to poor decisions. Overcoming "groupthink" requires that all members feel free to express themselves and that no one is subconsciously bullied into compliance. Everyone should feel *obligated* to express his dissent with team decisions, and have his opinion heard. A good team leader will actively seek dissenting opinions as the group moves toward decisions. Many times, a single opposing thought will change the course of the team's direction and strengthen its decision.

Groupthink and other team dysfunctions are frequently caused by team imbalances. The most common problem is decisions overly influenced by Dominators—team members who are outspoken and persuasive. Obviously, sales teams have a high incidence of Dominators. That goes with the territory. They are the best and worst of team dynamics. Dominators are the rainmakers, the lightning-in-a-bottle types who bring leadership, experience, and salient ideas to the team process. At the same time they can intimidate and railroad team decisions. They frequently have hidden agendas. Many times, they expect the team to follow their lead, and exhibit resentfulness when they don't get their way. The leader has to ensure that Dominators have their say, because their input usually is invaluable. But other team members have to be prompted to speak up even if it means going against the Dominator. This give-and-take, done in a constructive way, is vital to effective team decisions. You can address this through ground rules that let Dominators know up front that everyone's input is valued but no one can expect to get her way. Encourage your people to agree to disagree. Make team discussions like friends who have differing opinions but are able to talk without animosity or invective. Encourage diverse ideas while seeking team consensus. Remember that consensus is not unanimity. It doesn't mean everyone agrees with the decision, but they do agree to accept and facilitate it. This especially applies to Dominators.

One additional step the leader can take to bring out the best in Dominators is to have side discussions with them outside the meeting environment. Thank them for their input and leadership, and ask them for their opinions on the team process in general. Let them know you appreciate their going along with decisions with which they might not agree. These side talks will let them know you recognize and appreciate their abilities. In the long run, this will help reduce any bitterness they might feel from the failure to "sell" the team on their ideas.

In reality, many sales team meetings are about as organized as a street fight. Salespeople have strong opinions, like to voice them, and tend to "sell" them. It gets chaotic quickly if the leader doesn't step in to direct traffic, minimize friction, and maximize inclusion from the reps. Don't let outspoken reps hijack the meeting, and make sure everyone has a voice in the decision. It's important to build overwhelming agreement from team members while recognizing that some will not concur with the team. To address dissenters, establish a fundamental team value that encourages compromise and a "team player" attitude.

That is, you might disagree with the play (or decision) but you'll give it your best to make it work. In the same vein, dissuade reps from taking a rigid position and "selling" it to the team. Team building requires an open exchange of opinions, with participants remaining receptive to other ideas. Discourage team members from "owning" ideas. Encourage them to stay flexible and consider other positions. Develop the habit of laying all ideas on the table and selecting the best ones that a majority of the team can support.

In spite of your best intentions, you'll find reps who won't participate in the process—especially in the early going. Hopefully, over time, you'll gradually win them over. However, there will be those who simply don't get it or won't get it. Honestly, there's not a lot you can do with these people other than monitor them to minimize any negative impact on the team and make sure they are complying with group decisions. After all, no one has the option to pick and choose which team decisions they follow. In the long run, you'll find the "lone wolves" moving on to sales jobs that match their temperament. As this occurs, it gives you the chance to hire replacements with team skills that will reinforce effective team building.

You'll also find team "loafers"—those who fail to pull their share of the workload. The best way to handle this problem is by making it transparent. At the first meeting, address it and get it out in the open for all team members to scrutinize. Make it a reportable offense, and make sure all team members hold each other accountable for pulling their weight. Peer pressure is a powerful tool that will help prevent loafers.

On the positive side, "early adopters" will help drive the team process from the outset. They might be natural team players who instantly see the value of team building. Some will go along with you out of loyalty. Others might have been burned in the past by self-absorbed managers, and welcome a different approach. Hopefully, your "early adopters" will include leaders from your Unseen Team, those reps who informally, but effectively influence team dynamics. The best way to engage them is at the pre-planning stage, giving them an early role in your efforts. Regardless of their motivation, be sure to cultivate your "early adopters" by keeping them informed on a one-on-one basis and making sure they know how much you appreciate their efforts.

Tips for Team Building

Create a buzz. Successful teams show excitability and cross-pollination. Develop this beehive aura by setting an objective or a vision that challenges your team, one that actively involves them in making a meaningful contribution to the company. The second part: Continually encourage cross-pollination of ideas. Team members should be talking among themselves outside the meeting, exchanging ideas and concepts. It's not so much the quality of ideas that is initially important, it's the pattern of communication that counts. After your team members are discussing team topics informally among themselves outside the meeting room, you'll begin to feel the buzz.

Make team contributions a part of your formal appraisal system. Financially reward active team members. Similarly, consider informal rewards such as gift cards to team members for outstanding team performance or for such things as "idea of the week."

Team building is a face-to-face process. Meetings are necessary. Allow out-of-town members to join via video conference, but continually emphasize the need for attendance at team meetings. The face-to-face relationships create the buzz and team trust.

Share the team experience. Invite your boss to team meetings for the credibility it adds. Employees from other departments, even customers, can add a valuable perspective to meetings.

Guest speakers add a refreshing change of pace.

Foster a tactfully honest environment in which team members can address issues without offending others. This takes work, but the key is for all members to be considerate of each other, perhaps being critical of ideas without being critical of the person attached to the idea.

Have audiovisual equipment available for members to exhibit video and Internet visuals to the group, as well as connecting to outside sources of information. Be sure to have the ability to project online connections and use Internet searches extensively for team questions. A great deal of research is available immediately from Internet searches to expedite problem solving and group decision making.

As the manager, step back and let things happen. Don't ask for reports and updates from the team, but do ask that they keep each other updated. Let them lead the process. You can informally stay abreast of team activities through casual conversations with team members, but let them decide how to inform you in between meetings.

Team cohesiveness is stronger when an external threat or competition exists. Threats from competitors or even economic threats to job security can help develop this "us against them" attitude.

The biggest challenge in team building is getting your people actively involved. To accomplish this, keep reminding the team about the power of synergy—that is, two plus two equals six—which far surpasses what individuals can do by themselves. This synergy makes individuals better salespeople. Better salespeople create stronger profits for the company. Stronger profits mean more money for reps and job security.

It will take some time to get all members onboard and active. Be patient. Sometimes a little command/control is necessary, insisting on teamwork and on adherence to ground rules.

Finally, establish your team dynamics at your pace in concert with your people. Don't rush the process. Don't force it. Begin slowly with small, insignificant tasks. In the beginning stages, it's better to underorganize than overorganize. Don't overwhelm your people or try to move too fast. Let team dynamics decide how fast you should go. It could take a year until everyone is comfortable with being open and sharing. Some will never get there, but make sure even the doubters are included.

Three Ways Sales Teams Enhance Managers' Success

As a sales manager, you're a problem solver. You create ways to maximize market opportunities. You inspire and motivate people. Notwithstanding your personal successes, the best sales manager in the history of sales can achieve only a fraction of what a high-performing team can do. Your team gives you the multiplier effect, a way to exponentially leverage the talents and experience of your people to build individual and group success. Here are three primary ways for a team to build successful sales:

1. **Problem Solving**—You're faced with dozens of problems every day that require time, attention, and energy. Take them to your team. Granted, you can't take them all for team consideration; there are simply too many. And some—such as personnel issues—aren't suitable for team discussion. Still, there are hundreds of problems your team can solve effectively with an economy of time and effort. The list of possibilities is virtually endless, including product pricing, customer discounts, sales objectives, commissions, and nearly anything with which the sales force has experience.

2. **Training**—Your team members can provide credibility and uniqueness to formal training. Ask the team to run a training session, using their experience on the topic to add realism and a deeper explanation of the subject. Your team can also develop training in needed areas that the manager might have overlooked. This process applies to any kind of training, including product, technology, and sales techniques instruction. The added benefit is that the best way for reps to learn is to teach.

3. **Planning/Organization**—Have your salespeople organize your next campaign kickoff, awards presentation, or social function. They know what to include to make events appealing, and things to avoid that reps find boring. It's usually best to ask for a small group of volunteers. Let them select their leader and develop the agenda with minimal guidance.

Things to Expect from a High-Performing Team

Optimal team performance is like an orchestra in which various instruments create a symphony. You know it when you hear it. You feel it. The numbers tell the story. Following are specific activities that you should expect to hear and see on a daily basis. In fact, you should consider these processes as a daily part of the sales rep's job:

Competitive intelligence. Your people learn a lot on the street about competitors' plans. They also gather information from reading and online sources as well. They should feel compelled to share this information with other reps and management.

Coaching sales techniques. Your reps should share their sales techniques formally and informally with each other. It could be in sales meetings or just mentioning it one-on-one with others.

Product applications. Your sales force probably develops innovative product/service applications every day. They should be disseminating these applications to you and other reps.

Best practices. Similarly, your reps should be educating each other in best practices ranging from pricing to administrative procedures.

Technology assistance. Your people should be helping each other figure out new applications, hardware, and such things as CRM and sales funnel processes. They know the shortcuts and should be sharing them.

Values confirmation. You should be hearing your reps repeating your team values and ground rules. The important thing is that they're discussing values among themselves, not just in front of you.

Encouragement. Your salespeople should be encouraging each other's success. Working with each other is powerful synergy. Working against each other is simply dysfunctional. It's possible to be competitive while being encouraging, that is, taking a "beat you at your best" attitude.

These functions have two vital parts. First, your reps should feel comfortable, even compelled, to instruct and educate others. You have to make this happen since it is not a normal course of action for salespeople. Not only do they need encouragement to share, but they also need instruction on how to share. They have to be careful not to come off as a know-it-all, and to avoid any air of superiority. The key is to impart knowledge in a friendly, helpful manner, one colleague to another.

Second, help your reps be receptive. It's easy to feel a little defensive when someone offers help or suggestions. Let your reps know that this is an expected part of learning: providing information and receiving it in a gracious way. It's a two-way process. And it helps everyone improve.

You'll have to reinforce this process through observation and follow-up. Make it an integral part of your sales culture in writing and in everyday experience. Include it in personnel assessments. Set an example yourself by willingly being taught by your reps. In fact, challenge them to teach you as well. After all, even the best can get better, managers as well as reps.

The By-Product of Teamwork Is Better Sales

The very things that make successful teams also create successful salespeople. Essentially, teamwork is a process of sales reps getting outside of themselves to collaborate and cooperate. Similarly, this is what good salespeople do with customers. They work together to identify and meet customer needs, to solve problems, and to help customers maximize opportunities. Team meetings, in which your people work together to solve problems and perform tasks, are coaching sessions in communications and interpersonal relations. When you enforce ground rules, your salespeople are receiving valuable feedback (as well discipline and self-awareness) that helps them ultimately connect better with customers. They learn from others how to express themselves constructively and how to moderate behavior that obstructs relationships. They learn on the spot when they're being obstinate or overbearing. Similarly, they learn the value of open and honest communications.

Team dynamics provide reps with a rare opportunity to learn about themselves. Customers don't have the time or inclination to give feedback. They simply buy or they don't. They won't tell you why. Training sessions and coaching are always valuable but they are infrequent. And they tend to be formal and impersonally unilateral—that is, the sessions emanate from a trainer or coach in a one-way manner that might inhibit active feedback. On the other hand, high-performance teams expect members to connect with each other productively. And the feedback is immediate. What better way to sharpen one's sales skills than by having to sell your ideas to your peers, who can be pretty tough customers?

Working in a team environment sharpens the things that make salespeople successful:

- Empathy—Being a successful team member means you have to understand others' opinions and positions. The process of walking in the shoes of your sales peers enables you to better comprehend your customers' needs and proclivities.

- Self-Awareness—Team communications is a mirror reflecting how well you're communicating. You learn quickly—from others' input—when you're being offensive or not getting your point across. This increased level of awareness helps reps remain nimble and communicative with customers.

- Assertiveness—The ability to express contrary thoughts in a diplomatic way is a valuable skill learned in team processes that applies to overcoming customer objections as well as customer fact-finding.

- Negotiation—Team members learn to promote win-win negotiations, giving a little to get a little. This is a valuable lesson that applies to customer transactions by helping reps prevent their own intractability and stubbornness.

- Openness—Remaining open to others' opinions and positions is a crucial part of team activities that helps reps be more flexible and attentive to customers.

- Conscientiousness—The peer pressure exerted in a team environment helps reps develop a sense of responsibility and accountability. They are judged every day by their colleagues on how well they perform their team tasks and duties.

- Agreeableness—Modesty, compliance, and altruism are all lessons learned in team dynamics that translate directly to interactions with customers.

Just as important, team processes help reps *balance* these characteristics. Top salespeople have the uncanny ability of knowing when to push and when to back off, when to talk and when to listen, when to be forceful and when to concede. Team feedback compels reps to build this ability, to recognize when they're over the top or not forceful enough. For example, in a team meeting the overly aggressive rep should hear, "You're being a little pushy and you're losing me." The dominating rep might be admonished with, "Do you mind if I express my thinking about this?" or "I wasn't done; may I finish?" The overly agreeable or nonassertive one might be encouraged with, "I'd really like to hear your opinion on this subject."

Care and Feeding of the Sales Team

A big part of team building is daily maintenance to continually build team momentum. Your employees are your warriors, your frontline soldiers. Make sure they are well-trained, are well-armed, and walk with a little swagger.

Needless to say, your people's trust in you is the key to all sustained sales management success (see Chapter 1, "First Step: Manage Yourself"). Then comes elements ranging from mentoring to ego affirmation. Here are a few.

Give and Get Respect

Respect your reps, no matter what. The more you give, the more you get back. Doug Cartland, author and speaker, said, "The basis for teamwork is genuine respect for each other and what each other brings to the table—a respect that goes beyond gender, race, economic status, even beyond ideologies and disagreements." Essentially, team building is based on nurturing and facilitating respect. The result is team success created by collaboration, communication, shared vision, and a mutual regard for each other's best interests.

Engage Your People

If you believe that your people are the key to your personal success, if that is the spirit and intent of your efforts, everything will fall into place. No matter how good a manager you are, you can't sail the ship by yourself. Unfortunately, the reverse is true—that is, a poor manager can single-handedly sink a ship. But to win, it takes all hands on deck, fully engaged in all elements of planning, policy, and procedures.

The Power of Asking

If there is a single word that's critical to teambuilding, it is "ask." Used for centuries by educators and psychiatrists, the Socratic method includes conceptual questions followed by probing questions. In fact, the Socratic method is at the center of "SPIN Selling," a popular sales technique used by many experienced salespeople.

Ask your salespeople what makes them successful. What makes them productive. What motivates them. What they need in order to be more successful. What works and what doesn't. In TQM circles this is known as the beginnings of process improvement. It starts by asking.

It doesn't have to be a formalized process. It can be as simple as asking your salespeople how to increase new business, and probing for examples and techniques. The simple act of asking is actually quite profound and complex. First, it tells the listeners that you respect their opinions. Respect energizes your people. Second, you're sharing in decisions that affect their lives; therefore, you're getting their buy-in. When a person owns part of a decision, she's more likely to make that decision work.

Caution: Asking means you don't have all the answers. Are you ready to admit it? Simply saying, "I don't have all the answers," is a powerful statement that will rally your people around you. Practice it. It's good for your soul. And, you know it's the truth. Also, it takes a lot of pressure off you. No longer are you the person everyone is looking to for answers. The simple act of asking shares the workload with your people. It allows managers to take a thoughtful, disciplined, interactive approach rather than shooting from the hip.

Having trouble meeting a sales objective? Ask the ones on the front line how to do it.

Planning? Setting objectives? Developing rates? Creating advertising? Overcoming competition? Ask and it will be delivered. Your people will surprise you with process improvements garnered from their years of experience. All you need to do is open the door and ask them to share.

General Colin Powell transformed questions into an art form. He said, "I'm sure you've heard the old stereotype about men not stopping for directions. That's fun to chuckle about, but in the business world if you don't stop to ask for directions, you'll sink—and bring the whole company down with you. If you see a problem, ask questions until you find solutions. If you don't know how to do something, ask someone on your team. Great leaders know that the right questions unearth problems and yield tremendous understanding about employees and customers."

We sometimes overanalyze and struggle to figure out people and systems. Why not just ask? It will save a lot of time, guesswork, and dead ends. For example, as managers, most of us have been like Sherlock Holmes trying to figure out what motivates subordinates. We spend hours looking for clues, analyzing their numbers, and observing how they react to sales contests. Wouldn't it be easier just to sit down one-on-one with them and ask, "In order of priority, what motivates you? What really turns you on as a salesperson? What can I do as a manager to keep you energized and motivated?"

Instead of a painstaking effort to solve the mystery of motivation, you've just done it in a half-hour session of asking the right questions. The added bonus is that you've just demonstrated that you care enough to ask. You've bought yourself a bit of loyalty.

The next step: Listen.

When you ask, make sure you write down every response made by your people. In front of the group, write it all down. Let them know you want every bit of their input.

Practice active listening: Follow up with questions and comments to let the speaker know you're engaged and interested in what he or she is saying. In group settings and individually, it helps to give your people your undivided attention. Look them in the eye as if there were nothing else in the room. Don't answer the phone; don't check your e-mail or text messages. Wherever possible, make responses that assure the speaker you are listening.

Accept the crazy, lame, and zany. Accept it all enthusiastically as if every word is worth framing. Be ready for comments you don't like, but be sure to be tolerant and nonjudgmental in order to keep the dialogue flowing. When you're looking for quality input, the manager's silence is golden. Give your people their moment, the ability to speak without being criticized or confronted.

The next step: Act.

If you've spent a lot of time asking and listening, it's all wasted if you don't finish the process with action. There are two components to this final step: taking action and ensuring that everyone knows about it. Every time you act on your team's ideas, you build a reservoir of trust while reinforcing the power and effectiveness of the team.

You can't act on everything, and team members need to understand that. Make it a clear ground rule. Not all suggestions are created equal; some are actionable and others aren't. The manager has to make a conscious effort to prevent team members from getting offended or dejected if their input isn't used. Let your people know it's like a firing range—you'll miss a lot of shots until you hit the bull's-eye.

Make sure your team knows that you've taken actions based on team input. Reiterate in team meetings and e-mails specifically the policy or procedural changes that have resulted from team input.

When you develop enhancements and innovations, be sure to give credit where it's due. Never take credit for the team's ideas. You will ultimately get credit for the ideas privately from your superiors, but make sure team members get the public recognition.

Limitless Selling

The human brain is capable of amazing feats when presented with challenge. It is estimated that people use, on average, only 10% of their brain. Using an additional 10% might be all it takes for your sales reps to accomplish not just goals but lifetime dreams.

Here are ways the sales manager can help activate that extra 10% brain capacity:

- Present challenging, record-breaking goals.
- Help reps believe in themselves, that they are capable of achieving extraordinary goals. The world thought it was impossible to run the mile faster than four minutes until Roger Bannister actually did it.

- Assist reps in identifying not just short-term objectives but life dreams (such as being president of the company or making $200,000 per year).

- Develop, in concert with the rep, a workable plan to accomplish the goals. Provide technical support, encouragement, tracking, and training to turn the thought into an aspiration into a reality.

- Keep them on solid footing, aware that there's a price to pay for achievement. It takes long hours, hard work, self-discipline, and learning new work habits.

Turn "know your limits" attitudes to "know no limits" selling. Obviously, extreme goal setting is not for everyone—some simply won't want to work that hard—but the active participants can make it worthwhile for themselves and you, the sales manager.

Tolerate Cockiness

It's okay for your salespeople to be outspoken and a little cocky. You want your salespeople confident and aggressive. It's a lot better than the alternative. We all need positive self-talk to drown out self-doubt. Salespeople especially need it to overcome the rejection and resistance they face daily.

Cockiness can actually have psychological benefits for salespeople. We all—especially salespeople—fight negative self-talk on a daily basis. A rep with a cocky demeanor might be cultivating positive thinking that expresses itself verbally. No matter how insufferably self-congratulatory they might be, reps with an air of bravado might be helping themselves to maintain optimism.

Research indicates that salespeople who are optimists are higher achievers and less prone to depression. Research done by Peter Schulman, published in the *Journal of Selling and Sales Management,* noted that insurance agents identified as optimists sold 35% more, whereas pessimists were twice as likely to quit in the first year of selling. "Pilot research in various industries—telecommunications, real estate, office products, auto sales, banking, and others—has found results similar to the insurance research. Optimists outsold the pessimist by 20 to 40 percent."

In fact, there is a school of thought that optimism can be learned and strengthened, leading to successful personal and professional endeavors. In his book *Learned Optimism,* Martin Seligman discusses how to become more effective by shaping your mental outlook. He is known for his five-point plan to develop one's optimism using "ABCDE" techniques.

"A" is adversity. This is an occurrence that creates frustration or defeat. For example, say a sales rep is angered by a customer who cancels three appointments in row, all at the last minute.

"B" is beliefs about that event, the mental recordings played about the event. In this case, the rep is thinking, "What a jerk! This customer has no manners and no consideration of my time."

"C" is consequences. The rep should make note of the emotions and thoughts pertaining to the customer and possible actions. Fueled by anger, the rep might consider dropping the account, not calling the customer again or even a vengeful tactic like setting up another appointment and then canceling it at the last minute to teach the customer a lesson. The ultimate consequence, of course, would be to lose the account, forfeit the commission, and take a setback in achieving objectives.

"D" is disputation, referring to the conscious act of the sales rep stopping the negative recordings and taking a moment to think clearly about the situation, and dispute negative thoughts. This is the "snap out of it" stage. During this phase, the rep might consider that the customer could be overwhelmed by events on the job. Maybe the business is about to go under and the customer is faced with one crisis after another. Or it could be a personal or family crisis that the customer is going through. Furthermore, the rep thinks, the customer probably does this to everyone so it's nothing personal.

"E" is energization, or the phase in which positive feelings of hope and optimism are created by halting the negative flow and focusing on constructive thinking. This gives the rep a chance to redirect thoughts. Instead of feeling angry and obstructionist, the rep decides to feel sympathetic and persist in setting another appointment. Psychologists call this process "sublimation," which means you are channeling unacceptable impulses such as anger into more acceptable ones such as sympathy. After all, the customer's inability to schedule appointments might be masking a problem that could be a sales opportunity for the rep. For example, if the rep finally gets the appointment, the rep's persistence has to impress the customer. And it gives the rep a chance to fact-find and build rapport with the customer, perhaps during a difficult time when the customer is looking for help.

Over time, the goal of "learned optimism" is to reduce negative thoughts and transform them into more positive, actionable responses. In this way a salesperson can move forward instead of being trapped in counterproductive thoughts and emotions. You know it's successful when this becomes the default reaction to adversity.

Along similar lines, researchers at the University of Kansas found that the simple act of smiling can help relieve the stress of difficult events. Test subjects were given demanding activities to perform, such as tracing a star with their nondominant hand by looking at the reflection of the star through a mirror. During this stressful activity, one group maintained a neutral facial expression, another group held a forced smile, and another had a natural smile. The groups with smiles showed lower heart rates and decreased self-reported stress levels than those with neutral expressions. Those with natural smiles exhibited the least amount of stress-related effects. The simple act of smiling—a form of learned optimism—can, in fact, have positive physical benefits especially during stressful times. As proponents of neuroplasticity assert, the brain can be reprogrammed by positive thoughts and actions to form beneficial habits and behavioral skills that make us stress resistant and optimistic.

At the end of the day, however, optimism means little without action. In the book *Good to Great,* James Collins described a kind of actionable optimism he called the "Stockdale Paradox." It's named after Admiral Jim Stockdale, who was the highest-ranking officer held as a Vietnam War prisoner of war. In captivity for eight years, Stockdale never lost faith that he would eventually return home, "I never doubted not only that I would get out, but also that I would prevail in the end and turn the experience into the defining event of my life, which, in retrospect, I would not trade." The paradox is that those who were optimistic without taking action were less likely to survive. They were likely to "stick their heads in the sand" and hope for the hardships to disappear. Stockdale faced the harsh reality of captivity, maintained optimism that he would get out alive, and developed such things as a tapping code for prisoners to communicate, as well as sending intelligence in letters to his wife. Stockdale found that it's important to be optimistic, but it's equally important to take action based on an honest, realistic assessment of the situation.

Build Team Confidence Through Ego Affirmation

In addition to building team members' confidence through positive self-talk and learned optimism, managers can use ego affirmation to strengthen salespeople's self-esteem or ego. It's a known fact that self-confident salespeople sell more. But you can't build self-confidence without first building sales reps' self-esteem. After all, self-confidence is simply one of many outward manifestations of the salesperson's inner ego system. Major influences on sales reps' self-esteem are significant-others such as family, friends, and, you guessed it, bosses. You, as the boss, have a huge impact on your people's self-image that rivals that of parents, friends, and spouses. This position gives you power to bolster their ego, which thereby improves their selling power.

Self-esteem is a mental muscle that requires exercise for maximal strength. The manager's role is twofold: To actively *develop* team members' self-esteem, and to help *maintain* healthy egos. For example, say you have a rep who sees himself as honest, resourceful, persistent, and hardworking. These are important values that compose his self-image. You can reaffirm these values by observing behavior and commenting on it. Tell the sales rep how much you appreciate him for working overtime to make a big sale. Or express how the rep's honesty led to saving a sale. Providing a verbal reward not only recognizes the behavior (what he did), but, more importantly, reinforces the rep's self-esteem (who he is). It's important that your comments are genuine and believable. Otherwise, you'll lack credibility and be viewed as patronizing or obsequious.

First of all, you have to know what values are the drivers in your salespeople's self-esteem. Ask them to jot down the things of which they are proud. The focus should be on values, "who they are" characteristics rather than "what they do," but can include skills as well, such as closing expertise or strength in fact-finding. If you prefer, make two lists: one of "who they are" values and one of "what they do" skills. Encourage your reps to list as many "who they are" items because you need to know the underlying values that create the skills. If a sales rep says he's a good rapport builder with customers, the underlying value might be empathy. Or, if he's a good closer, the underlying value could be persistence; or patience could be the driver behind overcoming objections. Be sure to keep the list short, perhaps the top five values. The longer the list, the harder it is for you to manage. In addition, by trying to focus on too many factors, you deflect emphasis away from the key components.

This list will help remind you of the things important to your reps, and help guide your comments and actions to build and maintain their self-esteem.

Ego affirmation helps develop salespeople's selling confidence, helping them to higher levels of self-assurance. But think of it another way. In the absence of recognizing sales reps' virtues, you get varying forms of resentment. A rep who works weekends and evenings but never gets acknowledged for hard work is likely to become embittered. It's just human nature for us to be proud of certain things about ourselves, whether it is intelligence or trustworthiness. We, either consciously or subconsciously, seek validation of these virtues from people important to us, especially our bosses.

Equally important in this process of observe-and-comment is what *not* to emphasize. A rep who sees himself as hardworking will not react well to being called lazy. If honesty is important to him, carefully avoid implying dishonesty. For example, if the rep is involved in a dispute with a customer, let the rep know you can count on his or her honesty, and then use fact-finding to unearth the truth. When it comes to discussing behavior or circumstances that are contrary to reps' self-image, handle it gingerly. Come at the issue in a way that does not threaten the rep's self-avowed values. Otherwise, the rep is likely not only to reject the message but also to discredit the messenger, you the manager.

When you have negative feedback for the rep, use the "sandwich" technique. Provide the criticism, preceded with and followed by positive information. If, for example, you have a customer complaint to discuss with the rep, start with, "You have a great renewal rate, which means you have a lot of happy customers. I'm always impressed with your patience and people skills. However, as you know, we can't please all the people all the time." Then after discussing the complaint, end with something like, "That's the bad news. The good news is that I'm really confident in your ability to win back this customer. You've shown me time and time again how persistent you are and how good you are with customer follow-up."

Prevent Sales Burnout

Your salespeople don't get burnout from hard work. Hard, challenging work is exhilarating and meaningful as long as you get a sense of accomplishment from it. Burnout comes from doing work at which you cannot succeed. You can have individual and/or team burnout. The first red flag to look for is failure to reach goals over a period of time. That's when burnout begins. If, like Sisyphus, you have people repeatedly rolling the stone to the top of the hill only to have it roll back again, it's time to explore the problem and seek solutions.

Two major causes of sales burnout are *frustration* and *boredom.* Frustration with failure to achieve objectives can drive any good salesperson into a tailspin. It takes more than a couple of bad weeks. Burnout results after repeated failure over months, even years. All salespeople are different and have varying degrees of tolerance to frustration. But a large contributing factor is the feeling of being overwhelmed by circumstances time and time again. These conditions could include a weak economy, changing industry patterns, competition, and other factors over which the salesperson has no control. This was a common occurrence in the economic recession that began in 2008, when a convergence of economic setbacks besieged sales teams for a number of years. The housing and mortgage markets tanked. Consumer spending plummeted. Unemployment soared. Unfortunately, some sales groups maintained inflated objectives without adjusting for market conditions. And sales floors became a breeding ground for burnout for frustrated reps who found it impossible to reach lofty goals in a train-wreck economy. The 2008 recession is an extreme example. Burnout can be caused on a more common basis by a frustrating mix of market conditions, personal problems, customer churn, industry changes, and just plain old bad luck. When conditions combine to prevent goal achievement over time, burnout can occur. Even the most resilient rep can contract it, and weaker ones are likely to suffer.

In addition to frustration as a causal agent for burnout, boredom also ranks high. Obviously, some reps are more easily bored than others. But when a person goes to work every day doing the same thing year after year with similar results and outcomes, burnout can rear its ugly head, especially for reps who have been doing the same job for more than five years.

Usually, we know when a salesperson is getting burned out. Many times, it is readily apparent. When it happens, there's a likelihood the person will focus on making the sale rather than really taking care of the customer. Burnout saps a person's energy and initiative; however, the pressure to reach sales goals remains. The result is a desperation, not necessarily to make sales, but to avoid losing sales. The difference between the two approaches is huge. Burnout can change a rep's attitude from aggressive/proactive to defensive/reactive. This might take the form of reps taking shortcuts or perhaps misrepresenting the product with "white lies." It's the "anything to get a signature" mind-set. Therefore, you'll see customer complaints rise. Such reps also will resist new training and show a general lack of accountability, blaming failure on everything but themselves. Burned-out salespeople usually have a "greener grass" mentality that impels them to look for new jobs.

Salespeople can wear a convincing mask that conceals burnout behind a smiling façade. In those cases, look for clues such as decreases in sales results, an increase in tardiness and absenteeism, or rising levels of irritability, inattention, impatience, apathy, argumentativeness, and cynicism. Burnout could present itself through an attitude shift from "get after it" to "who cares" and from "can do" to "can't do." If you're lucky, the sales rep might just come out and tell you he's getting burned out.

An integral part of handling burnout is an early detection system. Make sure you have "red flag" metrics that measure changes in salespeople's production. Spikes and valleys might indicate that individual reps are having problems. The easiest way to stay ahead of burnout is to investigate changes in sales production, behavior, or attitude. Just ask your rep what's going on. Probe. When you detect a potential problem, don't accept simple answers from the rep that it's just a run of bad luck. Ask more questions, even personal ones, that get to root causes. Find out whether the rep is unhappy with pay, procedures, pressures, or other job-related processes. Every minute you spending probing could save hours of problem solving later.

Burnout is complicated. It's not a problem the manager can fix overnight. In reality, the only person who can solve it is the victim. But there are things a manager can do alleviate burnout such as these:

- Provide reassurance that the rep is still a vital part of the team. Let him know you haven't written him off as a loser. You, as a manager, cannot fix the problem by yourself. But you can support the rep through this dark period if you decide to make it a temporary phase rather than a permanent condition.

- Establish challenging yet achievable objectives on an individual basis. If a rep is not meeting quotas over time, burnout is a probability. Set reachable goals, taking into account market and competitive conditions. Have the wisdom and courage to ratchet down objectives when conditions warrant it. Steady increases in objectives year after year might look good on paper, but they can take a toll on your salespeople. Create mutually agreeable objectives with each salesperson, giving each person custom tailored goals to meet his or her skill set. This will decrease frustration and increase their accountability for the objectives—after all, they helped set the goals.

- Place the appropriate emphasis on numbers. Even if sales reps are achieving objectives, they can get burned out from the constant, frenetic pace and overemphasis on numerical objectives. Make sure you're also emphasizing such nonnumerical things as customer service, sales training, teamwork, and career development. Don't hesitate to praise reps for a good sales presentation even if it didn't result in a sale. It sends a strong signal if you reinforce reps' efforts and techniques rather than boiling everything down to a "make the sale" mentality.

- Give burnouts a chance to excel. Contests and incentive programs provide a chance for low-performing reps to shine. They may be far away from quarterly objective, but they can still get the satisfaction of winning a sales contest. In addition, contests provide a fun diversion for the reps to break the monotony of the daily sales pace.

- Provide a meaningful diversion. Ask a rep to lead a training session pertaining to his or her observed strengths. Similarly, assign a special project such as drafting a new compensation plan. This not only provides a pleasant change of pace, but also gives a dejected rep an ego boost.

- Provide release valves. Break up the routine with guest speakers, motivational videos, special training sessions, team outings, and video conferences with leading salespeople. Try assigning a different person each week to be Special Events Chairperson, in charge of making sales meetings fun and interesting.

- Spend some one-on-one time. Sometimes it helps just to get away from the office. If you have a burned-out rep, spend a little nonsales time just to relate in a no-pressure environment. If you're in the market for a boat, grab the rep and go look at one, asking for his opinion. Go to a ball game or a home show or go fishing. This helps the rep feel valued as a person and shows that you haven't given up on him despite his poor performance.

Humor Can Facilitate Managerial Success

A Robert Half International survey found that 91% of executives studied said a sense of humor is important for career advancement, and 84% said those with a sense of humor did a better job. For sales managers, humor is a lubricant for social interaction with the sales team. It helps us engage. It promotes trust from your people. It helps us relax and communicate better.

Perhaps the best way to describe managerial humor in the sales arena is to describe what it's not. It's not sarcasm. It lifts up people; it doesn't put them down. It's not a way to convey racist or sexist attitudes in a cloak of levity. It is intended to make people feel comfortable, not awkward; and enriched, not belittled or intimidated. It is not an impulsive "Aren't I funny?" comment at the expense of others. Humor is serious business. When used appropriately, it has the power to inspire and elevate. Used inappropriately, it's a sledgehammer that can alienate and estrange.

A number of medical and psychological studies have shown that humor has significant health benefits. It has the ability to enhance blood flow and heart function. Laughter can also raise the level of infection-fighting antibodies in the body and boost the level of immune cells. It has even been shown to reduce the blood sugar levels of diabetics. In addition, humor promotes deeper, more restorative sleeping patterns. Humor can reduce pain, anger, depression, and anxiety. Successful leaders have the penchant for defusing stressful situations with humor, helping de-stress themselves and those around them. If stress kills, humor enlivens us.

Humor and self-confidence go together. The sales leader's antidote for tension, turmoil, and pressure is the ability to laugh at oneself or at one's situation. It sends a signal that this problem is temporary and surmountable. It's just a speed bump, not a mountain. A little laughter says, "I'm not hurt and we're ready to get back in the saddle," or, "That glitch wasn't even enough to slow us down." Your people rally around this kind of self-confidence. It's a release valve that emboldens them. It builds your credibility as a crisis manager and as a team leader.

In addition, humor can help you relate better to your team. Having the self-assurance to make fun of yourself is an instantaneous way of building rapport. It helps you get eye-level with your people rather than looking down on them. Self-effacing humor says you're one of them. You share their interests and relate to their problems. Similarly, when people are comfortable enough to make fun of you, it's usually a sign of acceptance and affinity. So relax and go along with it. Ironically, those who take *themselves* seriously are not taken seriously by *others*.

Humor can even help your reps get "in the zone" by helping them loosen up before a big presentation. You've seen it happen in football games before a crucial kick. One of the most pressure-packed situations in the game, a kicker's success is partially based on his ability to control his nerves. He knows that all eyes are on him alone. And the fate of the game depends on his sole action. Occasionally, you'll see a coach talking to him before the kick. Many times, the coach will tell a joke or use humor to help the kicker relax, to take his mind off the pressure. Relaxed minds perform better athletically and in sales. Consider the opposite effect, when a rep goes into a sales presentation thinking that everything is riding on this sale. If it fails, the rep might think his or her career is ruined. Can you imagine the pressure? Can you visualize how forced and unnatural the sales effort would be? Keep your people loose with humor. It helps them sell. And it helps them help each other stay relaxed and focused. In this way, humor is contagious among your team.

Here are a few of the other benefits of humor in your sales space:

- It helps you manage change. We all struggle with frequent changes in the sales business. Humor can make change less threatening and stressful. In effect, you're laughing in the face of adversity, letting your people know that you all are equal to the challenge. Doing so develops a flexible, creative approach to change that could otherwise seem overwhelming.

- Humor encourages open communication. Laughter can break down barriers between people, fostering honest dialogue between the manager and the team. Leaders who use humor emanate a sense of candor, self-assurance, and nothing-to-hide sincerity. In addition, humor can help soften authoritarian messages and enliven boring correspondence.

- It facilitates teamwork. Humor can defuse tense situations in group meetings, helping people retreat and consider others' opinions. In other words, it can create a pregnant pause allowing team members to retreat, reorganize, and reconsider. Humor builds camaraderie by sharing a laugh together (even if it's at your expense). It breaks down stereotypes, showing each other our unique humanness instead of a person playing the traditional role of a manager or a sales rep. Humor can also build an "us against them" sense of team unity and shared values.

Southwest Airlines, Ben and Jerry's Ice Cream, and even IBM have utilized various forms of humor in the workplace to help create relaxed performance and build cohesive teams. If nothing else, it makes the workplace a little more fun and less threatening, a place to which you look forward to going. You don't have to be a raconteur, comic, or joke teller to inject levity in the workplace. If you do have a sense of humor, use it. If not, a little extra effort can add some degree of comic relief to your sales team. Involve your reps. Most sales teams have plenty of comics and showboats who love to ham it up. Ask them to do skits at campaign kickoffs or do presentations at awards ceremonies. A funny introduction can enliven training sessions. As a manager, don't hesitate to tell a joke or humorous story at sales meetings. In addition, it helps to keep a humor file of quotes, jokes, and anecdotes.

Companies from AT&T to Cisco are making the workplace fun through such things as in-office scavenger hunts; "Fun Committees" to create monthly activities; sales incentives for the funniest sale of the week; and dress-up days for St. Patrick's Day, Presidents' Day, or Columbus Day. Keying on the ridiculous and absurd, these companies are making the workday more fun, and hopefully more productive.

Spouses Are Your Number One Support Group

Your sales team's most influential support group is spouses. Be sure to include them in social events, awards presentations, and other opportunities that make them feel part of the sales team effort. Send them notes thanking them for their support. Congratulate them as well as sales reps in awards presentations. Invite them to campaign kickoffs. Arrange spouses' luncheons or meetings aimed at aligning them with team sales efforts. Have a standing invitation to sales meetings for spouses to drop in at any time. Also, encourage them to call you, text, or e-mail anytime with questions or concerns.

A knowledgeable spouse can provide your sales rep with valuable support during hard times, and offer informed opinions when needed. In essence, by involving spouses you take the mystery out of your sales operations. You and your sales team become real people rather than just names. A well-informed spouse is able to understand—and hopefully support—your vision and objectives. In times of trouble, such as burnout or illness, a spouse can offer information and support to you to get the rep back on track.

Beyond the Basics

Don't forget the basics, the most important parts of a salesperson's work life: pay, security, and fair treatment. These are the baseline essentials to keep people on the payroll. Employees expect regular pay from a stable company that treats them fairly. You can't be successful without these basic building blocks.

When things go wrong, whether it be morale or sales failures, first go back to the basics. We often forget the basics, and look for new and novel ways to solve problems. Just get online and you have access to a vast array of management fix-its, fads, and one-size-fits-all sales management solutions. That's good and that's bad. The advantage is that you can get a lot of new and innovative ideas. The disadvantage is that it sometimes takes our eye off the ball and distracts you from the basics. Before implementing the latest management craze, go back to the basic foundation of employee needs (pay, security, and fair treatment). Then review the basics of sales effectiveness: training, preparation, and effective selling techniques.

Regardless of a sales manager's goals and aspirations, peak team performance will not develop without a strong foundation of fundamentals. It takes adept leadership to insist on the basics, and then go beyond them to tap into the power and resourcefulness of a sales team—to create continuously improving sales performance. Walk before you run. You won't inspire or motivate your team if they don't feel good about their working conditions or if they are ill prepared to sell effectively.

Is Your Gratitude Showing?

The simple act of showing gratitude to your salespeople and colleagues has powerful consequences. Though many of us might not hear many expressions of gratitude from the boss, 81% of us say that we would work harder if we did, according to a study sponsored by the John Templeton Foundation. The problem is that only 49% of men and 51% of women regularly thank those surrounding and supporting them. If only half of us, as sales managers, are regularly showing gratitude to our people, we might be missing an opportunity to get that little edge in sales productivity that can make a big difference in results.

In addition, showing gratitude can benefit your career. Shawn Achor, author of *The Happiness Advantage,* says that those giving thanks and praise to colleagues—especially in stressful times—are more likely to be promoted. "Write one quick e-mail first thing in the morning thanking or praising a member on your team. This surprisingly increases your feeling of social support, which, in my study at Harvard, was the biggest indicator of happiness." He also says, "Happiness is an advantage and a precursor to greater success. Every single relationship, business, and educational outcome improves when the brain is positive *first.*" Rather than waiting for success and goal achievement to make you happy, if you cultivate happiness during the struggles to reach your goals, you actually increase the chances of success. Achor suggests writing down, on a daily basis, three things for which you are grateful, as well as writing for two minutes a day about a positive experience you've had during the past 24 hours.

Remember, Team Building Begins One Rep at a Time

As noted in Chapter 1, knowing your reps individually is the beginning of team building. Developing their trust and loyalty is done through hours of individual interaction. Know what motivates them and what alienates them. Take advantage of every chance you get to ask about a rep's family, hobby, big sale, and so on. Take the time. Memorize their spouse's and children's names. The team won't follow you if the individuals aren't aligned with you. It's a given that you're not going to like all your people, and not all are going to like you. But knowing them will help you develop their potential as part of a high-performing sales team.

Teaching Moments Are Best One-on-One

If you take advantage of every opportunity to teach, your reps will have little opportunity to learn. Trying to teach all the time can actually create a deafness on the part of your reps, who simply ignore the noise. Over-teaching makes you look condescending, like a know-it-all. Teaching moments should be carefully selected when the time and environment are just right. Usually the best time is one-on-one with your reps when you can tailor the information in a way that opens their eyes and helps them arrive at solutions on their own with a little guidance from you.

Involve the rep in the moment. For example, if you just rode along with a rep on an appointment, open the conversation with, "How do you think it went?" Have her self-analyze her performance. This allows her to self-teach without being lectured by you. When it's time to offer your observations, limit your comments to a few specific things you noticed. Don't overwhelm the rep with your vast knowledge. A few concise remarks are easy to remember and have more impact than a number of detailed points. When it comes to teaching moments, less is more. And self-teaching has more impact than lecturing.

Timing is everything. If you accompanied a sales rep on an appointment that resulted in losing the account, this is not the time to teach. The rep probably will be in no mood to listen, but might be tomorrow. Likewise, if the rep just made a big sale and wants to celebrate, don't take the wind out of her sails with a teaching moment.

The key to teaching moments is not how much you know, but how ready the rep is to be taught.

And, when it comes to teaching, remember that the classroom is the *least* effective place to teach salespeople. Of course, a classroom setting is necessary because it's economical and delivers a lot of information to a lot of people. The problem is this: The things that make successful salespeople are the things that make them poor classroom students. Most top salespeople are not the studious type. They are adventurous, street-smart, task-oriented, and a little impatient, and have an obsessive sense of urgency. Sitting in a training class—when there are sales to be made and deals to get signed—can be a torturous ordeal for an enterprising rep. And no matter how good the trainer or how eager the salesperson is to learn, the ordinary salesperson is likely to be occasionally or frequently distracted by the reveries of ongoing deals or upcoming appointments. That's not to say to avoid classroom training. It's just a reminder that the best learning comes one-on-one at the right time from the right person (a sales manager/coach or a sales peer).

Training Beyond the Basics

The majority of salespeople in America receive two types of training: product training and sales technique training. Obviously, it's vital to know your product applications and how to implement, for example, six-step selling. However, a well-trained sales force needs much more. Make sure you are training your people on "softer" skills such as emotional intelligence (EQ), listening, negotiation, and body language.

Try to budget an individual training allotment for each rep to pick and choose training sessions that address personal needs. This allows your reps to go beyond group training and personalize a learning program to augment each person's individual skill set. It helps for the sales manager to arrange for e-mail notifications of new training courses from reputable Web sites, and forward these to the sales force.

Create a Mentor Program

Mentor programs are good not only for the mentee but for the mentor as well. It gives the mentee the value of the mentor's experience and knowledge. It gives the mentor a sense of ego gratification by using his sales acumen to help develop a sales rep. And unlike expensive training programs, mentoring offers one-on-one instruction free.

Essentially, a good mentor program provides the multiplier effect, allowing the sales manager to extend his or her influence with minimal time and energy.

There are hundreds of ways to establish a mentor program. The first step, however, is to determine your goals. Do you want to use it as a way to orient newcomers? Do you want to include reps with less than one or two year's experience? Are underperforming reps your target? How about a skills focus—tech-savvy reps paired with low-tech ones, or good closers with poor ones, for example?

The typical mentor program assigns experienced reps to mentor newcomers. Even after the newbie is oriented, the mentor relationship remains as an ongoing source of support for the mentee.

The critical step for any mentor program is selecting the right mentors. Obviously, underperforming reps with bad attitudes will poison the well for you. The best mentors have, first, a good attitude. You have to be able to trust that they are passing along not only good information but also a positive mind-set. Your mentors don't have to be superstars. They don't have to be rich in sales skills. In fact, they don't even need years of experience. All they need is a demeanor that represents your company well in addition to patience and basic communications skills. Managers instinctively know who their mentors are, and could probably jot them down in a matter of seconds.

The third step is simply to set the ground rules for the program, the objectives, and the procedures. Irrespective of how formal and organized the mentor program is, it helps to put in writing the goals, benefits, scope, and expected outcomes of the program.

Possible goals of your program might include the following:

- Supplement your training efforts by having a mentor reinforce sales skills and possibly pass along personal selling tips in a hands-on fashion.

- Help mentees learn procedures and shortcuts, as well as how to navigate administrative processes.

- Provide mentees with career development instruction from an experienced mentor who knows what it takes to rise in the organization.

- Establish another "go to" person for the mentee in addition to the manager for advice and questions. (Sometimes newcomers are reluctant to discuss certain issues or problems with the sales manager that a mentor can address.)

- Create an additional source of encouragement to the mentee.

- Expedite the onboarding process for new reps.

- Improve the rep retention rate by helping newcomers succeed faster.

After clear goals are set, the manager needs to define roles and responsibilities.

A role statement is as simple as "The mentor's role is to help the newcomer adjust effectively to the sales environment, and to keep the sales manager apprised of progress." Among the mentor's responsibilities are the following:

- Responding to the mentee's questions and comments

- Proactively providing information and updates, and "checking on" the new rep

- Meeting with the mentee at least one hour per week

- Assisting the manager in evaluating the outcomes of the mentoring process

After you've outlined the program in print, share it with mentors and mentees to make sure everyone fully understands the program.

Finally, evaluate the program. You can do this formally or informally, in scheduled assessments or checking as you go. The important thing is that you know the value of the program from the mentee's perspective (and from her sales results), as well as the mentor's views. Evaluation helps you make refinements needed to get the most out of the process, and make sure you are achieving your stated goals.

Insist on Honesty, Not Positivity

Sales is a minefield of rejection and surly customers. You're absolutely lost without a positive, hopeful mind-set. But, as a manager, don't insist that your people act like cheerleaders all the time. Allow—even encourage—them to express frustration about policy or managerial obstacles. Their comments can lead to process improvements and better sales. In other words, encourage a positive mind-set but insist on honesty. Don't get ensnared by a foolish insistence that your sales team be "positive" all the time while criticizing your people's complaints as being "negative." To a reasonable extent, let your people grumble and complain. If you insist that everyone be positive, you're insisting that they be dishonest and phony. Surprisingly, the more you allow and encourage honesty, the more likely it is that your people will complain less. And when they do complain, there could be fire behind the smoke, allowing you to discover issues that need to be addressed.

Encourage Your Reps to Vent

Give your people the freedom to speak their minds, to vent if necessary. Bradley J. Sugars explains the process as "WIFLE" sessions ("what I feel like expressing") in his book *Instant Team Building*. These sessions give team members "uninterrupted time to speak their thoughts without fear of recrimination." Seeking employees' opinions gives the leader an early warning system and gives team members an effective way to get problems out in the open instead of simmering behind the scenes. Remember, sunshine is the best disinfectant; openness with employees will prevent corporate bacteria and organizational rot.

Don't Wait for Me

After you've opened the door for honest input, add this twist: "Don't wait for me to solve all your problems and answer all your questions." That's partly what teammates are for.

Obviously, there are issues that only you, as a manager, can address. And you certainly don't want to discourage your reps from coming to you. But you (and your reps) can save considerable time and effort if your people have the ability to share information and solutions among themselves. In the same vein, when a rep brings you a problem, ask that he bring a solution. When he brings a complaint, ask for an alternative. Don't let your office become a dumping ground for problems and questions. Require your reps to be part of the solution, and you all benefit.

Daily Assessment Keeps Everyone in the Loop

Assess your people continuously. Give them sales reports daily so that they know their progress toward objectives, as well as their strengths and weaknesses, as shown in the numbers. In addition, observe and discuss their performance as frequently as practical, at least once a month. What do salespeople learn from their annual performance review? Nothing. They should already know everything there is to know about their performance on a consistent basis.

Get Close to the Action

Stay close to the sales process. Know your salespeople and how they spend their working hours. Know your customers and competition. Go with your reps on sales calls frequently. Being removed from the process makes us all poor leaders, prone to making decisions to achieve objectives while overlooking the details needed to get results. Active involvement helps managers make decisions based on reality, decisions that can be understood and followed rather than directions that cause confusion and consternation among your salespeople. In addition, sales reps respect "field generals" who lead the charge from the front lines rather than from behind a desk.

Make Sales the Priority

Make it easier for your reps to sell. Eliminate unnecessary paperwork, meetings, and nonsensical procedures. Remember that no company survives without the first step of any business transaction—making the sale. Everything else follows.

Help your people stay focused on the selling process. Selling is the only thing that's going to reach your objectives. Paperwork and administrative details do not. Here's a sales formula to remember: *Focus* equals *time* plus *energy*. Focus is not a renewable resource. It is a limited resource. There are 86,400 seconds in a day. That sounds like a lot of time; but you know how fast it flies by, and not one of those seconds is recoverable. The same holds true for focus. That is, if you borrow just a little of your team's focus to achieve more accurate paperwork, that's a little focus you just lost from sales. If you keep adding other things to focus on, you're rechanneling more and more time and energy from sales. In essence, you're asking your salespeople to start thinking more and more about things other than selling. The age-old statement of Confucius applies here: "The man who chases two rabbits catches neither."

Time and energy focused on selling brings cash in the door. No matter what your product, sales is where the cash flow starts. Make sure everyone in the organization knows that the cash from the sales process allows them to get a paycheck. Of course, everyone's job is important. But make sure the secretaries, clerks, accountants, and engineers know how they connect with and depend on sales.

Push, prod, cajole your support people to help your salespeople sell. For example, an increasing number of sales organizations are requiring their salespeople to use the Internet for reports, ordering such things as forms, making travel arrangements, and performing many of the functions that had been done in the past by secretaries and support personnel. The thought is that it's good for the bottom line because fewer secretaries are needed, having been replaced by cheaper online applications. The problem is that in our technological zeal to cut personnel costs, we are creating cyber distractions for sales reps; that is, we're asking them to do more clerical functions and less selling. Many times, the rationale is, "It only takes five minutes for the rep to log in and order a sales form." That might be true. However, is anyone looking at the aggregate number of five-minute functions your sales reps are performing? Little by little, these cyber distractions accumulate imperceptibly to the point where each of your salespeople could be spending an hour or more per day doing administrative work—the things that had been done by a $9-an-hour secretary. Would it be better to pay $9 an hour as opposed to $50 an hour for a sales rep to be doing nonsales activities? Is the savings of $9 an hour costing you more in the long run and distracting your salespeople from selling?

Be a Heat Shield

Take care how you pass information from your superiors to your subordinates. If you're feeling the heat, absorb it. Even if your boss just insulted you in every way possible, from your intelligence to your ancestry, don't pass along the invective to your people. Your people need to know what needs to be done, but threats, criticism, and anger will only distract them from getting things done. Look at it this way: How do *you* feel about the boss who just tore into you? Do you feel more productive and inspired or just angry, self-doubting, and scared of losing your job? That's how salespeople feel when the heat is applied.

Remember the Law of Opposite Results

Sometimes we get the opposite of what we strive for. Take, for example, a young swimmer in his first competitive race. Trying so hard to win, he abandons smooth strokes and flails away at the water, which actually slows his speed and drains his energy. The winner stays relaxed, maintains form, and glides to the finish line with steady, focused strokes. Opposite results occur, for example, with the manager who tries too hard to be "the boss" and loses the respect and trust of his or her people. Or the manager who wants to control the sales force, and ends up with a flimsy framework of rules and directives that reps ridicule. Or the manager who tries so hard to reach objective that one game plan is discarded for another until there is no game plan at all. You also achieve the opposite of the desired results when you are working such long hours that exhaustion erodes the quality of your work as well as your health.

Of course, trying hard is better than not trying at all. Many times, however, the manager needs to pause, relax, step back, focus, and look at the situation. Get an eagle's-eye view before acting and reacting. Make sure the pressure of goal attainment isn't rushing and contorting your decision making. And don't try so hard that you take on all the responsibility for decisions and outcomes. Sometimes we forget who's going to get us to our goals: our salespeople. There's no way of predicting opposite results and unintended consequences; they occur every hour of every day to the best of sales leaders. However, you can bet that if your goals and efforts aren't shared by your salespeople, your outcomes are not going to be what you expected. Frequently, the buy-in of your people is the single factor that separates a manager from a leader.

Carefully Criticize Your People

Criticize in private. No one wants to be criticized in front of others, no matter what they tell you. It breeds resentment toward the criticizer, and much of the message is lost anyway because the recipient is thinking of who's listening, what kind of response should be made to save face, and other factors. In private, you take away the distractions, helping everyone to concentrate on the message.

Listen to What Is **Not** Said

Sometimes the things people *do not* say are as important as what they do say. Listening to things unsaid is not a science. It cannot be taught. Rather, it's a predisposition to pause, reflect, and identify verbal omissions. Sometimes it can provide insight into your reps' habits and practices. On the flip side, sometimes things not said have no meaning at all, so be careful not to jump to conclusions.

Many times it comes as a "eureka" moment. For example, someone asks you whether a rep is married. You answer that you think so because he wears a wedding ring, but, now that you mention it, he never talks about his wife. You just never thought about it because it was never discussed. That sends up a red flag that there might be marital problems. Why else would he not ever talk about his wife? Now, you've established a hypothesis to test. You become more observant of signs that indicate marital discord. Later, you might discover that the rep is happily married, but is a private person who doesn't like to discuss personal matters. Or you might find he does have problems that explain absences from work and a lack of enthusiasm.

Frequently, it takes time and close observation to interpret things not said. In casual conversation, people talk about what's important to them. Salespeople, in particular, will usually let you know what they spend time doing and what they do well. On the other hand, you can assume that things they don't discuss are probably not as important to them. If a salesperson talks a great deal about being a good closer but rarely discusses preparation, it could be a signal to explore how well prepared the rep is for customer presentations.

Unsaid things are most helpful in providing clues to a person's beliefs and attitudes because these elements are otherwise hard to detect and assess. Let's take honesty, for example. The rep who tells you the occasional story of honesty with customers at least has the subject on his mind. On the other hand, a red flag might raise for the rep who never talks about it. People talk about things on their minds—obviously they *don't* talk about things they're not thinking about. In addition to integrity, unsaid things can provide insight into a sales rep's sensitivity to others, empathy, loyalty, trustworthiness, and other values instrumental to the selling process. Sometimes silence can be deafening.

A few additional verbal omissions to look for include these:

- **Look for changes from said to unsaid**—For example, you have a salesperson who had regularly told you about his or her personal plan to reach objective, including how many sales were in the pipeline. Though it was all very informal and not required, it revealed initiative, enthusiasm, and planning on the part of the rep. It occurred to you that it has been two months since the rep last provided one of these informal updates. Is there a problem?

- **Look for exceptions to things generally said**—If eight out of nine reps have mentioned that they like the new compensation plan but one says nothing, is the silence a sign of discontent?

- **Look for things said by your top sellers**—What things are they saying that low performers aren't? Are they discussing, for example, detailed preparation for sales presentations and innovative product applications? Are your low-performing reps talking about similar subjects? If you have reps talking more about compensation plans and vacation schedules than things that make them successful, those verbal omissions could be red flags of failure.

Selling Is an Art and a Science

Remember, selling is an art. Preparing to sell is a science.

Science is a branch of knowledge dealing with a body of facts or truths systematically arranged and showing the operation of general laws. It's a precise application of facts or principles. In sales, you scientifically gather facts about the customer. You learn selling techniques and such things as how to overcome objections. You study product attributes and benefits. You memorize pricing and discounts.

After you've prepared, the sales process becomes an art in which you use imagination, creativity, intuition, and passion to arrive at a desired result. In sales, the desired result is the sale. There are no formulas to create successful sales because the process involves the most complex of activities—human behavior. In transactions with people—with either your sales reps or customers—you're dealing with unknowns and unknown unknowns that require intuition over reason, and resourcefulness over theory. As a manager, don't rely on typologies, sales matrices, and canned strategies to facilitate successful selling. Do rely on your intuition and innovation to connect the disparate components of people, products, and buying behavior.

There are thousands of books, blogs, and consultants extolling the effectiveness of their particular formula for sales. Inasmuch as there is always something good to be learned from them, there's also a danger in dogged adherence to a formulaic approach. Take the six-step sales approach, for example. It's a valuable framework for selling in that it instills a disciplined methodology for the salesperson. However, it is *only* a framework subject to the vicissitudes of each individual situation. If the customer is ready to buy in the middle of the "presentation" stage, the astute sales rep will quickly forego the remaining steps and get the contract signed. The fact that sales is situational and unpredictable tells us to use "sales science" as a compass but sharpen our inner drivers (such as empathy and creativity) to provide the horsepower to get to our destination.

Make Pressure Work for You

From the day they start, all salespeople know that their income and eventual survival are based on their sales output. That is pressure. It's something that every healthy organization requires. Salespeople need pressure to keep an edge, to achieve objectives. However, too much pressure and the boiler steams and whistles and ultimately explodes.

The trick is to build a healthy head of steam without the pressure debilitating your sales force.

Mike Meseda, president of ADP Total Source, stated in the *Houston Business Journal,* "Job stress comes with a costly price tag...that includes accidents, absenteeism, employee turnover and diminished productivity." One of the chief ways to improve a stressful work environment, he says, is to "give workers opportunities to participate in decisions and actions affecting their jobs."

In fact, the World Health Organization estimates that the cost of workplace stress caused by overbearing management is more than $300 billion nationwide.

Pressure causes stress, and stress kills. Heart attack, stroke, high blood pressure, immune system malfunctions, decreased brain function, and even chromosomal damage are caused by stress. In an extensive study of primates, Dr. Carol Shively found that subordinate macaque monkeys have a higher incidence of plaque in heart arteries than alpha macaques. The stress of being a subordinate increases blood pressure, creating pits in arteries that fill up with plaque and reduce blood flow to the heart. In human terms, being a subordinate can be stressful and debilitating, depending on the amount and kind of pressure exerted by the boss.

Pressure also can disrupt sales performance. "Pressure raises self-consciousness and anxiety about performing correctly, which increases the attention paid to skill processes and their step-by-step control. Attention to execution at this level is thought to disrupt well-learned or procedurized performances," according to an *Inc.* magazine article quoting a study by Sean L. Beilock and Thomas H. Carr. In other words, excessive pressure can interrupt "flow," resulting in a debilitating kind of self-consciousness instead of performing smoothly, naturally, and automatically.

The "stress resistant" salespeople on your team are less susceptible to the ill effects of stress because they interpret pressure as challenge. For them, it's Go Time and Show Time. But it's likely that a majority of your sales reps feel the pressure and feel the stress. After all, sales is not like other jobs that create intermittent stress, such as a presentation every month or so, or a weekly deadline. Sales pressure is every hour of every day. The last thing salespeople need is a manager adding to the pressure by looking over their shoulder, making unreasonable demands or micromanaging.

Unhealthy pressure comes from the leader who says, "It's simple, you sell or you perish." Belaboring the obvious is the easy way out for the lazy manager. It puts all the burden on the salesperson. It lets the manager sit back, take an evaluative approach, and wait for the results.

This kind of inappropriate pressure sometimes comes from the manager who hasn't made the mental transition from a salesperson to a leader. You can't expect salespeople to do things the way you do or as well as you. You're the leader now, the strategic thinker, the problem solver, the big-picture person. Figure out a way to get the numbers without driving your people insane. Displace some of the pressure by sharing responsibility with your team to come up with solutions, instead of leaving your people alone to struggle toward objectives.

Another productive way of channeling sales pressure is turning the pressure into a bonding experience. This approach is characterized by the sales leader who says, "You know and I know that your future is dependent on your sales performance. And we're going to work together to ensure your survival and success. I promise I'll do everything I can to make you successful." Part of this process is ensuring that the sales team is prepared and confident. The sales leader uses role playing, training, and coaching to make sure reps are ready for all situations. The more practice reps get, the more self-confident they become, and the less stress they feel. This leader becomes the mentor, the go-to guy when there's trouble. This is the sales leader who, like a military general, has trained the troops extensively, and leads them aggressively into battle. This takes more work, more commitment, and more risk, but it generates a loyalty that galvanizes successful teams.

In fact, stress can be productive. You've heard of positive stress. That's what Larry Hunter, University of Wisconsin at Madison, and Sherry Thatcher, University of Arizona, found in a study of 270 bank sales employees. "We theorized and found that higher performance under stress occurred among workers who were more committed to their employer and who were more experienced in their jobs," states the researchers. In effect, these employees were able to actually use stress to improve job performance. On the flip side, stress had a negative impact on employees with low levels of commitment and experience. It stands to reason that the category of "high-commitment reps" will include a large number of stress-resistant people—those who are energized by challenge and are "in it to win it." Likewise, more experienced reps—those with plenty of practice—should be less susceptible to pressure. On the other hand, for those who are more vulnerable to stress and pressure, the question is this: How does the sales manager decrease pressure felt by reps by increasing their level of commitment and experience?

Increasing sales reps' level of commitment is no easy thing since it is greatly affected by their inner work standards. But a manager can affect reps' commitment in a number of ways:

- Managers can ensure that adequate financial reward is available through commissions, bonuses, and sales contests. These "extrinsic" rewards are important to keep reps focused and rewarded. (But keep in mind that money is not the only thing that gets your reps dedicated to the pursuit of objectives. In fact, as noted earlier, money might be a secondary motivator for many reps. And when bonuses and sales contests are over, reps' level of commitment might decrease.)

- Rep involvement, participating in decision making, intensifies commitment levels by increasing the salesperson's ownership of plans and procedures.

- When reps are held accountable for their results, their commitment rises because they are viewed as the captain of their ship, the master of their fate. Having no one to blame but themselves, reps are more likely to commit themselves to take the steps necessary for success.

- Reciprocal commitment is another concept that sales managers can employ. The sales manager who shows a strong commitment to the best interests of the sales team might, in turn, receive the reciprocal commitment of the sales reps. Simply put, it's another case of the Law of Reciprocity at work.

As for increasing reps' level of experience, the manager can use role playing and simulated sales situations in order for the rep to "experience" various situations before they actually occur. This tactic, obviously, is best deployed for less experienced reps as a way to compress as much experiential learning into as short amount of time as possible. In addition, it's beneficial to encourage newer reps to get as much "face time" as possible with customers to experience a variety of personalities and situations.

At the end of the day, there will always be pressure. Effective sales managers will do all they can to help their people to adapt and thrive under pressure. Moreover, we should wake up every morning and be thankful for the pressure to perform; without it there would be no reason to come to work. By all means, keep the pressure on. Every hour, every day. But do it subtly, through daily sales reports that keep everyone apprised of their progress, ranking reports that build healthy competition, sales contests, and one-on-one assessments to spotlight reps' strengths and weaknesses. For reps to be aware of objectives, they have to know that *you* are aware and attentive to those objectives. Focus, focus, focus on the excitement of winning—not the consequences of losing.

At all times, monitor your people for signs of excessive stress: absenteeism, tardiness, medical problems, customer complaints, comments from peers, mood shifts, even changes in appearance such as weight gain or loss and sloppy attire.

Look also at unexpectedly poor sales results, which can point to reps being stressed and distracted from selling. Even take a look at consistently high performance, which could be a sign of someone "gaming" the system. That's always the last thing a manager thinks about when outstanding results are reported, but occasionally, a rep will find a loophole and risk his or her job to meet quotas. Ninety-nine percent of the time, improved sales is a good thing; however, sudden, inexplicable improvements can occasionally indicate cheating. The necessity—in *all* cases of sales improvement—is for the manager to know why. First and foremost, the manager needs to replicate and expand legitimate success stories, incorporating them into best practices. The vast majority of successes are genuine, but it's always a good idea to maintain a healthy skepticism for those rare cases in which unethical behavior could be at play.

In a healthy environment, reps will put pressure on themselves to succeed. The good ones don't need additional pressure from the outside. The others? Well, that's the gray area that requires attention and observation from the manager to keep the boiler from blowing.

An added benefit of a manager's attention to pressure and stress among reps is this: Reducing stress in the sales team decreases stress on the manager. As stress declines, sales team focus increases, which enhances sales performance. With their eyes on the goal instead of obstacles, salespeople are more relaxed and likely to support their manager. As a result, the manager has more time and focus to exert on key managerial initiatives rather than putting out brush fires. In essence, it gives the manager all the health and performance advantages experienced by subordinates.

Positive Reinforcement Works

The goal of positive reinforcement is to increase the frequency of desired sales behaviors (customer alignment, strong closing, thorough preparation, overcoming objections, etc.). The opposite is negative reinforcement, such as reduced commissions, undesirable account assignments, demotion, suspension, or dismissal. All reinforcements are based on the desire to avoid pain and the desire to gain pleasure. Negative reinforcement decreases the frequency of negative behavior, and positive reinforcement should increase the incidence of positive behavior.

Research indicates that positive reinforcement has more power to influence desired behavior than negative reinforcement. Part of the rationale for this is that if you are consistently seeking pleasure, you will naturally avoid the things that cause pain. It stands to reason that if you are rewarding desired behavior, you should see less undesirable behavior and, therefore, a decreased need for negative reinforcement.

The key is to make positive reinforcement *personal* while making negative reinforcement impersonal or *procedural.* Positive reinforcement should be administered personally by you every chance you get, as soon as you can. Doing so not only rewards salespeople's desired behavior, but also builds rapport between you and your people. When negative reinforcement is required, make it an expected outcome of rules and procedures. For example, you should have a clearly defined set of consequences for failure to reach sales objectives. All reps should be aware of the consequences and, in effect, be in agreement with these conditions of employment. A sales rep who misses objective faces negative reinforcement as an outcome of the stated rules, not as a personal action of the manager. In effect, the impetus for positive reinforcement is a caring manager showing gratitude for a job well done. The impetus for negative reinforcement should be a company enforcing its stated procedures.

Sales managers have to reach a balance between overrewarding and underrewarding. If you make your reps work too hard for positive reinforcement, they'll probably be too exhausted to appreciate it. On the other hand, if your rewards are too frequent, they become expected and meaningless. Rather than looking for superlative performance to reward, you should be looking for examples of behavior you want to see repeated. If you have a rep who tends to underprepare for sales presentations, look for instances in which preparation was obvious and reward the behavior with the hope of it continuing.

Some of the personal actions of the manager to influence positive behavior should include these:

- Complimenting your reps in front of the group: "I just saw Kristen make one of the best uses of sales visuals to a customer yesterday...."

- Writing or e-mailing reps congratulatory notes. Put the notes in their personnel files.

- Sending notes to spouses congratulating their spouse and thanking them for their support.

- Adhering "You're Awesome!" stickers to contracts and paperwork sent to your reps. Having these stickers forces you to remember and to use positive reinforcement.

- Developing a Sales Hall of Fame to acknowledge your superstars. Post it, complete with photos, in a prominent position at the office as well as online through a Web site, Facebook, and other social media.

Reward team success in addition to personal recognition. Congratulate the team for small accomplishments like working together to develop a new and improved sales contract.

Use your sales reps' individual accomplishments to create role modeling, with comments such as, "I remember two months ago when Jerry took some big account losses and everything looked pretty bleak. But he kept on with optimism, made some new sales to make up for the losses, and he made objective." These anecdotes also become stories that are passed along and become part of the legend and lore of your organization.

Catch people doing the right thing and talk about it. Look for something good and build on it. Take, for example, a poor sales performer who has a laid-back, yet engaging approach to people. Focus on his way with people and how he develops customer alignment. Instead of excoriating his lack of results, reinforce his strength and build on it by showing him techniques to ask for the sale in a way that matches his personality.

Don't underestimate your importance as sales manager for inspiring your people. Remember that a positive comment from you might be the only encouragement a rep gets all day. Even a 15-second phone call to commend a rep for a sale can be a big motivator. (In fact, even if you don't have specific praise, just taking the time to talk and listen is positive in its own right.)

When possible, provide the positive reinforcement immediately following the act. The shorter the time gap between action and reward, the higher the impact the reward has.

Award your people's success with framed certificates, trophies, and medallions, and call special meetings or award ceremonies to distribute them accompanied by your congratulations. Do it in front of as many people as possible. And do it as fast as possible. Many, perhaps most, salespeople love to be the center of attention. Formal or informal ceremonies where your people can stand in the limelight are their 15 minutes of fame. Watch carefully how many of those certificates or trophies are placed on open display in your salespeople's cubicles or on their desks. They need those constant reminders of success, especially during the tough times.

Reward success with money, gift cards, things that have monetary value. These rewards are above and beyond your commission plan. They can be instrumental in helping you reach targeted, short-term goals. Inasmuch as some sales reps are primarily moved by recognition and a sense of accomplishment, all your people are moved by monetary rewards—especially when provided in front of an audience of their peers.

Make sure, when administering monetary rewards, that your people know exactly what they are being rewarded for. Make it simple and easily understood by your reps. We, as managers, sometimes overcomplicate the rules for bonuses and monetary awards to the point where reps are not really sure how they get paid or for what they are getting paid. Overcomplicated promotions are hard to track, are difficult to explain, and take managers' and reps' time to decipher. At the start of the contest or campaign, make sure everyone understands the time frame, and the rules for payouts (avoid complex formulas, emphasize simplicity). Then provide daily updates to keep everyone aware of their progress. Consider informal sales rallies every few days, taking a few minutes to report results; this generates continued excitement and constructive competition.

Look for Reasons to Celebrate Success, and Then Step into the Shadows

Considering the failures and rejection we face every day, we can't afford to miss any opportunity to celebrate. When things go right, celebrate success. It doesn't have to be formalized goal attainment. It can be going a week without any customer complaints or seeing a new sales technique being used by a majority of the sales team. It can be a zero-error day in completing customer contracts or it can be the success story of the week. Essentially, the manager defines success and how to celebrate it. Be creative. Always look for opportunities to throw a victory party, luncheon, or banquet. Bring in pizza or ice cream for the sales team to highlight achievements. Sponsor outings at the bowling alley, mini-golf course, laser tag arena, and other venues. Call your reps together for informal "stand-up" meetings to announce successful sales. Make even small successes a big deal. Don't miss a chance to recognize even minor accomplishments in meetings when reps have an audience to help them bask in the glory.

Rule number one: When things go right, don't take any credit. The credit belongs to the team. You—as a leader—are the facilitator, not the frontline warrior. It's their moment to shine, so make sure you stay out of the limelight.

And be sure *not* to thank your subordinates for success. It's their success, not yours. You never heard Vince Lombardi thanking his team for winning the Super Bowl for him. You and your team are partners, sharing equally in success. If, by chance, they thank you as their leader, that's great. But don't expect it, and don't seek it. Look for every chance to give your people *their* moment. And you, as their manager, should look for every chance to stand in the shadows and applaud.

Let everyone know what you're celebrating so that it can be replicated, whether it be meeting deadlines, making new sales, or simply maintaining a winning attitude despite setbacks. More importantly, make sure you've kept the recipe for success in your best-practices file.

Beware of Unintended Consequences

When it comes to sales incentives and rewards for your reps, remember, for every action there's a reaction. You hope the reaction is improved sales, but it doesn't always work that way. Always be cognizant of unintended consequences that could even undermine your sales. For example, let's say you're trying to get more sales closed per week to increase cash flow. You offer, for example, $100 to any rep who closes ten sales per week. Consider the downside risks. More accounts will be handled but less time might be spent per account, which could decrease your per-sale revenue. In addition, if you set the goal as ten closes, there's no incentive to go over ten, so you might have reps coasting when they hit the magic number; or they might "sandbag" results by applying any closes over ten from one week to the next week's results. Also, consider the long-term effects of a faster sales pace: Will some reps' results actually decrease because they feel rushed or get burned out?

Another unintended consequence is "cannibalizing" product sales. Anytime you provide incentives to your reps for selling a particular product, you run the risk of underselling other products. Overzealous reps can even do harm to other products as they sell what they're being paid for, and may deemphasize the product qualities of what they're *not* getting paid for.

Another question to ask yourself: What do you do after the incentive program? Did the program create the sustained selling behavior you intended or was it just a temporary uptick that disappeared when the payouts ceased? You can create a kind of incentive addiction cycle in which reps become dependent on short-term rewards, and fail to perform between incentive programs. Don't depend on an incentive program to permanently change your sales force's selling habits—it rarely happens that way. Incentive programs are great morale builders, but other than that, managers should accept incentive programs for what they are: short-term rewards that create a temporary selling frenzy but rarely have long-lasting impact.

Sales incentives are expensive and come with downside risks, as well as being time-consuming by requiring tracking, reporting, and additional administrative work. To increase the chances of a successful sales incentive, get your team involved in the planning. Discuss your objectives openly, as well as the downside risks and opportunities for reps to "game the system." Ask your reps what rewards work best for them: cash, trips, gift certificates?

After you begin the program, monitor the incentivized results—those results you're wanting to impact—but also measure other results that are not part of the incentive program. For example, are other product sales and cross-selling decreasing? Look at the whole sales scenario and consider the intended impact but also the unintended consequences. Taking a careful, participative approach with your reps will maximize the upside and minimize the downside risks.

Great Results Might Not Be So Great

A word of warning: Don't be mesmerized by good results. If you are achieving sales goals but losing sales talent consistently, you have a problem. The costs of recruiting and training might be negating your stellar sales achievements. If your turnover is 25% to 30% for first-year salespeople, you could have a problem. If it's 50%, you need help. Measuring turnover is a science of its own and takes into account turnover over time and turnover by performance level. For example, if you lose 10% of your top 25% performers annually, you have a big problem. On the other hand, if you lose 10% of your lower 25% performers, you're about right.

In analyzing turnover, the first place to look is management itself. Even though you're hitting your objectives, are you burning out your sales force? Are your salespeople alienated by pressure and drained by demands? Often, the success/failure syndrome is caused by managers who are overfocused on the numbers and neglect coaching and developing the sales force. "When salespeople get too fanatically focused on making their quotas, they can be driven insane by the numbers.... Ultimately, that creates this culture where if a sales team or salesperson doesn't hit their numbers, they're failing," says Jim Keenan, sales consultant. "That takes a lot of the fun out of selling and kills team morale pretty quickly."

"War Stories" Are Their Moment

Salespeople love to regale their manager with play-by-play accounts of their big sale or the account they saved. Many can't wait to get you on the phone or get back to the office and provide the glorious details. They don't realize that you don't have a lot of time to hear their story, and that you've already heard a dozen such stories from other reps. Although these stories can be boring and time-consuming, they are important for salespeople's mental health. This is their chance to momentarily forget the rejection and failures incurred on the sales battlefield, and become the hero of their own war story.

Take the time to hear them with enthusiasm (even if you have to fake it). Encourage the stories and send out a quick text or e-mail to share the story with your team. Above all, give them their moment. Do not make it a teaching moment by asking "Did you..." or "Why didn't you..." questions. And don't make it about you—one of those "I'm glad you learned from me" or "Didn't I tell you?" moments.

No, these are moments purely and surely intended for the rep to bask in the brief moment of achievement.

Don't Let Failure Get in the Way

Things will go wrong. No matter how good you are, your team will miss objectives, will miss deadlines, will just screw up. There are millions of ways to handle failure, but the best way is to make the most of it, remembering that failure is the best teacher. A real team builder will take the blame, explain the facts to superiors, make no excuses, and learn from failure.

In *Leadership Gold,* John C. Maxwell said, "My friend, management expert Ken Blanchard, is right when he says, 'Some leaders are like seagulls. When something goes wrong, they fly in, make a lot of noise and crap all over everything.' People with that kind of attitude not only refuse to take responsibility for their contribution to the problem, but they also make conditions terrible for the people who work with them."

Sales managers who blame reps for group failures weaken themselves in the eyes of superiors and subordinates. Superiors look at this kind of finger pointing as a lack of accountability and as an inability to solve problems. Subordinates consider it cowardice. Even though it's really not your fault that you didn't make objective, it really is your fault. After all, it was your objective. And, yes, there were many things you cannot control, such as the economy and the competition. But to your superiors, these are just excuses. Moreover, your superiors have the ultimate trump card, the "Why didn't you?" card—for example, "Why didn't you adjust for the economy?" or "Why didn't you know the competition better?" Whether or not they actually ask it, you know they are thinking it. (In fact, sometimes it would be preferable for the boss to shout and rant. Because it's the silence that's disturbing—also the silence of your name not being mentioned when the next promotion comes up.)

It's a lot easier to forthrightly explain the errors you made and what you've learned. Doing so will position you as one who can take the heat and benefit from failure rather than being a weak, ineffectual finger pointer. By the way, you'll notice that the word "superiors" is plural because failures will attract interest from your bosses' boss and on up the ladder. The hard irony is that reports of failures travel a lot faster up the organization than success stories.

Here are three steps to make a failure successful: Explain the situation to your superiors with no excuses, assess the problem with the team to make it a learning experience (not a punitive action), and come up with an action plan to resolve the problem and prevent it from reoccurring.

Most important is a complete team analysis. "Okay, people, we messed this up big time. And I don't want to go through this again. So what do we do to make it right? Where did we go wrong and what do we need to do to make the next objective?"

Stay the course. You started this as a team effort and it's vital to keep it that way. Do not perpetuate the kind of institutional ADD (attention deficit disorder) that emphasizes short-term fixes over long-term discipline and persistence. We all understand the extreme pressures on sales managers to produce—pressures that sometimes lead to knee-jerk reactions to fire people, and upturn procedures and policies ("decisions and revisions which a minute will reverse"). Frequently, we create bigger problems in the midst of a crisis by letting *urgency* drive our decisions instead of *priority*. As soon as the pressure starts to intimidate your people, you've begun a decline that will take a long time to turn around.

Many times, organizational fixes are necessary. This, of course, requires people and procedural changes. Some salespeople just aren't right for the job and they have to be moved out—hopefully, with grace and honor— so as to find their niche. In addition, procedures need to change, and change frequently to meet market conditions. The important thing about making people and procedural changes is making these changes proactively, not reactively, by building consensus with your team as you go. In other words, act quickly and decisively but keep your people involved to the extent that they feel a part of making the changes instead of being the victims. Dance with the one that brung you. Keep supporting and respecting your people and they'll make things work.

In *Semper Fi: Business Leadership the Marine Corps Way,* Dan Carrison and Rod Walsh describe how Marine Drill Instructors never give up on a recruit: "The Drill Instructor's mission is to bring each and every individual up to the standard of excellence demanded by the Marine Corps.... The Marine Corps doesn't weed out, it cultivates."

When things go wrong, there's a strong temptation for the manager to come in with his or her six guns blazin'; however, research and common sense suggest that a more effective way to handle corrective action is through collaboration with your team as opposed to the gunslinger's approach.

In a sales group, failures are inevitable, but defeat is optional. It's the manager's option to let failures overwhelm him or her, or to let failures teach the group how to sell better.

Letting Go: When Change Is Necessary

Just as important as it is to stick to your game plan is the ability to know when to make changes. A sales organization is like a tree, requiring nurturing, feeding, and pruning. Even though nurturing is the first priority, pruning is required occasionally. It's imperative to trim nonproductive reps. Some organizations trim the lower 25% each year. This strengthens the organization and helps those low-producing people find their aptitude or strengthen their skills to survive in another group. Whatever employment retention guidelines you have, make sure they are specific and understood by all your people. More importantly, ensure that everyone knows where they stand through frequent sales assessments, and make sure that there are no surprises.

Here's the tough part: If you have clear and easily understood retention guidelines, you *have* to implement them. You have to replace reps who are functioning below expectations. No matter how much you like the sales rep, to protect the integrity of your guidelines, you have to terminate, demote, or move the rep to another job. You are not doing a favor to underperforming reps by helping them do a job at which they are not good. They need to discover what they can do best, and it might be something other than sales. Guidelines that are not adhered to are not guidelines, and won't be taken seriously by your sales force. Even more dangerous, exceptions to retention guidelines can land you in court with job discrimination lawsuits.

On the other hand, it's a manager's job to develop his or her people to succeed. And there's nothing more satisfying than leading the transformation of a weak salesperson to a top producer. It's a lot easier and more cost-effective to improve the reps you have than to start off with new ones. Hiring and training costs for new personnel are exorbitant and drain an organization's budget. Usually, it takes a year to get a new rep up to full speed—that's a year full of mistakes and downtime. It also takes a lot of supervisory time and energy that could otherwise be spent more productively. In other words, fertilizing and nurturing is more productive than pruning.

The power of nurturing was studied by researchers from Colorado State University and Kansas State University. They asked a sample of 224 salespeople, from a variety of companies across the nation, what kind of management style enhanced their sales performance. The most effective style was "Dominant-Warm," which emphasizes collaboration, synergism, and empowerment of sales reps. This style incorporates such concepts as "I want the best plans possible. That frequently requires ideas from others. I don't have all the answers. Get people committed to their goals and they'll supervise their own efforts. Leadership is helping people do what they have in them to do. A leader develops people." An opposing style that was found to be less preferred is called "Hostile-Submissive," typified by "Planning is my prerogative. I make the plans; they carry them out. I make sure everyone knows what to do and how to do it. I call the shots. Most people want a strong leader to tell them what to do. My people know who's boss."

What's Your Legacy?

As you get older, your legacy becomes more and more important. When you retire or go to another job, how to you want to be remembered? Think of it this way: Imagine yourself as a next-door neighbor to each of your reps. Every day, when you came home, you'd run into their spouses and children. Would you be able to have a friendly chat with them based on how you treated their husband, wife, or parent at work? Or would they avoid you like the plague? People might or might not remember how many sales objectives you reached, but they will remember how you made them feel. Did your anger make them feel small and insignificant? Did your pride in them make them feel confident and respected? Always keep an eye on what you say and how you say it, but more importantly how it will make your reps feel; that's what will be remembered.

In summary, the proper care and feeding of your sales force will make the difference between commitment and indifference, enthusiasm and apathy. You can have hired guns who go where the money is. Or you can have warriors who believe in your vision and will follow you with pride and loyalty. Shaping these realities is the province of the sales manager. A good manager can make ordinary salespeople good and good ones great. A poor manager will make ordinary sales reps bad and great ones merely good.

Case Study #4: Using Teamwork to Increase New Business

Going into the team meeting, Brett wasted no time. "I've been in Dave's office and it wasn't pretty. We're way behind in new business and we've got to turn it around. This is full-court-press time, and I need everybody onboard," he said while distributing a report to the reps. In the highly competitive business of commercial janitorial services, Brett's 12-rep team was showing above-average customer retention rates. They were doing so well that new business prospecting had suffered.

"Here are the metrics—your individual new business, comparing last year to this year and your current progress to annual objective. Take a look at where you are and where you need to be. Overall, we're 10% behind the pace, even though a couple of you are above objective—good job, Lisa and Jim. We need to see a 10% increase from each rep. That comes out to fifteen thousand bucks per rep. I know that's challenging but that's what we need to get in the game, and—considering historical numbers—it's doable.

"The good news is that we're blowing out our cross-sell and up-sale numbers. And our customer losses are the lowest in three years. If we can get a handle on new business, this is going to be a record-setting year. If we don't, the good things we're doing aren't going to matter.

"Now don't get me wrong. I'm not saying this is all your fault. In fact, as I told Dave this morning, this is really as much my fault as anyone's because I've focused too much on existing accounts. But I also told him we will fix it. Now, we need to figure out a way to get us on target. Think about things that have worked in the past, things that we've never tried before, even things that didn't work but might work now. Think inside the box, outside the box, on top of the box. I don't care. At this point we need ideas to sift through.

"Do we have a volunteer to lead this? I know two or three of you have pretty good new business numbers...." Natalie Carter raised her hand, coming up front to the whiteboard to write down the reps' ideas. "Thanks, Natalie," said Brett. "I'll do the minutes."

It was a slow start. No one had an immediate comment. Natalie got it started by writing down one of her prospecting strategies, which was membership in a local purchasing agents' association. She then waited patiently for other reps to join the discussion. Janice Brandon said, "How about getting a list of new companies from the city clerk? Then we could split the list among us all."

"Good idea," Natalie answered. "We should definitely look into this and see what we can get. Any idea who we should call? Would you mind following up on this for the group?"

Gerald Brown raised a hand. "One thing that has worked for me this year is going online to Contractors for Hire to identify business prospects. There seems to be some potential there...."

"Another good idea," responded Natalie. "Is there a way we could divide those prospects for the team?"

Pen in hand, Brett busily jotted down the minutes, including all the suggestions as the other reps warmed into the session and offered their opinions. With a total of 18 ideas listed, Brett laid down his pen, saying, "Alright, we have some pretty good ideas. Now, Natalie, if you'll help, let's prioritize the top six ideas so we can focus on developing them fully."

After the team narrowed the list to six, Brett said, "We've made some progress in the last hour and a half, but we still have some things left to do. I know you have appointments, so I suggest we get back together in two days to finish. Here's what I'd like you to do in the meantime: All of you analyze the six priority issues and be ready to discuss your analysis. Also, be ready to volunteer for an assignment. Some of you have already said you'd be willing to do the follow-up work, and I think it's only fair we all have a share of the work. Discuss this among yourselves, and don't hesitate to see me if you have additional thoughts. One key question I would like for you to address is this: Can each of you do 10% in new business? Is it realistic to think that these ideas are going to get us where we need to be?"

In the subsequent meeting, the reps were fresh and came in with a game plan built around the six priorities, individual commitments to perform tasks (some more ambitious than others), and an honest assessment of their abilities to reach the 10% goal.

Addressing the team at the end of the meeting, Brett said, "I appreciate everyone's hard work and input. I know you've worked on this among yourselves, and I feel confident that we have a plan to reach our goal. I also know some of you are not as enthusiastic as I am, and I appreciate your honesty. I know that when you're at zero new business, it's hard to see how you can reach objective. But keep in mind that you're not in this alone—we all need to pitch in and help each other all we can.

"The important thing is that we have a plan. It's our plan and we're accountable for its success."

4

Fourth Step:
Becoming a Successful
Servant Leader

Even though it sounds like some touchy-feely management fad, servant leadership dates back to prebiblical times and is still energizing leaders around the world. It is a discipline, a tough-love approach requiring character strength from the sales leader and accountability from subordinates.

The concept is best defined by Robert Greenleaf, former AT&T executive, who coined the term in 1970: "The servant leader shares power, puts the needs of others first, and helps people develop and perform as highly as possible." It's a form of "reverse delegation" with proven bottom-line results in companies ranging from Southwest Airlines to Starbucks.

A recent *Harvard Business Review* article stated, "Leaders are shepherds, goes the conventional thinking, protecting their flocks from harsh surroundings. Not so.... Leaders who truly care for their followers expose them to the painful reality of their condition and demand that they fashion a response. Instead of giving people false assurance that their best is good enough, leaders insist that people surpass themselves. And rather than smoothing over conflicts, leaders force disputes to the surface.... But leaders who cultivate emotional fortitude soon learn what they can achieve when they maximize their followers' well-being instead of their comfort."

Servant Leadership requires the sales leader to expect, respect, and inspect.

Servant leaders *expect* their people to surpass their best, to constantly seek ways to improve their performance. They provide support, training, and resources for their sales team to get the job done. In return, they require accountability from the sales team to be successful. After all, the servant leader is a member of the team—a partner—but the accountability lies with the people who do the work, the sales reps.

Servant leaders *respect* their salespeople, their opinions, their skills, their professionalism, and their ability to succeed. They are respectful enough to listen to their people and humble enough to let their people take the lead when appropriate. (After all, it takes a big ego to be humble.) They are self-confident enough to share power and decision making with their reps. And they are wise enough to know that sharing creates a fusion exponentially more powerful than the efforts of any one manager.

Finally, servant leaders *inspect* results continuously to ensure that they are proceeding on the right track. As former President Ronald Reagan said, "Trust but verify."

Edward Hess, professor at the University of Virginia, has studied top-performing corporations throughout the country and found many of them being led by servant leaders whose management philosophies run counter to more traditional, authoritarian management styles. "Many people believe great leaders are charismatic, have a commanding presence, are visionary and educated at elite schools. Almost all of the leaders of the high-performing companies I studied had none of those traits," Hess said, emphasizing that they were more likely to be humble and subordinate-focused who lead by example and the "Golden Rule." Hess adds, "How servant leaders behave is a key to their successful leadership.... For example, treating people with dignity, being in the moment and not multitasking, not interrupting others, listening intently, smiling, saying please and thank you, acknowledging the contributions of others, admitting mistakes, apologizing, not having to be the smartest person in the room all the time, and spending time on the front line with employees and customers.... Servant leaders do not think that unless employees are watched like hawks, they won't work hard. They believe that if you create the right values and culture, normal people will do extraordinary things."

Twenty-five years before we started hearing about TQM (Total Quality Management), General Dwight Eisenhower was leading Allied forces in World War II as a servant leader, building decisions through compromise and consensus. Alan Axelrod quotes Eisenhower in *Eisenhower on*

Leadership: "The art of leadership is getting somebody else to do something you want done because he wants to do it."

As Supreme Allied Commander, Eisenhower's job was pulling together the U.S., Russian, British (and Commonwealth), and Free French armies into a unified fighting machine. He led one of the most successful military campaigns in history through participatory management. Getting input from all parties, he made sure everyone was on the same team as a valued player. He made the final decisions but gave everyone a voice and a role in the process.

Custom-Made Team Building

Eisenhower had an uncanny grasp of the complexities of team and individual psychology. He realized that "one size fits all" doesn't work in the human equation. Every person, every team is different, requiring custom-made communications, motivation, and rewards. Servant leaders carefully study their people and team dynamics. This isn't quantum physics; you don't have to be a scientist because there are no secret formulas for analyzing your people. Nor do you have to be a psychologist. All it takes is the ability to ask the right questions. Take a minute with every rep and ask what motivates him, what annoys him, how he likes to be managed. Ask your team to tell you how they prefer meetings to be run, who should be leading special projects, and the expectations they have of you, their manager. It takes time, patience, and energy, but the payoff is found in increased loyalty and decreased friction in the sales team.

By the way, when you use the word "team," make sure your sales team understands that it means people working together for a common goal. Using the word "team" in a business context is dangerous because of the sports analogy it conjures up. There's really very little in common between a sports team and a sales team. A sports team is a traditional command/control unit led by a coach who determines strategy and tactics. Therefore, coaching denotes a kind of autocratic guidance that works when dealing with teenage athletes. However, in the work world we are dealing with educated adults who are responsible for feeding families. This is serious business because people's lives depend on it. It certainly is no game, especially no sports fantasy. We can learn from sports such things as discipline, determination, and the will to win, but coaching a sports team has little to do the intricacies and demands of managing a sales force.

The Inverted Pyramid

"A leader is best when people barely know he exists, not so good when people obey and acclaim him, worst when they despise him. Fail to honor people; they fail to honor you. But of a good leader, who talks little, when his work is done, his aim fulfilled, they will all say, 'We did it ourselves,'" said Lao Tze in 500 B.C.

If you look at an organization as an inverted pyramid, you see the role of the servant leader. Instead of the CEO being at the top, he's at the bottom of the pyramid; the hourly workers are at the top and the managers in between are working for their people.

After ensuring that the sales team is well trained and well armed, the servant leader and the team create a common vision and objectives. Then, the servant leader turns them loose—with adequate monitoring of progress—to get the job done. Micromanagers not allowed.

The servant leader has to take chances for his people. This is not for the weak at heart. There are times when the leader has to turn things over to subordinates and show confidence in their ability. Then, the leader has to fight relentlessly to help them get where they are going. Salespeople always notice their leader's efforts for them, and even if they don't show it, they will remember when you went to bat for them. The payoff is developing that ever-so-important element of trust.

Zig Ziglar, legendary speaker and author on sales effectiveness, captured the essence of servant leadership by saying, "You will get all you want in life if you help enough other people get what they want."

Ethics and Servant Leadership

In "The Eight Elements of TQM," Nayantara Padhi said, "TQM is built on a foundation of ethics, integrity and trust. It fosters openness, fairness and sincerity.... This is the key to unlocking the ultimate potential of TQM."

Name any great military, political, or sports leader and the word "integrity" is a key part of his or her legacy. In sales management, maintaining integrity can be a challenge because the typical manager has spent a large part of his or her life selling. Not to say that there's anything dishonest about sales. In fact, the most successful salespeople build a reputation on ethics and truth. However, selling, like debating, requires a single-minded attempt to sell and defend a product, service, or idea. The salesperson has a single point of view with a mission to persuade the customer to buy. The servant leader's job is not necessarily to persuade sales reps to buy a particular point of view, but rather to provide the available facts to create a decision based on the team's knowledge and expertise. It's more a matter of *inclusion* than *persuasion*.

The challenge for you, as the sales manager, is to take off your sales hat when dealing with subordinates. You're not selling as much as facilitating ideas—taking suggestions and refining them. Reps know when you're selling. The moment you start selling, you lose your objectivity, and you lose your chance for team input and collective energy. Just tell the truth, the whole truth. Remember, you're a manager, not a salesperson. Lay all the facts on the table and have your team help sort them out and create solutions as partners.

In *Lead Like Jesus,* Ken Blanchard states, "People follow a great leader because they respect them, not because they have power." Sales reps respect honesty and fairness. Inclusion, rather than persuasion, will generate a positive environment for your reps and, in the end, better decisions.

In addition to better decision making, integrity also improves salespeople's job satisfaction, which leads to improved retention rates, according to a Baylor University research paper reporting results of a study of 501 salespeople. The researchers state, "As employees perceive organizations as more ethical, their intention to want to continue working there increases. We can therefore conclude that leaders who adopt a servant leadership approach will positively affect their followers' perceptions about the ethical standards of the organization and thereby increase employee job satisfaction as well as the likelihood of employee retention."

Top Leaders Have High Expectations

In addition to honesty, servant leaders have a sense of infectious optimism and expectation. Instead of pushing and prodding, they trust and irrepressibly expect the best of their salespeople by helping them develop into the best they can be. They understand that high expectations create a kind of self-fulfilling prophesy that leads their people to high achievements. In this regard, Joel Osteen, author and founder of Joel Osteen Ministries, tells the story of a high school that selected three teachers and told them they were the top three teachers at the school and were getting the top 10% of students for a special advanced studies program. At the end of the semester the students scored 30% higher than other classes' average. Then the teachers were told that they were part of an experiment, and that their students were actually ordinary students randomly selected. Everything else being equal, the big difference in student performance was expectation. The teachers expected these students to be the best and the brightest. That's what they became.

An important part of servant leadership is setting the bar high, expecting your salespeople to achieve high goals, believing they will, and preparing them to do so. Servant leaders not only do this through an ambitious vision for the team but also through their trust and confidence in the team to reach progressively higher goals. The servant leader's efforts help reps become motivated, prepared, and confident. Surprisingly, they too develop a sense of expectation of themselves. This shared expectation, between sales manager and sales rep, leads to a harmony of effort and improved sales productivity.

Leading with Grace Under Fire

In addition to high expectations, an element of graciousness is found in servant leaders. That is, the ability to provide subordinates with undeserved favor. It means trusting when others don't deserve to be trusted, giving loyalty despite being betrayed, showing kindness in the face of malice. The smart ones have learned that retaliation in the workplace never works for a leader, considering the polarizing effect it has.

As in some martial arts, sales managers occasionally have to go with the flow and use opposing momentum to work as a constructive force.

Aikido practitioners "blend" instead of clash with their opponents. They join with the rhythm and intent of the foe in order to devise the optimal response.

It's called "verbal aikido" by Luke Archer, author of *Verbal Aikido— Green Belt: The Art of Directing Verbal Attacks to a Balanced Outcome*. Here's how the concept applies to sales leadership: Instead of silencing the person confronting you, the servant leader listens, absorbs, and redirects the attack. For example, say a rep accuses you of revising a commission plan to reduce reps' earnings. The first step is "blending," to look for commonality with a response such as, "I understand what you're saying, but I can assure you that I'm on your side because I want you to earn as much as possible. The more you earn, the happier and more productive you are." The next step is to respond to the rep's "intent," which is to make money: "Help me understand why you feel your earnings might be reduced." With additional information from the rep, the sales manager is ready to redirect the attack with something like this: "Let's take a look at the commission plan and figure out ways to make sure your earnings are as good as or better than in the past."

Case Study #5: Servant Leadership in Advertising Sales

Brandon managed a district sales office for a national medical magazine published quarterly. His 12 sales reps were experienced, all having more than three years with the company; however, they were just learning how to sell Internet advertising in addition to the traditional print ads. This combination was extending the time needed on appointments, which was increasing the sales cycle.

This was not going to be a good meeting, Brandon thought as he spoke to his reps, beginning with the bad news. "People, we have a problem. This next edition goes to press in eight weeks and we have only 60% of our existing accounts handled. This is a big problem because it leaves our artists and printers only a couple of weeks to publish the next issue. It's already created a cash flow shortage of $290,000 short of what was budgeted. Worst-case scenario, if we miss our deadline with the printer, we have to pay $30,000 for every day we go over.

"Bottom line, chances are that my boss is going to bring in reps from other offices to help us. That means fewer accounts for you to handle, which means a smaller paycheck for everyone. He's already started calling around to arrange for help, even though I told him we can handle this on our own. I don't mind taking another run at him, but I wanted to discuss it with you all first.

"We need to do two things this morning. First, I need to know what the problems are, what's slowing us down. And second, we need to figure out a solution. And we need to do it quickly; otherwise, we're going to see some new faces coming in here to handle our accounts. Tell me, honestly, do we need the help or can we get it done ourselves?"

After a brief silence, one rep said, "We have some paperwork logjams and laptop problems that are slowing us down, but we can work around these problems. Look, I can't speak for everyone here but I can get mine handled without any help. And I really don't want someone else coming in and working any of my accounts. What do you guys think?"

Someone responded with, "Yeah, I agree. We can do it."

"Hold on," said Phil Weston. "We have more problems like administrative clerks who don't want to do their job and a sales funnel that's taking hours to deal with."

"Hey, Phil, chill out, man," replied a rep. "Nobody else seems too concerned about those things."

Brandon interceded, "Phil's got a right to his opinion. Remember the ground rules? I'm writing down these two additional concerns. Other comments? How about you guys who haven't said anything yet?"

"I agree that's there's a lot of things slowing us down," said Lisa Browning. "But we can deal with them. The last thing I want is help from the outside."

The room resounded with "I can get it done" and "We can fix it."

"Okay," Brandon said. "You're telling me that we can get back on track. I have a list of four roadblocks that we can solve. Is there anyone here who has any doubts? If so, let me know now, because this is my head that's going on the chopping block if I tell my boss we can get it done by ourselves."

With everyone agreed, Brandon added, "One more thing, one more very big thing. Despite the deadline pressures, I expect you to do a quality selling job on each account. We have to sell all our products and cross-sell as we normally would. No rushing through your accounts. We will not compromise our standards under any circumstance, and we'll make an honest effort to do the best we can with every customer. I might add, my tracking system will give us a daily look at the quality and quantity of sales. I guarantee you if either quality or quantity is being sacrificed, I will pull the plug immediately and bring in reinforcements. With this in mind, do I still have everyone's commitment?"

The reps agreed, and Brandon continued, "Okay, it looks like we have unanimous consensus. So tell me what you're going to do to get it done, how we're going to solve the problem. I can't guarantee that my boss is going to let us finish by ourselves, but when I ask, I want a good solid game plan and I want your commitment."

In an hour, the reps outlined a timetable, identified secretarial and database improvements that were needed, and established a weekly account review system that would make sure they were on track to reaching deadline.

"Okay," said Brandon. "This plan looks reasonable. You guys put it together; you all are committed to it. And you are accountable for its success. I'll support you in any way I can, but when it comes down to it, each one of you are the only people who will make this work. I'll polish up the plan and take it to the boss. If he agrees to it, I will tell you this—that everyone will be watching. Your results will be tracked daily, and the pressure will be on. So you'll have to give it your best. And you'll have to keep me in the loop if there's even the smallest problem."

The Servant Leader as a Problem Solver

As demonstrated by Brandon, servant leadership takes self-confidence coupled with a lot of planning and organization. Though he wasn't leading troops into battle, Brandon used his own brand of servant leadership to solve a substantial business problem.

First, he showed courage to take a risk for his team. He could have simply acquiesced to his boss's directions, but he made the conscious decision to seek an alternative that would not only benefit his sales team in the short-term but might set the stage for long-term process improvements. He refused to take the easy way out, even if it meant having to convince the boss. Then, in four steps, he addressed the problem and created a solution:

1. He identified the problem and defined it using specific numbers and metrics that left nothing in question. Sharing financial information—including profit/loss details—helps your sales force develop a full understanding of the issue and their stake in it.

2. He clearly illustrated the impact of the problem on the company's financial picture, on other work groups, and, more importantly, on the reps themselves. Giving the big picture—from the company perspective down to the impact on the individual rep—will increase the likelihood of buy-in from your sales force.

3. He probed to identify the source of the problem, seeking solutions from the sales force and developing a plan based on their input. Now, the problem and solution were no longer only the manager's burden but had morphed into a shared plan for which the reps had taken responsibility.

4. He summarized the solutions and made sure he had commitment from the sales reps to be accountable for implementing *their* plan, as well as setting the stage to track results of the plan. The value of tracking—or performance measurement—not only provides management with data to signal the need for midcourse corrections, but also emphasizes to the sales force that their efforts are important enough to be carefully scrutinized.

Communication Is Vital to Servant Leaders' Effectiveness

A joint study by researchers at Illinois State University, Ohio University, and University of Alabama found that sales reps ranked these four traits among the top attributes of effective sales leaders:

- Communications and listening skills

- Human relations skills

- Open communications
- Knowledge possession

The reps ranked these preferred attributes of an effective manager over such skills as selling, organization, and time management. In other words, the reps seemed to say that they functioned better under leaders who, first, had command over human dynamics such as communications. Of secondary importance were the more technical elements of the manager's job, such as selling skills.

Not surprisingly, the study found that sales managers had a different view of which attributes were the most important for effective sales managers, ranking coaching, selling, and organizational skills higher on their list. "Sales managers have indicated in previous research that it is important for them to have good selling skills." However, the study states, "no sales representative in our interviews directly discussed selling skills as an attribute of an effective sales manager."

Another difference in perception between managers and representatives was that representatives valued managers who recognized salespeople's individuality; managers did not acknowledge this value. The researchers state, "This result suggests the sales managers in our sample do not recognize treating salespeople as individuals as an important consequence that might ultimately affect job performance."

These differences in perception can create a chasm, alienating reps from the manager; however, the servant leader builds a productive team by communicating and understanding reps' needs while considering those needs in daily sales operations. Sales reps are more likely to follow leaders with egos big enough to serve and bold enough to lead. Ironically, the more they serve, the better they lead.

Servant Leaders Create Flow

As mentioned in Chapter 1, "First Step: Manage Yourself," we all have peak performance moments known in athletic circles as playing "in the zone." These are times when a person performs at his best in an effortless, relaxed manner. Athletes do it as well as salespeople, performing artists, attorneys, doctors, and other professionals. These moments of brilliance might seem spontaneous and unplanned; however, there is nothing accidental about them. In fact, you might have spent weeks, months, even years preparing for these moments.

These peak performances are called "Flow," a term used by Mihaly Csikszentmihalyi, author of *Flow: The Psychology of Optimal Experience*. The components of Flow match closely with TQM principles utilized by servant leaders who facilitate high-performing sales teams. These are the nine main components of Flow:

1. **Challenge-skills balance**—This is a state in which you feel confident that you are well prepared for the challenge you are facing. Servant leaders prepare their people through training, coaching, and positive self-talk, as well as technical and sales support. In addition to developing a sense of self-sufficient expertise, servant leaders let their people know that help is available from the sidelines, if needed.

2. **Action-awareness merging**—In this state, salespeople are completely immersed in the transaction. People are truly absorbed in things they enjoy and for which they have prepared. Servant leaders create a sense that this is "showtime" or "game time." It's the moment you have worked toward, so enjoy it and give it everything you have. When action and awareness become one, the action component becomes automatic. The actions of the salesperson's presentation are effortless and natural. He or she, for example, intuitively overcomes objections and uses the correct visuals without even thinking about it.

3. **Clear goals**—Salespeople who have clear goals and objectives know what is expected of them. A servant leader helps establish concrete, achievable objectives so that reps know exactly what is required in each customer presentation. In addition, the rep goes in fully aware that he or she is accountable for the results.

4. **Unambiguous feedback**—A continuous stream of feedback in the form of coaching, performance measurements, and team dialogue helps the rep refine efforts to meet objectives. The servant leader creates an atmosphere in which daily (even hourly) feedback is presented through updated sales metrics as well as ride-alongs from the sales manager. Some even arrange rep

ride-alongs with other sales reps to provide another source of feedback and encouragement. The servant leader also encourages constructive feedback from peers, one salesperson to another.

5. **Concentration**—This is hyperfocused concentration on what you're doing. Servant leaders enable this by minimizing distractions such as excessive paperwork, unnecessary rules/procedures, job threats, and any factors that shift the rep's focus away from selling. For example, you do not want a rep getting in the middle of a good presentation and start thinking such things as "Did I forget step three of the five-step process?" or "If I don't get a cross-sale today, my boss is going to kill me." It's similar to a basketball player saying to himself, "If I miss this shot, the coach is going to bench me." The result of these distractions is a type of performance anxiety that leads to failure.

6. **Sense of control**—This occurs when a salesperson realizes that, for example, she *owns* this sales presentation. At this moment, only she can influence the outcome of the sale. The servant leader creates a sense of self-sufficiency and independent decision making by reps, giving them a sense of control.

7. **Loss of self-consciousness**—Losing this sense of self occurs when salespeople are self-confident, so self-assured that they're not second-guessing themselves or overthinking what they're doing. Their focus is on the presentation and the customer, not on themselves. The servant leader facilitates this process by building reps' self-confidence through training, role playing, providing feedback, and encouraging positive self-talk.

8. **Transformation of time**—When you're in "the zone," you lose track of time because of your total focus on the issue at hand. An hour might seem like 10 minutes when the sales dialogue is flowing. (Hopefully, the customer feels the same way but the rep has to be sure during this moment that he doesn't overstay his welcome.)

9. **Autotelic experience**—This element of flow means that you are internally driven to succeed even without external rewards. You're doing something because you love to do it. Servant leaders encourage this process by providing an amiable work

environment, free of threat and intimidation, in which reps can ply their chosen trade. In this sense, the servant leader becomes a cheerleader, generating enthusiasm and promoting a love for selling. Of course, it helps to hire people in the first place who love to sell.

Experiencing Flow doesn't require all nine processes to occur at the same time. Also, not everyone experiences Flow. In fact, Csikszentmihalyi says a study showed that 12% of respondents never experienced it, and 63% said "often" or "sometimes," with the remaining 25% saying "rarely." Nonetheless, the servant leader, using TQM principles, has a natural tendency to automatically create an environment promoting Flow in the sales force.

Servant Leadership Improves Productivity

Despite an absence of research showing a direct link between productivity and servant leadership, ample anecdotal evidence exists. For example, leadership authors Michael Lee Stallard and Jason Pankau suggest that servant leaders improve productivity by increasing the level of "connection" with subordinates. "Most leaders focus on achieving task excellence alone.... What happens every time is that the failure to establish and maintain relationship excellence ultimately sabotages task excellence," say the authors. "Our research has identified a force in organizations that we describe as 'connection.' It is a bond based on shared identity, empathy and understanding that moves self-centered individuals toward group-centered membership.... Connection moves people to give their best efforts and align their behavior with organizational goals. It engenders loyalty and increases productivity, innovation and overall performance." They quote a study of 50,000 employees that indicated "connected" employees are 20% more productive than other employees on average.

Southwest Airlines, one of the premiere servant leader companies, has led the airline industry in productivity indices for a number of years. Herb Kelleher helped found the airline on the following premise: "Your employees come first. And if you treat your employees right, guess what? Your customers come back, and that makes your shareholders happy. Start with employees, and the rest follows from that."

Action Fast Print, according to *Inc.* magazine, implemented a servant leader approach with impressive bottom-line results. Instead of telling employees what to do, founder David Wolfskehl started a dialogue with employees, saying, "Today we're going to start talking about your problems and how I can help you." In the article he goes on to say, "Once I started asking how I can help, amazing things started happening in my organization. In a two-year period, we had a 30-plus percent improvement in productivity."

Admiral Vern Clark, Chief of Naval Operations, is credited for reenlistment rates that soared from 38% to 56.7% during his tenure with the U.S. Navy, according to servant leader researcher Michael Lee Stallard. "He encouraged people to speak up, challenge the assumptions, and make the Navy better each day," said Stallard. "He told people to dig into the data and don't be afraid of 'constructive friction' as they discuss differing points of view. This gave people permission to speak up and prove their case if they had ideas to improve the Navy."

Servant Leaders Improve Sales Retention Rates and Customer Engagement

The practice of servant leadership can also improve your retention rate, helping you keep your experienced salespeople. According to the Baylor University report mentioned earlier in this chapter, "In particular, this study reveals that adopting an employee-oriented approach will improve turnover intention, a common problem in sales...." By placing salespeople's needs as most important, "leaders who operate from this perspective serve as role models to their employees and reap the benefit of improved employee attitude and job satisfaction.... While it may on the surface appear counter intuitive to place employee needs as a top priority, even above company objectives, this study, as well as supporting research, demonstrates that servant leadership has myriad benefits to the organization and is an effective tool to retain employees."

In addition, this and other studies have shown that the servant leadership style also improves relations with customers, ostensibly having the effect of improved sales. According to the researchers, "Essentially, employees learn to treat their customers by observing how their managers treat them." Employees who are treated with dignity and respect tend to treat their customers the same way, as noted earlier with Southwest Airlines. Many successful companies take this contrarian stance of "employees first" rather than "customer first," believing that satisfied personnel create happy customers. This gives the servant leader a performance advantage that's particularly important in sales, in which customer satisfaction is everything.

5

Fifth Step:
Sales Empowerment,
Beginning with Ownership

We, as managers, are fixers. You know the drill. See a problem. Fix it fast. Move on to better things. Like psychic mediums, we see problems. Intuitively, we have solutions in mind. After all, there's a reason why we got to this lofty position on the management team—our education, experience, and accomplishment made us a cut above our subordinates. All we have to do is use our ample managerial skills to control our people, and solve the problem. Correct? Not exactly.

The more unilateral "I'm the boss" control you exert, the less control you get. What you get when your people feel pushed is push-back. This brings up the first step of sales empowerment:

Step One: Give Control to Get Control

An overcontrolling manager is limited to control of visible activities. For example, you can ask for reports on each of your reps' customer presentations explaining why a sale was or was not made. You can demand detailed, daily activity reports. You can require 16 appointments per week. At the end of the day, what you have are reports and activities. What you don't necessarily have are the *invisible factors* that compose high-performance selling—enthusiasm, commitment, and accountability.

The control issue revolves around extrinsic and intrinsic motivators. Extrinsic motivators come in two general categories: money and threats. Perform the desired behavior (meeting sales objectives, for example) and you get paid commissions, bonuses, and other awards. Failure to perform gets you fired. Extrinsic motivators are the currency of command/control management. On the flip side of the coin is intrinsic motivation, a form of psychological pay: feeling respected, feeling appreciated, believing that you are doing meaningful work toward an important vision. Intrinsic motivators—a key part of TQM and employee involvement programs—provide powerful and sustained progress toward success. If all you offer salespeople is extrinsic motivation, when it's taken away, you have nothing left. You'll see it happen when you offer a bonus to sell a particular product. Product sales increase, temporarily. Take away the bonus and sales drop. Intrinsically motivated salespeople work harder, consistently harder, because they are doing something they actually want to do. They believe that they are playing a vital role in the company, and they have a stake in its future.

"Most companies have it all wrong. They don't have to motivate their employees. They have to stop demotivating them," states an article in the *Harvard Management Update* by David Sirota, Louis Mischkind, and Michael Meltzer. "Incorporating a command-and-control style is a sure fire path to demotivation. Instead, redefine your primary role as your employees' expediter: It is your job to facilitate getting their jobs done. Your reports are, in this sense, your 'customers.'"

The combined complexities of globalization, increasing competition, expanding scope of supervision, exploding information technology, and rising customer expectations require more sophisticated, complex leadership strategies. The simplicity of command/control strategy will always be a part of sales management; however, modern markets require sales leaders to fully utilize and engage their people in reaching success.

Jack Welch, former General Electric CEO, said it succinctly: "To be blunt, the two quickest ways to part company with GE are, one, to commit an integrity violation, or, two, to be a controlling, turf-defending, oppressive manager who can't change and who saps and squeezes people rather than excites and draws out their energy and creativity."

Even if you don't believe in the philosophy and rhetoric of employee involvement, you can bet on one certainty: Sales reps will "game" the system when they're faced with unreasonable demands. They will find workarounds and loopholes to get managers off their back. Ironically, they'll do it so well that the manager won't know a thing about it. Giving your people the control and accountability to work out problems might not provide instant solutions, but it will get everyone working together with a unified sense of involvement. And it will decrease the likelihood of reps gaming the system.

A lot of the control issue boils down to simply using your power judiciously. Authority protects; it doesn't dominate. Confident leaders don't feel a need to defend their power. The good ones exude self-assurance and share their power. They are able to distribute it. As a manager, you are not their parent—these are grown adults with whom you're working. You are not their coach—they are not high-school athletes. And you are not their teacher—they are not school kids. You are their manager, and that is a sacred trust that includes a little teaching, a little coaching, and some parental nurturing; but it's done in a way that gives them professional respect. Remember, the more respect you give, the more you receive. Same for control: The more you give, the more you get. Yes, you guessed it, the Law of Reciprocity at work again.

How can you ensure that your salespeople aren't goofing off? You can't. You can check their phone calls, ask for daily activity reports, follow up with their customers, or even follow them to see how they're spending time; however, your lack of trust sends a message that is far more destructive than sales reps wasting time. Would you, as a manager, want your boss checking on you all the time? Would it make you feel like a trusted, productive employee?

This is where the prayer for serenity comes in: "God grant me the courage to change the things I can, the serenity to accept the things I can't change, and the wisdom to know the difference." Recognizing the things we can't change is liberating. That recognition frees a lot of time, effort, and worry to focus on things we can change.

Some of you might recall a study back in Psychology 101 in which two groups of students were given a complex math problem to solve. Both were subjected to noise and distractions while working the math. One group was given a device with a button to push that would immediately stop the noise and distractions. The other group did not have this device. Results? The group with the "quiet device" did substantially better than the group without it; however, no one even touched the device. The simple idea of having control over the situation gave them a sense of well-being and confidence, providing the *perceived* ability to overcome their distractions and achieve better results.

Put yourself in the place of a sales rep who goes into daily sales meetings, not knowing what to expect or what new plans and procedures are about to be thrown at them. It's like walking in on the wrong end of a firing range. The uncertainty is unnerving. The lack of input is frustrating.

Dr. Michael Marmot, University of College Medical School of London, has studied the effects of individuals' real and perceived control in the workplace. His Whitehall Studies have found that workers in the lower strata of an organization exhibit increased levels of stress-induced illness, partly because they have less control over their work lives, which increases stress levels. Conversely, having more control in the workplace decreases stress and absenteeism while increasing productivity. "Giving workers more involvement and say on the job not only makes them healthier but more productive," said Marmot.

This idea of subordinates having some control in the workplace caught on in the seventies and eighties in the form of Quality Circles, a TQM offshoot originally initiated to improve manufacturing processes. These circles included management and nonmanagement employees addressing process improvements as partners.

This partnership was addressed by Peter Drucker, in *Classic Drucker,* who said there are four steps to making substantial growth in productivity, including defining the task, concentrating work on the task, and defining performance. "The fourth step is...for management to form a partnership with the people who hold the jobs, the people who are to become more productive, by asking them what they think is the way to address both productivity and quality."

Back in the 1940s, as Edward Deming discovered, continuous process improvement was everyone's job—from the janitor to the CEO—to look for better ways of doing things. The results went far beyond process improvements. Employees were energized and felt a sense of ownership. Self-esteem rose. Loyalty to the company increased. Stress decreased.

Instead of being given daily marching orders and repeating their routines mindlessly, employees suddenly were being asked for their opinions. They now were being involved in decisions that affected their work lives. The result was increased enthusiasm, creativity, and belief in the company. The TQM principles that revolutionized manufacturing apply to sales because salespeople, though temperamentally different from salaried manufacturing employees, are still people. Providing even a modicum of control in the workplace energizes them by giving them a voice and a vote in their future.

For sales managers, sharing control can come in various processes and in varying degrees. Consider the following:

- **Objectives**—When setting group and individual sales objectives, do it in concert with reps individually and as a team. This helps ensure that objectives are attainable—no pie-in-the-sky goals that only frustrate sales reps. Collaboration in objective setting also means that reps are more likely to own the objectives, rather than looking at them as an arbitrary number dreamed up by people far away from day-to-day selling. In most cases, you, as a sales manager, already know your volume and profitability hurdles. With that in mind, go to your reps individually and shape objectives that are mutually agreeable, realistic but challenging. After the individual goals are set, go to your team to set group objectives. Objectives can inspire and motivate, as well as establishing reps' accountability for goal attainment.

- **Policy and Planning**—Frequently, company policy and planning are handed to the sales manager from above. It's simply not up for discussion. That's when you, the manager, need to *make* it up for discussion, in two ways. First, work with your superiors to get a voice in policy making. Let them know that your people—the implementers—can provide powerful input into the development and execution of policy. Second, get your people involved in creating policy changes or developing new policy that you champion and present to your superiors. (A by-product of this approach is the manager being viewed as proactive and therefore more promotable.) Facilitate creative thinking; that is, if your people don't like a policy or plan, come up with a better option. For hand-me-down policy coming from the top, work with your people to get their suggestions on implementation. If you can't change policy, at least you can involve your people in the best ways to execute it. The bottom line: Getting your people involved gives them a sense of productive control as opposed to blind obedience.

- **Pay**—Does your commission plan motivate your people? Does it provide incentive to sell the products you want to sell? Is it competitive with similar industries? Are your sales incentives (cash, vacation trips, "spiffs") on target? Discuss these items with your people. Get their opinions and suggestions. The discussion could shed light on problems and inconsistencies of which only salespeople would be aware. Consider a task force composed of reps to examine your pay structure and suggest alternatives.

- **Pricing**—Dealing with customers every day positions your reps as pricing experts. Getting them involved in pricing decisions makes a lot of sense. Are your products competitively priced? Are your reps losing sales to cheaper products? Are there value-added features or bundles to make your pricing more attractive to customers? Whether or not your pricing personnel want to hear it, keep pricing information flowing from your sales force to those who set prices.

- **Information Sharing**—Occasionally, you'll see the manager who hordes information, with the thought that information is power, and he who controls the information flow controls the work environment. The fallacy with this line of thinking is that the less your salespeople know about your operation, the more alienated they become and the less likely they are to use their personal initiative to support company goals. For example, on the surface, a single factor like rising production costs might seem inconsequential to a sales force. But if you look harder, you see that rising costs decrease profitability. Decreased profitability means it's less likely that the sales unit gets a bonus for the year. But how does the sales force impact rising costs? Maybe it's as simple as increasing sales by one unit per rep per month. In this way, the simple sharing of information gives the sales group the chance to actually improve the company's bottom line (and increase their take-home pay). Known as Open Book Management (OBM), this strategy provides employees with profit-loss information—including expense, cost of goods, and cash flow—that demonstrates ways in which employees can impact the bottom line.

More specifically, OBM can help sales reps overcome customers' pricing objections by providing exact financial details to discuss with customers. For example, the sales reps can respond with such data as this: "It costs us $177 to produce the unit and, like any business, we have to make a profit on it for us to stay in business; the profit, by the way, is approximately 10%." Or for the customer complaining about a price increase, the sales rep can answer, "Our operating costs increase 5% per year. Most of the increase is due to rising transportation costs and the price of gasoline." Reps can more easily overcome objections when they help customers understand that your cost structure is similar to theirs. In addition, OBM can also help your reps tell the quality story of your products. If your salespeople know, for example, component costs of production, they are able to compare your costs with those of competitors, emphasizing how your expenses on superior components lead to increased durability, reliability, and effectiveness for the customer.

- **Procedures and Everything Else**—Excepting individual personnel matters and disciplinary situations, the list of issues for sales rep involvement is virtually endless. A few of them are listed here:

  - *Reports*—Are the reps spending too much time completing sales reports? Can the reports be streamlined? Are the reports meaningful, having an impact on reps' sales techniques and tactics?

  - *Office Hours*—Are reps required to spend too much time in the office? What office hours are optimal to facilitate managerial needs while maximizing time spent selling?

  - *Meetings*—Are there too many or too few sales meetings? What types of meetings are helpful and which ones hamper sales reps' efforts? What changes in meetings would facilitate sales management and sales rep effectiveness?

  - *Training*—Are reps benefiting from training sessions? What would make sales training more valuable? Are there different topics and approaches that would improve sales reps' performance?

There are hundreds of other examples of and reasons for sharing control with your salespeople. The most important factors are, first, that salespeople do not like to be controlled—it's a suffocating, demeaning, and ultimately counterproductive feeling. Second, sharing control gets salespeople involved, energized, and accountable for their actions.

"Senior managers commonly fear that if employees participate in developing policies concerning hours of work, benefits, and a host of other human resources issues, they will be too lenient or generous," says Edward Lawler in *The Ultimate Advantage.* "In fact, research shows that when employees are involved in developing these policies, they often set *higher* standards than would be set by senior management."

There are times, however, when a manager goes overboard, giving too much control in the workplace. This happens when you have a "Best Friend Manager" in charge, a manager who wants to make everyone happy, and frequently lowers expectations in the process. Unlike the Best Friend Manager, a strong leader drives performance, challenges sales reps to do their best, and gets the most from subordinates in a way that makes them look forward to coming to work every day.

This is a huge paradox of sales management: Deep personal relationships and friendships drive the sales process but can hamper your management efforts. In sales, it's important to be accommodating and especially to be liked. However, in sales management, friendship with your reps creates big problems. "If you create or allow close personal ties with your subordinates...you will struggle as a manager," according to Linda Hill and Kent Lineback in their book *Being the Boss: The 3 Imperatives for Becoming a Great Leader.* "You won't be able to make tough but necessary people decisions or evaluate people accurately and give critical but helpful feedback. If you try to stay on good terms with everyone, you'll make exceptions for individuals that others consider undeserved or unfair. Relationships that are primarily personal can only produce disappointment for your people in the long run and make you much less effective." The authors go on to say that it's important to be human, caring, and close with subordinates, but in a way similar to your relationships with doctors, attorneys, and other professionals. You want them to care deeply about you but you don't need them to be your friends. You want them to provide the best possible service for you in a caring way. Likewise, that's the best approach bosses can offer subordinates—a compassionate but professional relationship. In the same vein, don't hire friends to work for you—that's a good way to demolish a friendship and reduce sales productivity at the same time.

Insisting on high output and quality standards might occasionally make people unhappy. Call it tough love or whatever you like, the truth is that it's better to be respected as a manager than liked. The basis for employee ownership/empowerment is fair, equitable, and professional treatment of your salespeople—this requires the manager to be a leader, not a friend.

Step Two: Develop Buy-In

Even the most responsible people among us feel the tiniest sense of irresponsibility when driving a rental car. After all, if you get a door ding or hit a pothole, it's not your car. At the end of the day, you turn in the car and walk away—no ownership, no accountability.

Is your sales force driving your product line like a rental car or do they own the process? Salespeople with a sense of ownership feel responsibility and accountability for results. Ownership creates a living link between the job and the sales psyche. It integrates your salespeople with your company, your products, your leadership. Without it, you have salespeople with no personal stake in your success.

How do you develop this sense of job ownership? Primarily, you have to believe that your people will determine the success of you and your company. You have to understand that the collective efforts of your people—their energy, enthusiasm, and creativity—is far more powerful than the ability of any lone manager. Owning a piece of the business, either figuratively or literally, helps unlock your people's potential.

A Stake in the Outcome, by Jack Stack and Bo Burlingham, outlines the importance of employee ownership: "There's a common belief, for example, that it's all about owning stock. Equity-sharing certainly plays a crucial role, but you don't get an ownership culture simply by giving stock to employees.... [For an employee] to be an owner, a true owner, you have to care," stated the authors in describing the difference between traditional employees and those who have become "owners."

These "owners" care about the business and about the ways in which they can positively impact the business. Additionally, the authors say, "Owners do not follow a job description. They don't just put in their time…they go beyond mere problem solving and look for creative, innovative ways to reach their goals."

No doubt, this ownership concept is not the traditional sales management model in which the manager develops objectives, provides product training, and monitors sales success. If you want salespeople to own their jobs, you—as the sales manager—have to loosen your grip, share decision making, and make them accountable for their actions. It's likely that the resulting increase in cooperation and enthusiasm from your sales team will more than make up for the initial discomfort you might feel in control sharing.

"Today's employees are looking for more than just a desk and a paycheck; they're looking for the opportunity to create, establish, and nurture an identity—a corporate identity, a work-related identity—of their own. They want something to be theirs," says Joyce Gioia, of the Herman Group, in "Finding Ways to Make Your Employees Intrapreneurs."

Intrapreneurship, a concept originally developed by Gifford Pinchot III, encourages your subordinates to handle their jobs like their own business. "Intrapreneur is short for intra-corporate entrepreneur. Within an organization, intrapreneurs take new ideas and turn them into profitable new realities. Without empowered intrapreneurs, organizations don't innovate. Yet many organizations waste their intrapreneurial talent…. Management is blocking legitimate intrapreneurial zeal with bureaucratic quibbling or industrial-age 'We know best' attitudes," says Pinchot in the book *Intrapreneuring in Action: A Handbook for Business Innovation.*

A recent *Time* magazine article described an intrapreneurial program at General Electric that has developed something akin to an internal venture capital firm that transforms employees' innovative ideas into new products and systems: "The result is that production cycles for projects like new oil drilling equipment or LED lighting systems are shortening dramatically. An idea that once took two years to test might go from paper to production in 45 days." GE also has a Web site where it posts problems and offers payouts for solutions.

How does this employee-input concept translate to your salespeople? Look at your sales force as they are today. Most are intrapreneurs whether or not they know it. Your salespeople are on the job every day, creating solutions for your customers, and improvising product applications to make the sale. All of these intrapreneurial actions are a part of a salesperson's everyday life—it's simply part of selling. The manager's job is to help the rep perform as a seller and think like an owner. An owner makes good decisions, takes accountability for his actions, and creates (and shares) process improvements that improve the bottom line. Following are four key ideas to convey to your sales team that will help them think like owners:

1. Salespeople are as important as shareowners and company executives in determining the success of your organization. In a sense, they are active investors who provide time, energy, and talent that generate cash-flow for the company.

2. Sales reps have a direct stake in the company's overall performance. The more successful salespeople are, the more successful the company is. And that means better pay, benefits, and job security for everyone.

3. Achieving success is incumbent on reps using their individual styles and skills, taking responsibility to actively shape the customer experience and to meet customers' needs.

4. Reps who think like owners are problem-solvers who create solutions and innovations, not only for themselves, but for the whole sales team and company.

In many respects, salespeople naturally operate like owners, especially when it comes to independent thinking and problem-solving. Routinely, salespeople are creating hundreds of best practices that go unrecognized and unshared. The manager's role is to identify, encourage, channel, nurture, and share these innovations among the team. Make intrapreneurial process improvements an integral component of your sales culture. Go a step further: *Expect* them from your team; make it part of their job description.

Take care to balance the energy of your sales intrapreneurs—your sole proprietors, your lone mavericks—by using your team as the incubator for intrapreneurial zeal. The key is to allow individuals autonomy while encouraging, magnifying, and optimizing their efforts through team dynamics.

For example, in team meetings, go around the table and ask for new and better ways your people are doing their jobs. Accept banality, celebrate ingenuity. No matter how insignificant the ideas, encourage, encourage, encourage the interchange of new concepts, improved processes, and innovative sales techniques. Also, hasten your team members to cross-pollinate their innovations with each other, to share ideas formally and informally. Reward idea sharing with monetary awards, certificates of accomplishment, and congratulatory notes from upper management. The result of your efforts is the message that your salespeople are vital to the success of your firm, that you depend on their collective efforts to build a winning sales team. This, in turn, creates a sense of ownership on their part that builds loyalty, trust, and accountability. In this sense, collaboration creates a multiplier affect that significantly expands the power of intrapreneurs.

On an individual basis, here's the ultimate job-ownership scenario: Sit down with one of your best performers and tell her, "I want you to handle your accounts like it's your own business. Your accounts total $250,000 in billed revenue. Your job is to bring back a 10% total increase in sales at the end of the year. No excuses. You have the resources of this company behind you and I'll make sure you get all the help you need. Of course, you'll be expected to follow company policy and procedure. I will track your sales and ask that you regularly inform me of your plans and progress."

You've just built job ownership using three building blocks:

1. **Responsibility**—The salesperson, as owner, now has responsibility for the success of the endeavor. Support is available, but make no mistake, it's the rep's responsibility to use her skills and talents to achieve success. The rep is solely responsible for two things: a full understanding of her accounts, the personalities, processes, and needs of each; and how to effectively couple your product line with customers' needs. No one—other than the rep—is going to get this job done. In all reality, who else *could* get the job done? There's not enough hours in the day for the manager to deal with each account.

2. **Accountability**—The sales manager has now established the rep as an owner who is accountable for specific results. No excuses. Regardless of the economy, the product line, or the level of sales support, the salesperson is fully accountable for failure or success. It's important to link accountability to measurable objectives (in this case, a 10% return) to which the rep and manager agree and that they fully understand.

3. **Authority**—The rep, or owner, has authority to make decisions within the boundaries of corporate policy. Accountability without authority is failure in the making. However, it requires careful thought to establish the appropriate level of authority for sales reps. It's always a judgment call by the manager, considering that some salespeople are more ready than others for making autonomous decisions.

This scenario is extreme intrapreneurship. For many sales managers, it sounds foolish to turn over decision making to reps. But is it? Think of how many commission-only sales reps and manufacturers reps you've known. Aren't they essentially extreme intrapreneurs? They operate with little or no supervision. They know their product and they realize what it takes to survive without the daily assistance of a sales manager.

Realistically, not everyone is interested in, or capable of, the pressures of total job ownership. It takes the right spirit and skill set to succeed. The true intrapreneurial spirit yearns for success, is full of initiative, ambition, and self-discipline. Combine these characteristics with sales skills, product knowledge, and people savvy, and you have a sales intrapreneur.

Many of your salespeople are going to have one or the other: an entrepreneurial spirit without the skill set, or sales skills without the spirit. The ones full of high-spirited ambition, usually new reps, might need training and grooming. Keep their fire-in-the-belly burning but loosen the reins gradually, carefully monitoring their judgment, decision-making ability, product knowledge, and sales skills. Little by little, give them more latitude to, for example, negotiate prices with customers, apply special discounts, make contract changes to close a sale, or resolve customer complaints on the spot.

Also, remember that some of your experienced reps might have an entrepreneurial spirit but simply have lost their fire over the years.

Perhaps they have redirected their enthusiasm to hobbies or part-time business pursuits. Reclaiming these potential intrapreneurs can help invigorate your sales force. One of the best ways to reenergize burned-out sales reps is to get them engaged in a new and challenging endeavor that tests their abilities. Intrapreneuring will do just that. It might just shake them out of their lethargy and give them a reason to wake up and get to work. Ask them—as experienced salespeople—to use their expertise to help lead the intrapreneuring effort. Putting them out in front as a leader or mentor could help restart their sales career.

On the other hand, there are the ones who have ample skills but who are content to take orders and wait for instructions. There's nothing wrong with this. In fact, this could be the profile for the majority of your team. You're not going to change them overnight, maybe not at all. You can, however, create a sense of job ownership by, first, ensuring that they are accountable for results. With that accountability, provide enough latitude for decision making to avoid the accountability-without-authority pitfall. Set decision-making boundaries. Encourage them to act decisively. Support their decisions. As they make progress, extend their decision-making boundaries.

Second, treat them like subject-matter experts. They are. No one else knows their customers better, and understands how to link your product line to buyers. Your expectations of your salespeople are similar to the "you become what you believe" theory. That is, if you want to become a successful salesperson, you dress, talk, and act like a success. Behaving like a success activates your subconscious and conscious actions to move you closer to your goal. The same line of thinking applies to a manager's expectations of subordinates: They, to some extent, will strive to become the kind of person you perceive them to be. If you treat them like a subject-matter expert, they are likely to acquire at least some of the skills to support your perception. On the other hand, if you treat them like an incompetent, chances are you'll get what you expect.

Essentially, every one of your people is an intrapreneur to some degree. You, as the manager, will ultimately determine their level of intrapreneurial success. Give your people support, training, and stretch objectives, and get out of their way as much as possible (considering that some require more supervision than others).

A word of caution: The real intrapreneurs, though possibly only a small percentage of your sales force, will test you. They will try new things that fail. They will cross boundaries. They will, at times, infuriate you. But they will get the job done. Chances are they will be your superstars. That's what job ownership is all about.

Step Three: Empowering Your Team to Success

Empowerment means giving power to your subordinates, empowering them to make decisions that will improve sales operations. In *The Three Keys to Empowerment,* Ken Blanchard says, "Literally, for companies to succeed in the new world of business, team members must feel that they own their jobs and that they have key roles.... When asked what they want from people today, leaders almost universally respond, 'We want people who are problem solvers, who take initiative, and who act like they own the business.'"

In considering an empowerment program, there are no requirements for how much or what kind of power you give—you decide that according to your particular situation. The biggest fear that sales managers have is that they will lose control. The simple fact is that the manager sets the agenda, establishing decision-making boundaries and the operating parameters. Subordinates who think empowerment is a blank check to do whatever they want soon discover that the concept actually puts more accountability pressure on them than a traditional command/control system. For example, the salesperson who has been empowered to negotiate pricing with a customer within specific profitability guidelines has fewer excuses for not making the sale. How many times have we heard a salesperson say, "The customer has a budget and our price was too high. If only we didn't have to stick to fixed prices." In other words, "It's not my fault I lost the sale; it's the company's fault." When you empower sales reps to negotiate rates on the spot (as long as they hit profit targets), they now have no excuses.

Giving up power is never easy, but remember the Law of Reciprocity. The more you give, the more you get. Power is not a fixed-sum quantity. The total amount of power increases as it is shared.

In command/control sales hierarchies, the manager spends a lot of time creating rules and reports, monitoring compliance, and dispensing reward/punishment. Compliance becomes so important that, at times, it overshadows achievement. In this scenario, the underlying thought is that the manager knows how to reach objectives, and if everyone follows instructions, success is a certainty. If, by chance, failure results, it becomes an exercise in finger-pointing—the sales reps saying, "It's not my fault; we were following orders," and the sales manager saying, "You didn't follow instructions well enough."

An empowering manager is focused on the bigger picture, leading the sales effort as a partner with his or her subordinates, implementing innovations and winning in the marketplace. It gives the sales manager freedom to plan, providing a bit of the hunter mentality to go where the prey will be rather than where it has been. At the same time, the reps are spending their time and effort on learning, and sharing creative ways to sell. Empowerment shifts the accountability paradigm from sales manager to sales rep. When there is no one to blame but yourself, the rep finds ways to succeed. In this way, empowerment is liberating for a sales manager.

Case Study #6: Sales Empowerment, One Step at a Time

"Now, let me make sure I'm understanding this." Alan took off his glasses, looking at Jason in disbelief. "You want the reps to set the market plan and rates for the Baltimore campaign—the big one, the one that makes or breaks our year?"

"Yes," Jason answered confidently. "And I suggest that they establish bonus payouts and awards, and do the kick-off ceremony too."

Alan paused to let his words take shape, "Man, I don't know.... In the past, the managers have always done this. They're used to it, and it gives us control on the money issues. To tell you the truth, I guess we've never trusted the reps with the big issues, they just don't have the experience."

"I hear what you're saying," interjected Jason. "But keep in mind, I'm not proposing giving away the store or taking away our decision-making authority. We'll set the parameters for who makes what decisions. And every step of the way, we'll work as a team, the reps and the managers. So there are no surprises. The reps get the benefits of managers' planning experience, and the managers get the benefit of the reps' street experience. Of course, you, as the head honcho, have the ultimate decision authority.

"Here's the payoff," Jason continued. "This is instant buy-in. It would be a program that the reps help build. That means they'll work it and defend it. They certainly can't complain about something they put together."

"So, what are you goin' to do?" asked Alan. "Call everyone together in a room and just hash it out?"

"No, Alan. We'll make it an orderly process. We'll set up a committee of five managers and five reps who represent the whole office. Their job will be to get everyone's opinions and keep them informed every step of the way."

Alan shook his head slowly, "I just don't know, Jason. This goes against everything I've learned in twenty years of sales management. I don't know if we're ready for it, especially the other managers."

"How about if I do some spade work, and see if we can get some support from the managers?"

Alan replied, "Support is not what you're looking for here. Just see what the level of resistance is. If you don't get chased out of the building, I'll talk to you about it. But I do *not* want my managers kicking down my door about this."

Jason spent the next two weeks selling the idea to the other four managers, encountering varying degrees of apathy and antagonism.

"This won't work," said one of the managers. "These bozos can't even learn our existing marketing plan, much less develop one. The more power you give them, the more they'll want. They already think they can do anything they want. They're loose cannons. We gotta keep these folks under control or they'll run amok—you know, anarchy in the hallways."

"We can always call in the National Guard," Jason said with a chuckle. "But I really don't think it'll get that bad. The idea isn't to turn over control to the reps. It's just to give them a chance to be heard, to give us their ideas. It's a controlled environment, everything subject to management approval. The main idea is to get them involved rather than fighting against us. Get them to feel ownership in the plans. Here's what it can do. First, it'll save you a lot of planning time because we'll have a team doing it. Second, it will reduce your complaints from reps, because they'll have a hard time complaining about something they created. It may even improve sales by using their ideas—they can sell their own plan to customers better than one that's been forced on them. Who knows, we might even learn something from their experience on the streets.

"It's kind of like a cross-country trip. Give them a turn behind the wheel, let 'em show what they can do, and give us a little rest."

At the end of the second week, Jason was back in Alan's office. Alan spoke in a measured, deliberate cadence, like a judge delivering a sentence. "Not everyone likes your idea. Some hate it and most are in the middle of the road. I can honestly say that no one is too excited about it, but as bad as our numbers were last year, and considering that the economy's not any better this year, I've decided to give it a try, as long as there are no surprises. I want to be posted on every step of the way. Remember, I have ultimate accountability for anything coming out of this process, so make darn sure I don't get blindsided."

The first meeting included Jason, four other managers, and five sales reps who had canvassed all the reps for their ideas. On a nearby easel, the Ground Rules were handwritten:

1. Everyone has a voice.

2. All ideas and suggestions are equal.

3. Keep every manager and every rep well-informed continuously (no surprises).

4. Alan has the final approval power.

With Jason serving as facilitator and referee, the monthlong process started with two meetings per week. Each meeting was followed by briefing sessions to make sure all reps, managers, and staff were aware of the group's progress and could add their ideas. No surprises.

Four weeks later, the plans were finalized. It was time for the kickoff. Standing before the reps, managers, and staff, Alan smiled and began, "Before we get started, I want you to know, I didn't have anything to do with this. If it doesn't work, it's not my fault." He and everyone broke into laughter. "On a more serious note, I want you to know how much I appreciate the time you all spent coming up with this plan. The marketing plan and commission plans are similar to last year, but we have what I think are a number of improvements. The key thing is that it's *our* plan, and now is the time to execute it to the best of our ability."

Alan then turned over the meeting to a group of managers and sales reps to explain details of the plan, from pricing to advertising to sales bonuses. When the meeting was over, as they walked out, Alan turned to Jason. "Well, how do you think it went?"

"Fine, I think everyone feels like they've had their say, and that's the important thing."

"I guess so," answered Alan. "You know, I was kind of surprised that nobody suggested any real drastic changes, no idiotic ideas. In fact, the pricing and commission systems are pretty much the same, and the objectives they set are probably more aggressive than what I would have come up with."

"The difference," replied Jason, "is that everyone had a chance to change anything they wanted to change. We listened, made some changes. And now, I think we're going into the campaign like a team. The reps are part of the process."

The Benefits of Empowerment

The *New York Times* recently reported that the U.S. Army is now asking 140,000 personnel—privates to generals—to rewrite seven field manuals providing instructions on various phases of Army operations. Officers behind the effort said the goal is to tap the experience of battle-tested soldiers rather than relying on researchers and specialists away from the front line. The Army, like many modern corporations, is engaging foot soldiers to establish procedures and policies. In addition to getting good information, this process increases what researchers call "self-efficacy," the self-confidence that people feel when their ideas are heard. This self-confidence is the fuel that drives successful salespeople. And successful salespeople are less of a drain on the sales manager. They don't need a lot of supervision. Essentially, they are self-managed sales reps, depending on the degree to which the manager develops them.

They can become, as mentioned earlier in this chapter, extreme intrapreneurs using the concepts of responsibility, accountability, and authority as the framework for their sales efforts.

Traditional command/control hierarchies simply exhaust managers and salespeople. The more control points—rules, reports, paperwork—the more monitoring required by a sales manager to ensure compliance. Also, it takes a lot of energy to create and re-create the many control points that keep your reps organized and marching in step. As for salespeople, command/control causes a sense of powerlessness that leads to apathy, at best, or resistance, at worst. Either way, it creates people who just don't care or people who will undermine the rules, "game" the system, or subvert sales simply to make a point.

Salespeople, independent creatures that they are, will likely take exception to the manager who tells them what to do and how to do it. The subconscious message from the manager is, "I'm the boss. I know more than you do. Do what I say and you'll be successful." The receiver of this message has a number of ways to respond—none of them productive. It's related to cognitive dissonance theory, which says people feel uncomfortable when presented with two contradictory ideas simultaneously. Think of it this way: Most of us in sales believe we are pretty good salespeople. If we didn't, we wouldn't last very long in this demanding profession. With this belief in mind, the "do it my way" manager presents a contradictory belief to the salesperson, the belief that the salesperson needs managerial direction to succeed. The result is simple: The salesperson rejects the manager's belief, as well as the value of the boss' directives. Doing so helps the sales rep reach a cognitive balance by decreasing the dissonance. The rep's real opinion of the boss might be along the line of "This guy doesn't know what he's talking about because I'm good and I know it. I do know how to sell." It's probable the rep will undermine the manager's orders one way or another, rejecting the boss as being out of touch with reality. In this way, the boss creates a sales group devoid of passion, one that shows a phony kind of enthusiasm merely intended to keep the manager off their back.

Similarly, cognitive dissonance occurs when we expect our reps to be self-starters, full of initiative, but, on the other hand, we expect them to suppress that enterprising spirit to submissively follow managerial commands. You can't have it both ways. That is, you can't expect your reps to be full of initiative on one hand but blindly obedient on the other. An empowering manager decreases reps' dissonance by allowing them to be part of decisions that affect them, letting them know that their ideas are valuable, that their experience is coveted, and that they are talented and competent. The empowering manager realizes that, when it comes to decision making, reps are better at participating than obeying. The actual truth is self-revealing, that is, that salespeople—through performance monitoring—discover their own strengths and weaknesses, without a lot of managerial direction. These lessons are the ones remembered.

A side benefit of empowerment is trust. In the *Journal of Personal Selling & Sales Management,* Karen Flaherty described results of a scientific study of sales managers and reps from companies selling medical equipment, supplies, and pharmaceuticals. "Results indicate that empowering salespeople is an effective way to increase performance. Managers who grant salespeople the freedom to make decisions and demonstrate a genuine concern for salespeople are more likely to be viewed as trustworthy." In effect, because the manager trusts the salesperson, the salesperson will trust the manager in return.

Studies of sales teams suggest that empowering sales reps leads to increased self-confidence, which improves sales performance. In "To Empower or Not to Empower Your Sales Force," a joint project conducted by researchers from the University of Houston and the University of Connecticut, the authors say, "An increase in a salesperson's self-efficacy increases his or her belief in being successful within the selling situation. This feeling of success allows the salesperson to be more comfortable and to use selling techniques that may not be typically used."

Empowerment is an orderly process that forces salespeople to analyze their own skill set and overall job performance. The manager's responsibility is to partner with reps to facilitate and monitor results, as well as setting boundaries. How much latitude do the sales reps have in making decisions? Can they negotiate customer rates? Can they provide refunds and make billing adjustments to customers? Can they set their own sales objectives? How do they report progress toward goals? How much power should be provided to the reps? On some issues—like pay/commission—does the manager simply want input from reps, leaving the final decision to the manager?

The answer is that it depends on the manager, the sales climate, and the individual reps.

In a typical sales environment, a manager will need to use a wide variety of tools ranging from command/control directives to complete sales rep empowerment, depending on the individual and the situation. Obviously, not all phases of sales operations lend themselves to complete empowerment. For example, you might have a product for which the margins are so thin that the price is nonnegotiable. Therefore, you might ask for salespeople's feedback on pricing issues but provide no decision-making authority on price setting at the sales rep level. Likewise, some reps are better prepared to be self-managed than others—clearly, a new rep is less likely to be autonomous than an experienced one.

As mentioned earlier, sales empowerment is best implemented one small step at a time. For example, give your sales reps the power to negotiate the price on one customer contract per month. After a couple of months, monitor the results, make necessary changes, and extend it to three contracts per months. You get the idea. Start small, market test the idea, and gradually roll it out in a way with which you and your people are comfortable.

Empowerment Means Better Decision Making

After you get the ball rolling, you'll find that empowered sales reps help managers make better decisions and, equally important, avoid bad decisions. In the book *Turn the Ship Around!* a U.S. Navy captain unknowingly issued an impossible command, and his crew tried to follow it anyway. When the crew was asked why no one challenged the order, they responded with, "Because you told me to." Realizing the potential downsides of command/control, the captain and author—L. David Marquet—created an empowerment program that transformed the USS *Santa Fe* from worst to first in the fleet.

As he and others have found, employees empowered in decision making help managers in various ways. Here are three primary ways:

1. First, the employees provide a checks and balances system for the manager that prevents poor decisions from being implemented. If you or your boss gives an order that just won't work, an empowered rep will tell you why it's a bad idea, and probably provide a workable option. This, at times, can keep you from shooting yourself in the foot, especially during busy times when you can't devote a lot of time and thought to all of your decisions.

2. Second, it sharpens your decision making by involving your reps before implementation. When they're part of decision-making, your salespeople can identify obstacles and opportunities that the lone manager might not see. Simply put, their knowledge of the marketplace will add value to decisions.

3. Third, giving them the ability to make decisions—within boundaries—on the spot with customers can save sales and create happy customers.

Fundamentals of Developing a Self-Managed Sales Team

"Self-management is an idea whose time has come," writes Joe Petrone in *Building the High-Performance Sales Force*. "When managers treat their employees like children, when they require them to ask permission for every action they take or decision they make, the employee never learns how to manage themselves and their time. Managers no longer have the time to closely monitor their employees. Only by empowering salespeople to take responsibility for themselves will they develop the skills and maturity needed to become self-managing."

Petrone's Progressive Goal Management system empowers sales reps by allowing them to set their own goals and rate themselves on goal achievement. The sales manager's job, through "partnering for performance," is to provide feedback and help reps stay focused on reaching goals. "Instead of acting as a dictator or controller, he or she acts as a consultant and coach," writes Petrone.

Compared to many professions, salespeople should most easily become self-managed. They are independent-minded, operating most of the time without supervision, and accustomed to the pressures of meeting objectives. However, some reps are more prepared for self-management than others. In fact, some will want no part of it. It's important, at the start, to reiterate that you're not abandoning them. You'll continue to provide the necessary—if not the same—level of support as in the past. You'll be available for coaching, ride-alongs, and all other forms of sales management support. The difference is that the reps will have more freedom to design their direction to attain goals. Here are the five basic steps to develop self-managed reps:

1. **Explain your goals in developing the program**—Your goals might include the following:

   - To provide more selling time for reps to be successful
   - To improve reps' responsiveness to customers by providing more flexibility in sales transactions
   - To give reps more custom-tailored development to advance their sales skills and career progress
   - To create viable, long-term financial goals for sales reps
   - To provide the sales manager more time for developing a vision and planning to achieve the vision

   This is a good time to let your reps know that they are the CEO of their own company, accountable for their results. Also, clearly explain your role as a facilitator and support person, and their role as an independent sales force.

   At the same time explain expectations: what they can expect from you, and what you expect from them. For example, your expectations of the reps might include these:

   - Meeting objectives
   - Submitting reports and paperwork in a timely fashion
   - Making good business decisions, within the boundaries of reps' authority
   - Showing responsiveness and follow-through with customers
   - Adhering to company policy, procedure, and code of conduct

Sales team expectations of you might include these items:

- Training and dissemination of product and market information, especially best practices
- Giving timely responses to sales team questions and needs
- Facilitating customer complaints and problems
- Providing long-term planning and sales strategy
- Representing sales team concerns to upper management
- Coordinating and ensuring sales support from other departments

2. **Develop individual sales objectives jointly with each salesperson**—Arrive at objectives that are ambitious but fair and achievable, with which the salesperson is comfortable. Objective setting should include financial goals: How much money does the rep want to make this year and subsequent years? Then translate the dollar goal to total sales needed, breaking it down by the day, week, or month. For example, say the rep wants to make $150,000 per year. There are hundreds of ways to break down the income goal into actionable steps. One way is an if-then approach, starting with basic assumptions:

   - If the rep's revenue base is $400,000, the rep will need to generate 10% of his assigned revenue base, which equals $40,000 ($400,000 × 10%) in net increased revenue needed.
   - If the historical average account loss is 6%, the rep will have $24,000 in anticipated losses ($400,000 × 6%). Adding $24,000 needed to cover losses brings the total net needed to $64,000.
   - If the historical average increase to existing accounts is 7%, the rep will gain $28,000 in projected increases ($400,000 × 7%).
   - Then the rep will need $36,000 in new business revenue to reach the goal ($64,000 − $28,000 in average revenue increase).

   A sample breakdown of action steps might look like this:

   New Business Objective: $36,000

   1. Number of sales needed at average of $360 per sale = 100 sales or 2 per week.

2. Number of appointments needed for 100 sales = 400 appointments or 8 per week.
3. Number of phone calls needed to set 400 appointments = 1200 calls or 24 per week.

The two additional targets, using this scenario, are maintaining a 6% or better loss per customer and a 7% or better increase per customer.

When sales activity begins, the projections will change to real numbers, and will commensurately change sales requirements. For example, if the 7% increased revenue projection decreases to 6% in real-life sales, the new business goal increases to 10% to make up for the shortfall. It's important to make sure reps have the latest metrics so that they can continuously maintain focus on the various elements (new business, increase to current accounts, and account loss) that make up their progress to objectives.

In addition to setting joint objectives with specific action steps, an additional step is to ask the rep for a *business plan* that includes a timetable and specific details on products to be sold, cross-selling considerations, targeted customers, sales techniques, sales cycles, quarterly sales projections, prospecting strategy, new versus existing business tactics, and other factors that are needed to accomplish sales objectives.

3. **Sales support needed**—Ensure you have agreement on what and how much sales support is needed to achieve the rep's objective. Specify support needs, such as the following:

- *Training*—This should include traditional product and sales training but also individualized, custom-tailored training specific to the rep's needs. For example, the rep might need focused training on setting appointments or compressing the sales cycle. The manager should consider an individual training budget for each rep to pick and choose pertinent training courses.
- *Technical assistance*—If possible, specify how the rep obtains technical help to sell the product. This should outline who is available in what situations and how frequently the

help is available. Assigning technical people to individual reps—where possible—can reduce reps' anxiety and develop a team rapport between sales and technical groups. The rep should know, for instance, whether he or she can call on a technician to go on sales calls or only on closes, or whether technical help is available only for big sales.

- *Administrative support*—Outline what help is available for paperwork and data input issues. Again, this might be rudimentary, but it helps to state the obvious to make sure there is a complete understanding of how the sales rep gets help when needed and who is available to help. In essence, it's a reminder to the manager to make sure that ample clerical support is available. At the same time, it assures reps that they're not going to have to fend for themselves.

4. **Establish ground rules**—Make sure everyone understands behavioral boundaries and program expectations. Define and explain such issues as the following:

   - Sales reports and paperwork required at specified times.
   - Required attendance at group meetings and individual meetings.
   - Retention guidelines for reps failing to make objective.
   - Limits of reps' authority to make variances in pricing and contract details.
   - Ethical guidelines, code of conduct, company policy/procedure.

   Stick to the ground rules without exception. If you fail to follow through on your rules, no matter how much you like or dislike a rep, your ground rules are meaningless.

5. **Develop tracking**—Develop a system to provide daily reports and feedback to reps that keep them informed of progress. If possible, provide statistics that show the amount of sales achieved and amount left to go, as well as the aggregate number of appointments and sales conversions. These diagnostic metrics will tell reps if they're not making enough phone calls or setting enough appointments, for example.

How Teamwork Facilitates Self-Managed Salespeople

These two concepts seem at odds: the *independence* of self-managed salespeople and the *interdependence* of sales teams. Actually, a robust sales team can strengthen self-managed sales reps by serving as a catalyst to solve problems and promote understanding.

First of all, it takes the heavy lifting from the sales manager. Making changes to the sales routine creates trepidation and unrest in any sales force. Without a supportive team, the manager is the sole source of problem solving, cheerleading, monitoring, and affirmation. That's a time-consuming burden. A high-functioning team can ease the transition by taking some of the load off the sales manager. An effective sales team will share information and support among each other, making transitions smoother and easier on the manager.

A sales team also can prevent a feeling of isolation among individual reps. A good sales team creates a "we're in this thing together" camaraderie and works collaboratively to make it succeed.

With proper grooming and training, a sales team becomes the facilitator of the beliefs and values of the program. A sales team that is fully engaged with the sales manager reinforces the manager's agenda. Through daily interactions, salespeople are able to remind each other of the practices and principles of the new process.

Finally, the team serves as a feedback mechanism, giving the manager insights and suggestions to fine-tune the program. This input not only helps to keep the process on track but also creates innovations that solve problems and generates opportunities.

6

Sixth Step: Success Through Performance Measurement

"When we ask chief sales officers and sales leaders how they measure sales performance, 60% say they don't measure it at all. Of the remaining 40%, a majority depend solely on a single trailing indicator, performance against quota," says Dave Stein, author and sales consultant. That's not surprising considering that performance measurement, to many of us, is like flies at the picnic. We're so focused on everything that goes into making the sale that measurement can be an annoying buzz, something we tend to ignore or wave away. If you have the gift of analysis, congratulations. That's usually not a strength of salespeople or managers. It's safe to say that we're less likely to be "numbers" people than "people" people. Even though performance measurement is simple mathematics, it is an acquired skill, a discipline that takes time to perfect. After it has been learned, it's a process that accomplishes more than just tracking sales. It provides insights into your reps and customers that enhance sales. It streamlines and optimizes sales managers' efforts in everything from goal setting to strategic development to customer retention. And, at the sales rep level, it can boost morale and self-confidence. As in most things, moderation is the key, that is, establishing the proper metrics to tell you what you need to know. Any more than that and performance measurement can actually become a distraction, an end in itself that turns sales into a numbers game.

This chapter on performance measurement is divided into two parts:

1. Daily sales team measures to prevent micromanagement.

2. Customer metrics that create sales opportunities.

Daily Measures to Prevent Micromanagement

Look up "micromanagement" on Google, and you'll find more than three million results (four times the number of results two years ago). Thousands of books, Web sites, magazine articles, and blogs seek to cure one of America's most prevalent workplace problems. Not only is it one of the top reasons for employee turnover, but it's also known to decrease productivity and increase absenteeism.

In the sales arena, instructions or directives beyond the monitoring of objectives, deadlines, and standards probably amount to micromanaging. Micromanagers will tell their sales force how to set up their files, how to set appointments, and what they should be doing during the sales day. Of course, nothing is wrong with instruction, but micromanagers insist on compliance, turning what could be constructive coaching tips into rigid rules. Telling your salespeople what to do and how to do it—this is the province of the delusional manager who thinks he or she can reach an imaginary sales paradise where everyone performs just like the boss.

Chances are that sales reps know as much as or more than most managers because they are out there exclusively selling every day. They can be micromanaged to function the way a manager wants them to; however, that carries a high cost in the form of lost creativity and loyalty. Salespeople, by the very nature of their job, have to be self-starters and operate with a high degree of initiative and autonomy. They will resist micromanagers. In fact, a salesperson who doesn't resist is probably a salesperson you don't want. You don't want a sales rep sitting around waiting for instruction. You want someone aggressively and creatively selling your product.

Sometimes, micromanaging is necessary, especially with problem employees who can't or won't follow guidelines or who are underperforming. Some need the help, but micromanaging has two unintended consequences: It takes valuable management time; and it conditions your people to follow instructions rather than being innovative and proactive. Micromanaging also fosters a tendency to systematize and treat everyone the same way, instead of recognizing individuals' strengths and weaknesses.

There's an element of self-fulfilling prophesy in micromanagement. That is, the micromanager doesn't trust his or her people to work without close supervision. Therefore, because of this lack of trust, the subordinates become untrustworthy, incapable of making decisions or improvements on their own. After all, with someone looking over your shoulder most of the time, why would you risk doing anything but what you're told to do? It's a lot easier to just take orders, go home at 5 p.m., and forget about your work. Conversely, if you expect that your employees are productive and professional, there's a likelihood that they will live up to that expectation. There are exceptions, and you will be disappointed occasionally. But occasional disappointment is better than the continuous frustration you get from subordinates who are openly or covertly fighting micromanagement.

"Try not to create too many rules," said J. Donald Waters in *The Art of Supportive Leadership*. "It has been wisely said that 'too many rules destroy the spirit.' Rules and precedents are, of course, much less trouble to work with than the daily flow of creative action. They kill the life, however, of any worthwhile ventures."

Rules can become the wrecking ball of the lazy manager. This kind of manager finds it easier to design rules that apply to the entire sales force than to take the time to handle the daily nuances and needs of the individual salesperson. General Motor's CEO, Mary Barra, simplified an onerous employee dress code from a ten-page document to two words: "Dress appropriately." Smart leaders, like Barra, recognize that their employees are responsible adults capable of making good decisions. In other words, they can be trusted. The message inherent in this trust is liberating and motivating, especially when you compare it to the cynicism and distrust lurking behind the creation of unnecessary rules. There will be lapses in judgment by employees, but it's easier to manage these exceptions than to spend the time and energy to create and enforce arbitrary rules that might apply to only a few people or situations.

A sales force needs structure and guidelines; however, rules can become a substitute for taking the time to solve an individual's problems. For example, if a sales team's results are below objective, the lazy manager will impose procedures to address team performance—such as remedial training sessions for everyone—rather than addressing individuals'

---

sales performance. The problem with that is that inflexible guidelines frequently waste time, as well as distracting and undermining the confidence of your good performers. Before establishing a rule that applies to everyone, ask yourself whether the problem could best be solved by attention to individual sales reps.

It's ironic that in the sales profession—the most entrepreneurial, unbureaucratic of all corporate endeavors—we often find micromanagers hiding behind policy, unable to create commonsense solutions to problems.

Take a look at the rules, procedures, paperwork, and meetings in place for your sales team. Are you using up valuable sales time with unnecessary approvals, paperwork, and reports? Is the output of all nonsales activities worth the time it takes? Is either management or the sales force learning something valuable from all nonsales actions? Bottom line, does it result in sales?

In 1990, when Lou Gertsner took over the reins of a troubled IBM, he studied why sales had dropped precipitously. The culprit, he found, was excessive paperwork. Sales reps and managers were being slowed with piles of unnecessary paperwork that had to be filled out daily. Whether intended or not, the sales force was being micromanaged by an avalanche of forms demanding unnecessary data that had little bearing on making the sale. Gerstner assigned the paperwork to assistants and got his salespeople back into the field selling. Within a year, IBM was making its comeback as a leader in the industry.

As an antidote to micromanagement, consider performance measurement, that is, establishing a system to measure *important* performance functions ranging from sales objectives to number of appointments to deadlines. These indices can also include new business, increased sales to existing accounts, or loss of accounts. Daily reports should capture these key statistics and be shared continuously with your salespeople to keep on the right track. It's as simple as the old adage "If it doesn't get measured, it doesn't get done."

A good performance measurement system allows the manager to target strengths and weaknesses of salespeople, prevent problems in advance, and create training and remedial programs based on individual needs. Equally important, it will prevent micromanaging.

It all comes down to measurements that clarify the organization's mission and strategy by reinforcing the right behavior, according to General John Michael Loh, United States Air Force, in *Leading People* by Robert H. Rosen. Challenged with leading 235,000 people, Loh established a measurement system: "You want to measure outputs and productivity.... We have 162 output measures across all our businesses, and every quarter I look at the results, and ask if we are measuring the right thing."

The result was a database that allowed Loh to push responsibility and control down the line, to switch from a command-and-control model to one of empowering personnel at all levels. "I realized that as your responsibilities grow, and you become head of a much larger organization, you can't have control.... To think you can direct and control activities from the top is incorrect. It's a false concept of leadership.... The crew of a B-52, with nuclear weapons onboard, goes off and is expected to perform their mission halfway around the world and come back safely and land. I can't be with them on that mission. I need to have a certain amount of trust and confidence in their ability to do the work."

The same concept applies to sales, from the standpoint of measuring output that gives salespeople the responsibility and accountability to do their jobs. For the cynics among us, consider this: When salespeople are empowered, when they are given authority and accountability, underperformers can't blame the boss. The numbers don't lie. Essentially, it shifts the blame from the boss to the subordinate.

The more a manager directs and commands, the more accountability he or she takes on. Tell sales reps what to sell, when to sell it, and how to sell it, and you give them an excuse for failure: They're doing it your way, and if it doesn't work, it's your fault. Give reps an unbiased look at their performance through the lens of good metrics. Explain the analytics thoroughly and help them determine their strengths, weaknesses, and changes needed to improve. Let the numbers do the talking; they'll speak louder than any words you can say. A self-taught lesson will stay with a sales rep more effectively than a manager's sermon. Your reps will get it, drawing their own conclusions about their performance. Your job as a manager is to facilitate support and training in response to the statistics. This gives reps information and the freedom to use it as they elect. The decision is theirs and the accountability is theirs.

First Priority, This Is a People Thing

The most important component of your measurement system is not the numbers. It's the spirit and intent of your metrics. We all know managers who establish reporting systems to impose their will on their reps, to keep them in line, to establish themselves as The Boss. These managers focus their reps on numbers rather than selling. Used correctly, a good reporting system empowers a sales force by helping them learn about themselves, their techniques, and their planning and organization. It tells them whether they are good closers, whether they're better on the phone or face-to-face, or whether they need to improve their cold calling. Taken as a learning tool, performance measurement gives the sales manager a way to continuously improve the sales force. All in all, it's pretty easy to select key performance metrics. It's not rocket science. In fact, performance measurement is the simplest of all management functions. If you've mastered basic arithmetic, that's all it takes. The real challenge is applying the metrics to energize and develop your sales force rather than distract and intimidate them.

Types of Key Performance Metrics

Every sales manager should have a list of Key Performance Indicators that tell the sales story on a daily or hourly basis. It goes without saying, a good reporting system is required, be it a sales funnel, a CRM system, or any process that provides daily analytics. The statistics included in your reporting should continually be tweaked to ensure you're measuring *only* what needs to be measured and to reflect changing market conditions.

Sales indices come in the form of "hard" metrics that are Output Measures and "soft" metrics that are Activity Measures. Output Measures are the end result of all selling activity. They are fixed measures of revenue requirements for the organization. These are the bottom-line numbers—total sales revenue, total new business revenue, renewal revenue, and so on—that demonstrate a sales group's ultimate success or failure.

On the other hand, Activity Measures reflect how a sales group gets to the bottom-line numbers. These are more instructive in nature, providing guidelines for reps to achieve their key performance metrics.

Ranging from appointments set to closes per week, Activity Measures are instrumental for getting and keeping reps on track to reaching objective.

Output Measures

Depending on your product and industry, Output Measures are usually simple. They are the revenue generated by new customers or existing customers defined by revenue or product:

- **New business acquisition**—Number of sales, revenue per sale, cold call conversion rate, lead-provided conversion rate.

- **Existing business sales**—Renewal rate, increased revenue per sale, and revenue loss.

- **Product or service unit sales**—Revenue per unit, conversion rate by unit, sales cycle by unit, unit sales by rep, unit sales by account type.

Activity Measures

Activity Measures show the activities performed to reach bottom-line output, such as number of appointments, outbound phone calls, and cold calls. When presented as a guideline, they are useful and enlightening; when presented as a demand, they can be counterproductive. For example, you will have reps who "sell big." These elephant hunters aren't too concerned with the quantity of appointments they make but rather the quality. They will have fewer cold calls, fewer customer presentations and closes; however, their sales revenue might be at the top of your team. An activity objective requiring them to set a given number of appointments per week is counterproductive to what makes the big game hunter successful. As a guideline it's fine; as a fixed objective it won't work to anyone's satisfaction.

Activity measures should be instructive in nature, not coercive. For example, if it takes 100 calls to get five appointments, your reps have a valuable guideline that helps shape their level of daily activities and expectations. If you insist that they make 100 calls per week, you set up a rule that will automatically penalize your elephant hunters or your "spurt" sellers, who might make 50 calls one week and 150 the next week.

In addition, you established a "my way or the highway" approach that robs reps of their autonomy and creativity. Output measures such as Net Revenue and New Business objectives are usually fixed and inflexible because they reflect the financial needs of the organization, but how reps get to those output measures should be left to their individual initiative.

Following are selected activity measures that can help keep your sales force on track:

- **Outbound Phone Calls**—The number of calls it takes to get an appointment or customer presentation/demonstration. The conversion rate of calls to appointments will show the effectiveness of the rep's phone pitch.

- **Cold Calls**—Similar to outbound phone calls, this measures the rep's ability to get appointments/presentations in a face-to-face manner. Similarly, a conversion rate of cold calls to appointments is appropriate here.

- **Appointments**—The number of one-on-one customer meetings it takes to get a close. The conversion rate of appointments to closes is an indicator of the rep's closing ability.

- **Closes**—The number of closes needed to reach revenue objectives. Important indices include rate of closes compared to presentations, revenue per close, and time needed to close.

- **Sales to Objective Gap**—This metric identifies how much difference exists between a rep's current sales total and the objective. Gap metrics identify current booked revenue, opportunities for closes, and prospects that need to be closed.

- **Sales Cycle**—It's helpful to know how long it takes to get the close and to answer such questions as these: Do longer sales cycles result in more revenue per sale? What types of accounts are taking too long to close? What reps are consistently showing shorter sales cycle and what's the impact on their total sales revenue?

- **Cross-Selling and Up-Selling**—Statistics on the number and value of cross-sales and up-sales can be beneficial: What percentage of total closes included cross-sales and up-sales? How much revenue was generated by each sale? Did cross-sales or up-sales increase the sales cycle? What differences exist in cross-sales and up-sales between types of accounts and reps?

Using the Numbers—Aha versus Gotcha

After you have your specific metrics and reporting system perfected, the next critical step is using it effectively. Try to make it an "aha" moment for your reps, a moment of self-revelation that leads to your reps' improvement. Provide reports regularly so that your sales force can have a guidepost to measure their daily activities. Frequently discuss results one-on-one with your people to make sure they are interpreting the numbers effectively. Instead of giving your interpretation of metrics, ask your reps for theirs. In some cases, you'll need to offer "assisted self-revelation" by adding your analysis to make sure reps are getting the full impact of the numbers. However, in general, reps will learn more when they develop their own insights rather than being instructed. After the manager is sure the rep sees the connection between metrics and sales actions that influence those metrics, the next step is developing an action plan to address weaknesses shown by the numbers.

In addition, when sending out reports, always rank order them by rep so that the reps can compare themselves to each other. This creates an understated kind of competitive edge because no one wants to be at the bottom. And everyone wants to be on top.

Above all, don't fall into the micromanagers' game of using the numbers to play "gotcha." This game consists of rigid goals for each index with punishment for noncompliance. Unfortunately, this approach turns performance measurement into a torturous process in which salespeople are more intent on escaping pain than learning. (Remember that negative reinforcement never works as well as positive reinforcement.) Gotcha measures might improve your reps' sales techniques but build resentment that leads to turnover and disloyalty.

Perhaps the toughest part of performance measurement is that your metrics will—and should—weed out the nonperformers. However, instead of being viewed as a "gotcha" process, good metrics should be seen by the manager and rep as a fair and objective practice that reflects reps' abilities independent of a manager's personal opinion. Worst-case scenario, when it becomes obvious that a salesperson has to be terminated, there should be no trace of surprise because the numbers told the story some time ago. It's never easy to part ways with a salesperson, but when you have clearly defined objectives and an effective measuring system, it's easier for you and the rep. In fact, a low-producing rep will see the writing on the wall and be sending out résumés well before the fateful day.

Stretch Your Objectives, but Don't Overstretch

A critical part of performance measurement is setting objectives that advance instead of impede continuous sales improvement. Reasonable stretch objectives are a good way to keep your people challenged and moving forward. A recent study by Steve W. Martin showed the effectiveness of stretch objectives in successful sales organizations. He noted that 75% of high-performing sales teams raised their 2014 annual quotas more than 10% over 2013. Only 25% of average-performing groups raised their goals 10%, compared to only 17% of low-performing sales teams.

The singular power of stretch goals is to help your sales reps step out of their comfort zone to develop new strengths and skills in response to your elevated expectations. If you expect more, you usually get more.

There is, however, a downside of stretch objectives. When stretch objectives are too ambitious, they lead to high failure rates (as high as 90%) that can demotivate salespeople.

Goals are motivating to salespeople only when they receive positive reinforcement for reaching them. Realistically, how many managers blow out their stretch objectives? Very few. The problem is that sustained failure over time erodes reps' confidence, rendering them progressively less effective. Moreover, unattainable goals diminish sales managers' credibility because they are viewed as the creators of meaningless, self-serving objectives.

The trick is to set attainable stretch goals. Smaller, incremental stretch goals are the most effective. Two years of achieving 5% increases is far better than two years of unsuccessfully trying to reach 10% per year.

Even though some will say that shooting for 10% and attaining 5% is progress, keep in mind that it's still viewed as a failure by your sales force.

Effective stretch goals can be created in two steps:

1. **Establish mutually agreeable goals**—Get your reps involved. Their input brings real-world wisdom, and their active involvement will help pave the way for goal attainment. In goal setting, openly discuss with your reps the following issues that directly affect objectives:

   - The importance of stretch objectives in expanding salespeople's skills
   - Historical sales results and progress toward objectives
   - Your organization's revenue requirements and financial needs
   - Product availability, new products, and different applications that affect sales
   - Reps' expected account losses and gains
   - Economic and industry trends that have an impact on sales

2. **Develop an action plan to achieve goals**—Stretch goals without an action plan is like a home builder without blue prints. Your action plan should be developed one-on-one with your reps in writing. Here are the key factors in developing your plan:

   - Break down objectives into sales per day, week, and month. Also segment goals into daily and weekly calls needed, appointments, and closes required.
   - Designate training required to meet the specific needs of the rep.
   - Establish a coaching plan that the manager implements for the rep's development.
   - Create a list of the salesperson's commitments for self-improvement.
   - Determine the measurement metrics needed to track the rep's progress toward goals.
   - Schedule follow-up meetings to keep the rep and manager apprised of the rep's efforts.

Case Study #7: Successful Performance Measurement in Industrial Sales

It had taken four years but, finally, Diane could see a change in sales results. Her 12 sales reps had nearly doubled the number of new accounts, morale was higher, and she was spending more time developing and planning sales. It hadn't always been so good. In fact, before the turnaround, she had come face-to-face with managerial mediocrity.

As branch sales manager for a regional petrochemical supplies firm with seven other branch offices, she had spent years carefully training her reps to do their job the way she had done hers. She was, in fact, an all-star sales rep with national awards, and she worked hard to shape her people to be as successful as she was. She trained her reps to set up filing systems, gave them phone scripts, and checked their daily calendars. She mandated how many phone calls a day were necessary and what days the calls should be made.

Unfortunately, it did not work. Her team results were average, nowhere near her level of success as a superstar rep. Overall turnover was a little higher than average at 30%, but the turnover rate for her best salespeople (those in the upper 25% of sales) was a worrisome 20%. Aggregate conversion rates, as well as new business generated, were average. In other words, her team was middle-of-the-road, not bad at all but not even close to the top.

Diane's average team results were a constant source of annoyance—as a top salesperson, she wasn't accustomed to being an also-ran. She had always excelled at everything she did. When she took the manager's job, she had fully intended to be the best. It was frustrating, and it was bewildering. She wasn't really sure what she needed to do to get out of the rut.

One day, a first-year rep, Emily, came into her office and asked a simple question: "Do you mind if I set up my own filing system? I've always had a way I like to file my accounts and I can't quite get the hang of your system."

"I don't think that's a good idea," said Diane. "If I let you do it your way, then I've got to let everyone do it their way."

Emily responded, "Is that such a bad idea? We are adults and have our own styles. It's kind of like your telling me how to arrange my purse. Sometimes you just can't manage personal style."

Though Diane quickly dismissed the conversation, Emily's words came back to her a couple of weeks later when she was talking to the branch manager of the leading sales office in the company. "Sometimes," Diane had said, "I think my reps have learning disabilities. They just don't get it. I show them every day how to sell and how to manage their accounts the way I did for years, but it all goes in one ear and out the other. It's like they don't want to be successful."

The other branch manager said, "Everyone has their own way of doing things, but the key word in our office is 'quantify.' I don't measure them against myself. We have a set of metrics that measure bottom-line results. I can tell you on a daily basis who's performing, how they're performing, and why they're performing. We keep it simple. In our sales funnel we measure three new business outcomes: number of leads, appointments, and sales conversions. For existing business there are also three metrics: cross-sells, increases, and account losses. These six criteria lead us to the overall metric that every rep is judged against: net sales per rep. It's all done by smartphone so we have near-instantaneous reports. The key thing is this: They don't need me looking over their shoulder because the numbers don't lie. It gives them the freedom to plan their work and work their plan according to their abilities. If a rep wants to set fewer appointments and take more time on each call with the intent of making more revenue per appointment, that's okay. Not only does it give them more latitude to work at their optimal pace, it gives me more time to plan and direct rather than babysit."

The words "you just can't manage personal style" came back to Diane. Little by little, she began to use metrics as the team's performance measurement as opposed to measuring them against *her* personal selling style. Instead of spending precious management time checking their filing system and appointment calendars, she focused on metrics that reported their bottom-line outcomes. The reps became more creative and goal driven, and the top producers stayed longer. Equally important, Diane became more of a planner and visionary—a leader.

Selling Smart with Sales Opportunity Metrics

When considering your key metrics, think in terms of *Who's Selling* and *Who's Buying*. The Who's Selling category, or Key Performance Indices, tells you everything you need to know about your reps' selling habits and practices, and the Who's Buying metrics identify customer sales opportunities in the marketplace.

Regardless of the metrics model or combination of models you use—CRM, SFA (Sales Force Automation), sales funnel, pipeline management, scorecard, or hybrid model—the important thing is the breadth and depth of your data. Key performance metrics pertaining to your reps' sales results are not enough. Your metrics should include customer data that generates sales opportunity intelligence to guide your sales team to the right customers with the correct sales pitch. Customer opportunity metrics are the foundation for strategic development, establishing separate sales strategies to target buyers with different needs, interests, and budgets. A critical offshoot of these analytics is customer segmentation, which differentiates your high-yield customers from the rest. The focus is on *who is buying what, how much, and when?* Effective customer segmentation helps your salespeople aim at customers who are likely to buy. It helps them refine their efforts to cross-sell and up-sell existing customers, as well as selling better to new prospects. And, equally important, it helps your sales reps avoid low-yield customers.

You know, intuitively, who your best customers are. You get plenty of anecdotal evidence every day from your sales team. Customer segmentation helps you statistically verify and expand what you might already know, providing more insights in addition to illuminating new customer segments of which you weren't aware. Following are key customer segment metrics your data base should provide:

- Best-selling products and services by customer segment

- Average sales cycle

- Seasonal variations in sales

- Conversion rate of cross-sales and up-sales

- Account losses and trends by segment

- Effect of discounts on sales

- Historical trends that show product maturity and sales attrition
- Who the decision makers are
- Effect and necessity of technical support
- New business metrics by segment

Understanding your individual customers is good but not good enough. By capturing and extrapolating client data to customer segments, the sales manager moves from singular account tactics to meaningful sales strategy. The first challenge is to *capture* the appropriate data. After you develop a baseline of customer data, it's possible to run cross-tabs to identify, analyze, and develop methods for selling to customer segments. Customer contracts can provide the lion's share of customer data. It's relatively simple to expand your customer database by simply adding a box to check on the contract such as identifying the transaction as a cross-sale or up-sale, or by specifying a discount amount and type. More elaborate information might require customer questionnaires or having a research consultant gather additional customer detail.

After you have developed a customer database, you should be able to run cross-tabs and data sorts that identify vertical and horizontal segments. Vertical segments are primarily types of business based on SIC codes such as computer dealers, metal manufacturers, or telecommunications firms. Vertical segmentation is most common, but horizontal segments also can yield sales opportunities. Horizontal segments include, for example, engineers, accountants, human resource personnel, or information technology managers. Examples of cross-tabs that can be run to unearth productive customer segments might include the following:

- Total sales of a specific product by industry with high cross-sale probability and low account-loss rate
- Specific product sales to new business in a particular industry with short sales cycles
- Highest sales per account by industry by season
- Products reaching maturity by industry and by up-sale potential
- Segments that have highest conversion rates when discounts are offered

- Customers by industry whose up-sale potential increases with technical support

- Accounts with engineers having cross-sale potential who buy in the early stages of product introduction

- Accounts with human resources directors who have outdated computer systems

There are thousands of ways to segment your customer base and even more cross-tabs that can be developed. The crucial activity is to translate the information into actionable plans. The details will not only tell you whom to target with what products where and when, but also suggest *how* to make the sales pitch. Good data helps develop a solid value proposition as well as visuals and sales aids. It also provides information that helps establish reps' credibility with customers by providing industry-specific details. Many sales managers have used customer segmentation to assign sales reps to specialize in specific, high-potential industries such as medical, retail, or industrial.

Here are the three steps to create a successful sales strategy:

1. **Study your customer base**—Review your sales statistics to determine which customer classes are yielding the biggest and most profitable sales. Which are requiring the shortest sales cycle? Which ones are best for cross-selling? Which ones generate repeat sales?

   Ask your sales team for input. What customers do they recommend focusing on? Which ones have the money to spend? Which ones will buy consistently? Which ones match up well with our product benefits? Where do we have competitive advantages? Which ones are financially stable and well-positioned in their industry? Which ones are immune to economic downturns?

2. **Identify your target customer as narrowly as possible**—Your target has to be a customer class large enough to yield ample sales but small enough to understand. Your "black bass" preferred customer class (see Chapter 1, "First Step: Manage Yourself") shares enough in common that indicates where and how they feed and when they're biting. This lets you customize your sales pitches and develop product/service applications that make

sense specifically to them. Also identify secondary targets and prioritize them in order of potential. At the same time list low-potential customers that are best avoided.

It's not enough to say your target customer is, for example, high-tech manufacturing companies. Break it down. Your real high-potential focus might be on purchasing agents for such companies with sales over $10 million who are located in Missouri, Oklahoma, Kansas, and Texas. Secondary targets should be identified to further delineate your customer base.

As another example, say you're a security systems firm. Don't stop with simply identifying your target as retail businesses. Segment them. For instance, your sales statistics show that the best sales production is coming from jewelry stores located in the southern part of the state, with annualized sales between $5 and $20 million. The best-selling product is a new version of video surveillance and their peak purchasing months are September and January. Most of your sales to jewelry stores have been made with a 10% or more discount.

Now you've developed a target based on your sales results that guides your sales team not only in handling your existing top-drawer customer class but also in targeting new business prospects. Your segmentation has provided the who, what, where, when, why, and how of your sales strategy.

The final phase of the identification stage is to have your sales team analyze and reality-check the customer segmentation. They will bring the street smarts to further refine and illuminate the metrics.

3. **Develop Customer Matchups**—The third step is usually the easiest: aligning your existing products and services with your target customer needs. It also includes creating innovative product/service applications that might apply individually to your target. Matching up also includes special pricing and discounts that serve as attractive bait for your black bass customers. It also helps create tactics to differentiate you from your competition, as well as sales techniques aimed at your target's decision makers.

Using the security systems firm example, your customer segmentation helps you do the following:

- Create customer brochures and other visuals with targeted messages emphasizing safety and crime prevention in the jewelry business, as well as specific ways your systems have helped jewelry stores in the market area. These messages also should be used in sales presentations as your USPs (unique selling propositions).
- Design product applications specifically for your primary customer class. Since video surveillance is the top-selling product, you find a vendor who can provide a new twist to the application: remote, 24-hour video surveillance from a smartphone. Since your competitors don't offer it, the application has potential for up-sales and for selling jewelry store prospects who aren't yet your customers.
- Determine appropriate discounts that have proved successful for your target segment. Because the majority of video surveillance sales to your target segment include a 10% or greater discount, you know up front that such a discount is necessary to make the sale.
- Establish a selling schedule that directs your sales efforts. You can plan your sales contests, selling aids, and other logistics to prepare your people for the peak selling months of September and January.

The result is a sales force with direction and resources to sell effectively. They can talk the lingo and push the right buttons to close sales. And they are credible to their customers because of their targeted sales approach, as opposed to salespeople who use a one-size-fits-all approach.

Over time, your sales strategy will change with market and industry trends. A continual review of your sales analytics and sales team input will tell you when strategic shifts are needed. Day-to-day tactics will, and should, change according to input from your sales team and your metrics. The key is to be informed and flexible, sticking to your strategy as long as it's viable and shifting your tactics to meet the daily needs of the marketplace.

Red-Flagging Your Database

Customers change and markets adjust. Sometimes quickly but many times as slowly but surely as the hour hand. Your database should have a red flag capability to alert you to new opportunities and challenges such as these:

- **Product maturation and sales attrition**—As a product matures, sales will eventually decline. Sometimes technology changes or competitive thrusts will decrease product sales. Your database should alert you to these changes. Running cross-tabs by industry and product will illuminate where the sales attrition is occurring and how long it has been transpiring.

- **New customer segments**—Occasionally, a new high-yield customer class will develop. Perhaps, unbeknownst to you or your sales team, an industry might be going through changes that make one of your products particularly attractive. In addition to industry changes, new prospects can be created by demographic, social, and economic shifts. Variations in interest rates, for example, can create a host of new sales targets in the housing construction industry by shifting emphasis from single- to multi-family building. Your database should reflect these kinds of opportunities as well as the "who, what, where, when, and how" of the segments.

- **New product applications**—Perhaps your products are being used in new and innovative ways by customers. Increased product sales into new segments might indicate unintended applications by customers that present sales potential. Historically, people have found innovative uses for products that created huge sales opportunities. For example, Minoxidil was originally used to treat high blood pressure but was found to be a catalyst for hair growth; WD-40's sales potential expanded from the defense industry as a corrosion preventer to widespread consumer use for lubrication and a variety of other purposes; and texting began as a way for cell phone companies to notify customers of phone system problems. Segmentation metrics—coupled with your sales reps' observations—can alert you to unexpected product applications that might be generating a new class of prospects.

- **Pricing trends**—Another red flag situation is imbalances in pricing and discounts. If your statistics have shown a historical balance between discounts offered and sales made, a sustained imbalance shows customer resistance to pricing. Your existing discounts, for example, might not be enough to facilitate sales. Cross-tabulation will tell you whether it's a broad-based problem or industry-specific.

Sales Segmentation Is a Team Effort

Encourage your reps to think in sales segmentation terms. Your people are a valuable component of your segmentation efforts by providing anecdotal evidence of new and emerging segments, as well as changes occurring in existing segments. Much of sales reps' informal discussions address their account transactions, and can lead to a kind of collective consciousness of trends in particular industries. For example, you might have one rep mention a couple of big sales to dentists. Another rep responds similarly, the word spreads, and soon your people have identified a new, high-potential segment.

This can be a gold mine for the manager who's listening or, even better, who's *seeking* this kind of information from salespeople. The manager can then run cross-tabs to discover more about, for example, dentists such as preferred products, revenue per sale, sales conversion rates, discount sensitivity, and peak buying seasons.

7

Seventh Step: Continuous Improvement, Maintaining Success

Having a successful year is good. Having two in a row is even better. Beyond that, success becomes the stuff of legends— those who succeed year in and year out. How do you replicate success year after year?

Obviously, it takes a steely will to win and a stonewall refusal to lose. It takes people skills, market knowledge, and hundreds of other managerial factors that coalesce all at once. But there seems to be one thread that runs through many successful sales management careers: an effective *process* that guides the sales team every year in problem solving, objective setting, opportunity analysis, rep development, and many other important sales functions.

In the TQM world, it's called continuous improvement, a systematic process that involves teamwork, rep involvement, empowerment/ ownership, and performance measurement. Sometimes performance measurement is mistakenly confused with continuous improvement. Performance measurement is a part of continuous improvement, just as multiplication is a part of algebra. The difference is that performance measurement is an *activity* whereas continuous improvement is a *system*. It's a step-by-step approach that the manager and sales reps employ as a team to overcome obstacles and maximize sales.

In the way continuous improvement has proven successful in manufacturing and industrial firms, it can be effective in sales groups as well. The key is to develop a process led by sales reps that is orderly, consistent, and organized. Unlike manufacturing and industrial processes, the sales process does not have raw materials that are shaped and refined into a final product. Contrary to sales activities, manufacturing has measurable input and empirical output, every step being easily quantified. Instead, with sales, you have a plethora of intangibles in the sales process such as personalities and motivation of buyers and of sellers. This volatile, unpredictable mix of human dynamics adds a complex layer to continuous improvement that is much harder to measure than in manufacturing/industrial concerns. Despite the procedural differences, the fact remains that sales performance can be analyzed and measured in a way that ensures incremental improvements in your sales results year after year.

There are hundreds of ways to establish a continuous improvement process. Two effective ways are Six Sigma and the Deming Cycle. Remember that both of these are metric-centered processes that require a great deal of buy-in from your team. The process might require additional time and effort on their part, and they have to believe it's a worthwhile endeavor. They need to know, for example, why they have to submit additional reports and what's in it for them. They also need to be part of the process, offering their guidance, input, and direction. Your people are instrumental in determining what needs to be measured and how to measure, as well as when and how to refine your metrics over time.

As you and your team develop your indices, keep in mind that metrics can be addictive. It's easy to get mesmerized by the metrics and forget that sales is the most human of all human processes. It's one person relating to another to meet each other's needs. Statistics can help explain this complex process but should never be given enough energy to direct the process. In other words, metrics enhance and facilitate the sales process but do not supersede it.

Achieving Success with Six Sigma

Developed in the mid-1980s by Motorola, Six Sigma is a manufacturing phrase meaning that 99.999% of products are free of defect. The Six Sigma process has expanded to be used by nonmanufacturing concerns throughout the world. Though used sparingly in sales operations, Six Sigma offers powerful potential as a structured approach to problem solving. Five elements characterize the application of Six Sigma: define, measure, analyze, improve, and control. Here's how the process works:

1. **Define**—Make sure you clearly define the process and problem. For example, if your sales cycle is too long and you need to compress it, define exactly what it involves, where it starts and ends, and the important steps in between. Defining the problem or process ensures that everyone has a common understanding of the issue from the outset. It also provides insight into the solvability and metrics needed for success.

   For example, a simple definition for a sales cycle problem could be this: "Our average sales cycle is two weeks longer than the industry average. The sales cycle begins with the sales lead and is followed by the first customer contact, the initial appointment, follow-up appointments, and the contract signing. Some of the key issues impacting the sales cycle are customer knowledge of the product, discounts, and promotional offers, as well as technical assistance during the buying decision period." In essence, the first step is to establish *what* is to be measured. The second step is *how* to measure it.

2. **Measure**—After the problem is clearly defined, you measure the activities and results that are instrumental to solving the problem. For example, you design a way—through CRM, sales funnel input, or other paper or online reports—for your reps to note the dates of first customer contact, the first appointment, and contract signing. Reps will also indicate on sales reports or post-purchase questionnaires can be used to show the level of product knowledge held by the customer and other factors such as promotional offers and technical assistance. The key to initiating the measurement step is to make it as streamlined and simple as possible. Here's where your team needs to weigh in because they will have to take time to provide details they haven't given in the past. If you already have a sales funnel or a similar reporting system, you have a head start that should require minimal extra effort from your reps.

3. **Analyze**—After you've established your measurement procedures (hopefully with a minimum of moaning from your team), the hard part is over. Now, you should have a stream of data to analyze and problem-solve. Using the sales cycle example, you now have the following data:

- The dates of each contact with customer, from setting an appointment to signing the contract
- The presence of items that affect the sales cycle, such as product knowledge of the customer, discounts/promotional offers, and technical assistance

This information allows you to evaluate issues that compress or extend the sales cycle. For example, if you look at the shortest transactions, you can see how the presence of technical assistance affected each transaction. You can also evaluate the effect that discounts—such as limited-time offers—have on closing the sale more quickly.

4. **Improve**—A comprehensive analysis of your metrics gives you assumptions or hypotheses to test. Now you're ready to make improvements in the process. Using the sales cycle example, you observed that higher levels of technical assistance—having your technical people confer with customers—were associated with the shortest transactions; therefore, you increased the level of technical assistance provided to customers and found that the sales cycle has been shortened by 20%. Similarly, perhaps a 15% customer discount for closing the sale in 30 days might significantly compress the sales cycle in the majority of sales where it was used. The point is that, now, you are not just guessing and hypothesizing. You have black-and-white statistics on every sale made to clearly demonstrate what factors influence the sales cycle.

5. **Control**—The final step is making the change a part of everyday operations. This last step has two parts: First, you should make permanent changes to procedures and revising forms and practices as well as employee training and incentives to ensure continued success. For example, you make sure employees are fully trained to understand and implement the new process. Incentives might be needed to encourage employee engagement in the change. This is also a time to reinforce the value of the metrics to the sales force. It should be an easy sell because you now have a road map of effective selling techniques that your salespeople can use daily. The statistics will tell them, for example, when to

bring a technical specialist into the transaction or what kind of discount should be offered to hasten the buying decision. Take care at this point to make the connection between data and sales practice. Give your salespeople specific examples of how to use the findings to improve their sales and put more money in their pockets. Provide the WIFM (what's in it for me). Give them "bottom line" statements like, "If you offer a 15% limited-time discount during your initial appointment, there's a likelihood that you'll close the sale two weeks earlier than normal. That means you can make ten more sales per year that can translate to an average of $15,000 more income for you per year."

The second part of this final step is that you should implement metrics that continuously monitor the new procedures to ensure that they are yielding the expected results. Never assume that programs working today will work tomorrow—after all, you have competition as well as changes in technology, the market, and the economy that create a constant need to monitor your metrics and make changes when needed. Using the example of discounts impacting the sales cycle, you might find that the timing or amount of a discount can lose its effect over time. The third year, your numbers might show the need to test a larger discount to effectively speed the sales close. You will see fluctuations on a daily and weekly basis. The key is to watch for quarterly trends that indicate the need for process refinements and changes.

Using the Deming Cycle for Improved Sales

Closely aligned with Six Sigma, the Deming Cycle focuses on team-oriented, continuous improvement. Originated by W. Edward Deming, the guru of process improvement, the Deming Cycle is characterized by PDCA: plan, do, check, and act.

"Plan" is the first and most critical component of the process, sometimes composing 50% of the total effort. Here are the key steps of this first phase:

1. **Collaborate**—Get the right people involved, from sales reps to managers to administrative and support staff. Make sure everyone

has an equal voice and is encouraged to speak up. Involving the right people will provide insights and ideas from all perspectives, ensuring quality and comprehensive input. Equally important, it gives your people (especially sales reps) a sense of ownership of the process. This is particularly important because they will have to make an extra effort to make the process work. For example, they will have to spend more time completing sales reports and attending meetings. It's a good idea to address this up front and clearly explain the payoff.

2. **Summarize the problem or market opportunity**—For example, "Our new business has dropped off by 20% the past year." Define the problem simply and specifically with metrics that clearly explain the situation.

3. **State the impact of the issue**—"A reduction in new business revenue has decreased the company's profitability, pressuring us to cut expenses and perhaps lay off employees. Take-home pay for sales reps has decreased by 15% on average."

4. **Describe the current situation**—"We are presently using the same procedure for acquiring new business that we have used for the past ten years. Sales reps are provided prospect lists, Mondays are designated as new business target days, special discounts are designated for new business accounts, higher commissions are paid on new business...."

5. **State the objective in statistical terms or as where the group numbers need to be**—"Total sales revenue is $10 million, our new business the past year is $2 million. Our target for new business this year is $2.6 million, which amounts to $90,000 per rep."

6. **Explain possible causes of the problem**—"Our numbers show a reduction in revenue per sale for new business accounts across the board. Also, we're seeing fewer new business acquisitions in the service sector that has traditionally accounted for 45% of our new business." This is the step where good data analysis is vital. It's also a time to hear from the group, especially the sales force, to get the "street" perspective on the causes of the problem.

7. **Brainstorm solutions**—After you've thoroughly analyzed the issue, it's important to get everyone's input on solving the problem. Rely on the frontline salespeople—they are an invaluable source of creative problem solving (that's a big part of their job day to day). Nothing is sacred. Discuss changes to existing practice, policy, and procedure. Consider pricing changes and commission revisions.

8. **Create solutions to be tested**—Initially, narrow and prioritize the solutions, and then start with a small-scale study to address the top-priority solution first; for example: "Since new business acquisition in the service sector is so important to us, we'll establish a limited-time, 20% discount to stimulate service sector sales. We'll test it for a quarter, and then decide whether we continue it." In marketing parlance, test-market the solution before rolling it out.

9. **Establish a measurement system to test the fix**—Begin the metrics process with a statement like, "All service sector sales will have a special discount code noted on the contract when uploaded into the system. This will provide total sales, amount of revenue per sale, and number of sales per rep."

The second step of PDCA is **"do."** Now it's time to implement the change, to make sure that all sales reps and support staff are informed and engaged in this process improvement. The steps include these:

1. **Training** to ensure that sales personnel understand the rationale for the test and that the discount is coded and applied correctly.

2. **Daily monitoring** by sales management to address problems as they occur.

3. **Regular updating** on implementation progress to keep all parties (managers, reps, and support staff) informed of potential problems or refinements that might be needed.

The third step is **"check."** This is the point where the metrics are evaluated:

1. **Review** the test frequently, daily if possible. Analyze results and identify what you are learning.

2. **Communicate** the metrics to all parties to maintain interest and enthusiasm.

3. **Ensure** that the measure is achieving what you want to accomplish.

The final step is **"act,"** or take action based on what you learned from the test:

1. **If the program was successful,** standardize it for permanent implementation.

2. **If it was unsuccessful,** go through the process again with a new approach.

3. **Make sure** that all concerned parties stay well informed of the resulting actions.

4. **Continuously monitor** results year to year to make sure that the solution continues to work. Make refinements as necessary to meet market changes.

Sales Excellence Is the Core Value of Continuous Improvement

Regardless of what process you use—Six Sigma, the Deming Cycle, or your own hybrid method—the underlying principle of your efforts should be sales excellence, not goal attainment. After all, accomplishing sales goals can be an empty endeavor. You know, reach the goal, get the trophy, and then move on to the next one. When we strive for sales excellence—becoming the best we can be—we establish a permanent mind-set, a continuous quest to improve ourselves first, and then reap the rewards such as attaining sales goals, higher pay, and recognition and awards. Aristotle said, "We are what we repeatedly do. Excellence, then, is not an act but a habit." It is a habit formulated by sales managers who seek long-term achievement over short-term fixes in all phases of their continuous improvement program. With this in mind, successful sales leaders encourage their people, on a daily basis, to observe, learn, practice, and prepare. The result is better salespeople who actively create an improved organization.

The continuous improvement process is meant to address a broad spectrum of sales problems and opportunities, both long- and short-range in nature. However, to get the most of the process, one should think in terms of long-range, sustainable improvement. For example, to attain a short-term goal, you might begin your team process with a question like, "How do we reach this year's sales objectives?" The long-range counterpart of the question might be, "How do we become a best-in-class sales force in our territory?" By establishing a process to become best-in-class, by focusing on sales excellence, you preemptively set the stage for sales goal attainment. In effect, you have created a long-term procedure that will reach short-term goals year after year.

A large part of reaching sales excellence is asking the right questions during the continuous improvement process. For example, let's say your team is considering the use of product discounts to stimulate sales. Instead of beginning the process with a question like "What kind of discounts should we implement to improve sales?" the preferred question should be "How do we increase sales through customer incentives including but not limited to product discounts?" The latter question will open a dialogue on other ways to boost sales such as value-added strategies that increase customers' perception of a product's value. Or product positioning that shows your advantages over competitors' offerings. By focusing on product quality, your sales team might avoid the downside risks of discounting which could destroy the perceived value of your product in the eyes of customers. In the same vein, product promotions—limited-time offers, buy-one-get-one incentives, and sweepstakes—can give you a temporary uptick in sales but can "cannibalize" other product sales and devalue customers' image of your product. An effective continuous improvement process can provide alternatives such as innovative product applications and inventive customer segmentation that might work better than product promotions.

Another example is using continuous improvement to address sales rep incentives. Instead of "What rep incentives should we use to boost product sales?" try a more comprehensive question like "How do we motivate reps to sell more product?" This "how" question might create unconventional, but effective, options to bonuses and gifts that provide fewer downside risks such as "incentive addiction" (when your reps sell well during incentive periods and coast when no inducements are offered). Alternatives to incentives might be training that includes targeted USPs (unique selling propositions) or applicable best practices. It could even include developing "pride of salesmanship" as a principle of your sales culture. These options can be used with or instead of traditional rep incentives to promote sustainable sales excellence in your organization.

Much of the process begins with asking the right question (using the phrase "including but not limited to...") and letting your team arrive at effective solutions. In addition to asking appropriate questions, your team should—formally or informally—conduct a root cause analysis. In other words, do more than simply identify obstacles and roadblocks to effective sales; dig and probe to ensure that you discover the root cause of problems. We all are guilty of creating simple metrics that state the "what" but not the "how" of sales issues. We sometimes spend so many hours analyzing the obvious—key performance metrics, sales forecasts, and revenue requirements—that we fail to look deeply beneath the surface. Using the product discount example previously noted, your sales might be lagging not because of price, but because of low perceived value. Your metrics might not tell you that, but the sales team process should identify these types of root causes by assimilating the observations, experience, and knowledge of your team members.

After you've identified the underlying root causes, you have a blueprint for solving the problem with training, coaching, preparation, and other follow-up actions.

Tips for Implementing Continuous Improvement

Following are ideas that will help you initiate and sustain successful continuous improvement for your sales team.

Think Deep and Wide

Continuous improvement can be used in various sales processes; everything is fair game for refinements. Think in terms of direct sales activities, as well as all activities that affect the sales function. Here are a few examples of things you should consider:

- Improvements to commission plans
- New product introductions
- Sales campaign planning
- Administrative logjams and slowdowns
- Enhancements to sales funnels and CRM systems
- Customer segmentation
- Implementation of new sales policy and procedures
- Sales training and rep development

At the Same Time, Think Small

As your team begins to address issues, focus on small tweaks and refinements. Don't overwhelm your people with radical changes, especially in the early going. Making small changes helps your sales team build confidence in the process, increasing their comfort level as you go. After they are more experienced, you can progressively increase the scope and significance of process improvements. However, no matter how proficient your team becomes, don't try to tackle too much at a time—small changes should always be your default position. Small, incremental changes over time result in large, significant improvements.

Avoid "It's Not My Job" Thinking

Continuous improvement is everyone's job. Encourage your salespeople to be process-improvement detectives, always looking for a better way to do their job as well as others' jobs that affect sales—clerical and administrative staff, in addition to marketing, accounting, human relations, and other departments. This means your salespeople need to take the blinders off and assume responsibility for improving not only themselves but the organization as a whole.

Invite Others to the Process

Think of all the departments and personnel that affect your sales team—get them actively involved in your process improvements. Even if you're addressing a sales-specific issue, such as cross-selling particular products, you might benefit from the input of a technician who installs the products. This cross-pollination not only helps in a technical sense but also builds rapport with nonsales personnel who can assist your selling dynamics. Invite others to your meetings, even give them a standing invitation or an official place at the meeting table.

Make It Your Own System

Don't get hung up on the methodology of Six Sigma or the Deming Cycle. If necessary, take parts and pieces of them and fashion a process that works for you. The important thing is that you and your people learn to recognize problems and solve them in a logical fashion. How you get from point A to point B depends on your personal management style and your sales ecosystem.

Conclusion

Leadership, the Sales Management Buffet

We're all different. We all have different personalities, goals, talents, experience. Every situation is different. There are no formulas, no textbook or instruction manual that will get you through the maze of managing salespeople.

It's interesting to see how sales managers in the same corporate environment—with identical objectives, products, and policies—will take vastly different approaches to managing. Some will actively learn new management skills, reject the status quo, take some risks, and succeed. Others will fail by continually doing the same thing over and over, expecting different results. Others doggedly stick to the adage "If it ain't broke, don't fix it" instead of "If it ain't broke, make it better." In the tumultuous world of sales management, things will get broke. That's guaranteed. It could be the gradual attrition of market changes on what was once a successful sales strategy, or it could be the sudden impact of an economic crash. To succeed, one has to—as hockey great Wayne Gretzky said—skate to where the puck is going to be, not to where it is.

Think of the real leaders you have known, those who have transcended from managers to leaders and who have been successful year after year. It's likely that, at some point in their careers, they moved from being a tactician to being a visionary, seeing the big picture, doing the right things, as opposed to only doing things right; from being a boss to being a partner with their people; from monitoring to allowing self-monitoring; from requiring obedience to asking for job ownership.

Learning to lead a sales force is like going through a buffet line. You pick and choose what works best for you at a particular time in a specific situation. Next month, chances are, everything changes and you start again.

The key is to keep your track shoes on, stay nimble, and treat every situation on its own merits. There are times—hopefully few—when command/control is the order of the day. Used sparingly, it can provide structure and boundaries as employee involvement develops. Use a mix that works for you and keeps your salespeople feeling respected, inspired, and energized.

Situational Leadership, as described by Ken Blanchard, Patricia Zigarmi, and Drea Zigarmi in *Leadership and the One Minute Manager,* embodies different styles for different people and different tasks. The product, sales territory, personality, and experience of the rep and hundreds of other factors should change your approach to the situation. As Blanchard and Zigarmis state, "There is nothing so unequal as the equal treatment of unequals."

As your personal management style evolves, consider the following five critical needs of salespeople:

1. **Structure**—A sales force needs clear-cut guidelines such as office hours, business attire, deadlines, objectives, and the rules of the road expected of them.

2. **Challenge**—Your reps need the challenge of stretch objectives to help inspire and motivate them. Expect them to be better than the best they can be.

3. **Respect**—Perhaps the most basic and universal need of sales people is respect. They desire to be treated like professionals in a trusting partnership with you.

4. **Involvement**—Your people want to be involved, to provide input on issues and decisions that affect them.

5. **Support**—If they say it or not, your people need your time and attention, training, and all the resources available to make them successful.

If you forget everything else from this book, the two basic but key ideas are these:

1. **Ask**—The simple act of asking your team for their ideas, suggestions, and feedback will begin a process of employee involvement that can pay huge dividends.

2. **Law of Reciprocity**—Everything you give will be returned to you. Maybe not in the same amount, maybe not at the same time, but if you give your people respect, thoughtfulness, and support, you will get it back.

References

Chapter 1

1. Dr. Wayne W. Dyer, *Excuses Begone!*, Hay House, Inc., 2009.

2. Charles Green, "Why Trust Is the New Core of Leadership," *Forbes*, April 3, 2012.

3. Ken Blanchard and Don Shula, *The Little Book of Coaching*, Harper Collins Publishers Inc., 2001.

4. Gregory A. Rich, "The Sales Manager as a Role Model: Effects on Trust, Job Satisfaction, and Performance of Salespeople," *Journal of Academy of Marketing Science*, Vol. 25, No. 4, 1997.

5. Geoff Colvin, "Great Job! How YUM Brands Uses Recognition to Build Teams and Get Results," *Fortune* magazine, August 12, 2013.

6. "America's Best Graduate Schools: Top Business Schools," *U.S. News & World Report*, March, 2007.

7. Rolph Anderson, Rajiv Mehta, and James Strong, "An Empirical Investigation of Sales Management Training Programs for Sales Managers," *Journal of Personal Selling & Sales Management*, Summer, 1997.

8. Samuel B. Bacharach, "How Leaders Reinvent Themselves," *Inc.* magazine, January 2, 2014.

9. Rebecca Webber, "Reinvent Yourself," *Psychology Today*, May 6, 2014.

10. Alvaro Fernandez, "Top 15 Insights on Neuroplasticity, Brain Training, Emotions, Cognition and Brain Health—Ready?" Ezine @rticles, www.ezinearticles.com, April 30, 2014.

11. Leonard Wong, "Developing Adaptive Leaders in Iraq and Afghanistan," *Harvard Business Review,* January 23, 2009.

12. "When It Comes to Business Leadership, Nice Guys Finish First," Green Peak Partners, www.greenpeakpartners.com.

13. Paul Tough, "What If the Secret to Success Is Failure?" *New York Times Magazine,* September 14, 2011.

14. Aimee Groth, "Student Test Scores Show That 'Grit' Is More Important Than IQ," *Business Insider,* www.businessinsider.com, May 28, 2013.

15. Sharon Jayson, "Bad Bosses Can Be Bad for Your Health," *USA Today,* August 5, 2012.

16. "Survey Shows 48% Would Fire Their Boss," Badbossology.com, www.badbossology.com, June 15, 2004.

17. "Survey Shows Bosses Still Driving Turnover," Badbossology.com, www.badbossology.com, April 21, 2004.

18. Charles H. Green, "Sales, Narcissism and Therapists," www.trustedadvisor.com, April 19, 2011.

19. Sue Barrett, "7 Signs that You Are in the Presence of a Sales Narcissist," Barrett Sales Blog, September 1, 2011, www.barrett.com.au.

20. Ken Blanchard, "I'm OK, You're Not—It's All About Ego," How We Lead, Conversations on Leadership with Ken Blanchard, www.howwelead.org, November 13, 2010.

21. Travis Bradberry, "Emotional Intelligence—EQ," *Forbes* magazine, January 9, 2014.

22. Dacher Keltner, "The Power of Kindness," *UTNE Reader,* May-June 2008, www.utne.com.

23. Arthur C. Brooks, "Does Money Make You Happy?" *The Christian Science Monitor,* June 24, 2008.

24. Workplace Bullying Institute, "The WBI Definition of Workplace Bullying," www.workplacebullying.org.

25. Max DePree, *Leadership Is an Art,* Crown Business, 2004.

26. John Maxwell, *The 21 Irrefutable Laws of Leadership: Follow Them and People Will Follow You,* Thomas Nelson, 2004.

27. Philip Kreindler and Gopal Rajguru, "What B2B Customers Really Expect," *Harvard Business Review,* April 1, 2006.

Chapter 2

1. David DiSalvo, "Move Over Extroverts, Here Comes the Ambiverts," *Forbes* magazine, April 10, 2013.

2. Steve W. Martin, "Seven Personality Traits of Top Salespeople," *Harvard Business Review,* www.hbr.org, June 27, 2011.

3. Kibeom Lee, Ph.D., and Michael Ashton, Ph.D., "The HEXACO Personality Inventory—Revised," www.hexaco.org, August 15, 2014.

4. Harris Plotkin, The Plotkin Group, "Measuring People's Full Potential," www.plotkingroup.com.

Chapter 3

1. RogenSi, "Courage to Act: 2012 Global Mindset Survey," www.rogensi.com.

2. "Say This! Certain Words, Uttered Frequently, Might Make You Rich," *Men's Health* magazine, January/February, 2015.

3. Kathleen Hurson, Ed Musselwhite, Craig Perrin, and John H. Zenger, *Leading Teams: Mastering the New Role,* Business One Irwin, 1994.

4. Michael Shammas, "These Are the 10 Most Psychopathic Jobs in America," *Huffington Post,* April 8, 2014.

5. Thomas N. Ingram, Raymond W. LaForge, William B. Locander, Scott B. MacKenzie, and Philip M. Podsakoff, "New Directions in Sales Leadership Research," *Journal of Personal Selling & Sales Management,* Spring, 2005.

6. Fernando Jaramillo and Jay Prakash Mulki, "Sales Effort: The Intertwined Roles of the Leader, Customers, and the Salesperson," *Journal of Personal Selling & Sales Management,* Winter, 2008.

7. Patricia Sellers, "Car Talk (and More!) with Mary Barra, GM's New Chief," *Fortune* magazine, February 6, 2014.

8. The Conference Board, "Job Satisfaction: 2013 Edition," www.conference-board.org.

9. Gallup Business Journal, "How to Tackle U.S. Employees' Stagnating Engagement," www.gallup.com, June 11, 2013.

10. Lou Holtz, "Setting a Higher Standard," *Get Motivated Workbook,* Get Motivated Seminars, Inc., 2006.

11. Kenneth R. Bartkus, "Group Cohesiveness and Performance in the Salesforce: The Impact of Active and Passive Mechanisms of Direction," *Journal of Professional Services Marketing,* Vol. 13 (1), 1995.

12. Terry L. Childers, Alan J. Dubinsky, and Steven J. Skinner, "Leadership Substitutes as Moderators of Sales Supervisory Behavior," *Journal of Business Research,* Vol. 21 (4), 1990.

13. Steven P. Brown and Robert A. Peterson, "The Effect of Effort on Sales Performance and Job Satisfaction," *Journal of Marketing,* April, 1994.

14. Ajay K. Kohli, "Some Unexplored Supervisory Behaviors and Their Influence on Salespeople's Role Clarity, Specific Self-esteem, Job Satisfaction, and Motivation," *Journal of Marketing Research,* November, 1985.

15. Charles D. Kerns, "The Positive Psychology Approach to Goal Management," *Graziadio Business Review,* Pepperdine University, Vol. 8, Issue 3, 2005.

16. J. Donald Walters, *The Art of Supportive Leadership,* Crystal Clarity Publishers, 1987.

17. Steven P. Brown, William L. Cron, John W. Slocum, Jr., and Don VandeWalle, "The Influence of Goal Orientation and Self-Regulation Tactics on Sales Performance: A Longitudinal Field Test," *Journal of Applied Psychology,* Vol. 84, No. 2, 1999.

18. "Favorite Quotes," Atlas Senior Living, www.atlasseniorliving.com.

19. General Colin Powell, "A Leader Worth Following," *Get Motivated Workbook,* Get Motivated Seminars, Inc., 2006.

20. Peter Schulman, "Applying Learned Optimism to Increase Sales Productivity," *Journal of Personal Selling & Sales Management,* Winter, 1999.

21. "ABCDE model (Learning to be Optimistic)," Positive Psychology Resources, www.centerforconfidence.co.uk.

22. Stacey Kennelly, "Smile! It's Good for Your Heart," *Greater Good,* University of California at Berkeley, www.greatergood.berkeley.edu.

23. Jim Collins, *Good to Great: Why Some Companies Make the Leap...And Others Don't,* Harper Business, First Edition, 2001.

24. Jacquelyn Smith, "Ten Reasons Why Humor Is a Key to Success at Work," *Forbes* magazine, May 3, 2013.

25. Robert A. Emmons and Michael E. McCullough, *The Psychology of Gratitude,* Oxford Press, 2004.

26. Shawn Achor, *The Happiness Advantage: The Seven Principles of Positive Psychology That Fuel Success and Performance at Work,* Crown Business, 2010.

27. Shawn Achor, "5 Ways to Turn Happiness into an Advantage," *Psychology Today*, www.psychologytoday.com, August 23, 2011.

28. Bradley J. Sugars, *Instant Team Building*, McGraw-Hill, 2006.

29. Mike Meseda, "Stressful Work Environments Can Stress Company Budgets," *Austin Business Journal*, March 13, 2005.

30. Catharine Paddock, Ph.D., "Stress Linked to Harmful Fat and Heart Disease," *Medical News Today*, August 5, 2009.

31. Jeff Haden, "Be Graceful Under Pressure: 7 Tips," *Inc.* magazine, www.inc.com, June 13, 2012.

32. Larry Hunter and Sherry M. B. Thatcher, "Feeling the Heat: Effects of Stress, Commitment, and Job Experience on Job Performance," *Academy of Management Journal*, 50, (4), 2007.

33. Jim Keenan, "3 Tips for Helping Reps Avoid Burnout," OpenView Labs, www.openviewpartners.com, April 8, 2013.

34. John C. Maxwell, *Leadership Gold: Lessons I've Learned from a Lifetime of Leading*, Thomas Nelson Inc., 2008.

35. Dan Carrison and Rod Walsh, *Semper Fi: Business Leadership the Marine Corps Way*, AMACOM, 2004.

36. Joseph A. Bellizzi and Robert E. Hite, "A Preferred Style of Sales Management," *Industrial Marketing Management*, August, 1986.

Chapter 4

1. Ronald A. Heifetz and Donald L. Laurie, "The Work of Leadership," *Harvard Business Review*, December 1, 2001.

2. Edward D. Hess, "Servant Leadership: A Path to High Performance," *Washington Post*, April 28, 2013.

3. Alan Axelrod, *Eisenhower Leadership: Ike's Enduring Lessons in Total Victory Management*, Jossey-Bass, 2006.

4. Nayantara Padhi, "The Eight Elements of TQM," iSixSigma Newsletter, www.isixsigma.com, February 10, 2015.

5. Ken Blanchard and Phil Hodges, *Lead Like Jesus,* Thomas Nelson, Inc., 2005.

6. Fernando Jaramillo, Douglas B. Grisaffe, Lawrence B. Chonko, and James A. Roberts, "To Keep Your Agents: Consider Servant Leadership," Keller Center Research Report, Baylor University, December, 2010.

7. Luke Archer, *Verbal Aikido: The Art of Directing Verbal Attacks to a Balanced Outcome, Volume 1: Green Belt,* CreateSpace, March 29, 2013.

8. Dawn R. Deeter-Schmelz, Daniel J. Goebel, and Karen Norman Kennedy, "What Are the Characteristics of an Effective Sales Manager? An Exploratory Study Comparing Salesperson and Sales Manager Perspectives," *Journal of Personal Selling & Sales Management,* Winter, 2008.

9. Mihaly Csikszentmihalyi, *Flow: The Psychology of Optimal Experience,* Harper Perennial Modern Classics, July, 2008.

10. Michael Lee Stallard and Jason Pankau, "To Boost Productivity and Innovation, Fire Up the People You Lead," Robert K Greenleaf Center for Servant Leadership, www.greenleaf.org.

10. Leigh Buchanan, "In Praise of Selflessness," *Inc.* magazine, May 1, 2007, www.inc.com.

11. Michael Lee Stallard, "Servant Leaders Outperform Because They Connect," Helping Leaders Create Cultures That Connect, www.michaelleestallard.com, October 18, 2010.

Chapter 5

1. Michael Irwin Meltzer, Louis A. Mischkind, and David Sirota, "Why Your Employees Are Losing Motivation," *Harvard Management Update,* January, 2006.

2. Dr. Michael Marmot interview, "In Sickness and in Wealth," PBS, Produced by California Newsreel with Vital Pictures, 2008.

3. Peter Drucker, *Classic Drucker,* Harvard Business Review Press, 2006.

4. Edward E. Lawler, III, *The Ultimate Advantage: Creating the High-Involvement Organization,* Jossey-Bass, 1992.

5. Linda Hill and Kent Lineback, *Being the Boss: The 3 Imperatives for Becoming a Great Leader,* Harvard Business Review Press, January, 2011.

6. Jack Stack and Bo Burlingham, *A Stake in the Outcome,* A Currency Book Published by Doubleday, 2002.

7. Joyce Gioia, "Finding Ways to Make Your Employees Intrapreneurs," The Herman Group, www.retentionconnection.com.

8. Gifford Pinchot and Ron Pellman, *Intrapreneuring in Action: A Handbook for Business Innovation,* Berrett-Koehler Publishers, Inc., 1999.

9. "GE Makes a Big Bet on Manufacturing," Rana Foroohar, *Time* magazine, November 20, 2014.

10. Ken Blanchard, John P. Carlos and Alan Randolph, *The Three Keys to Empowerment,* Berrett-Koehler Publishers Inc., 1999.

11. "US Army Announces Test of Wikis to Revise Tactics, Techniques and Procedures," News Release, US Army Battle Command Knowledge System, June 30, 2009.

12. Karen Flaherty, "Enhancing Salesperson Trust: An Examination of Managerial Values, Empowerment, and the Moderating Influence of SBU Strategy," *Journal of Personal Selling & Sales Management,* September, 2003.

13. John Mathieu, Adam Rapp, and Michael Ahearne, "To Empower or Not to Empower Your Sales Force?" *Journal of Applied Psychology,* Vol. 90, No. 5, 2005.

14. L. David Marquet, *Turn the Ship Around!*, Portfolio, May 2013.

15. Joe Petrone, *Building the High-Performance Sales Force*, AMACOM, 1994.

Chapter 6

1. Dave Stein, "Sales Performance Masurement," EyesOnSales, www.eyesonsales.com, July 29, 2008.

2. J. Donald Walters, *The Art of Supportive Leadership*, Crystal Clarity Publishers, 1987.

3. Patricia Sellers, "Car Talk (and More!) with Mary Barra, GM's New Chief," *Fortune* magazine, February 6, 2014.

4. Robert H. Rosen, Paul B. Brown, *Leading People: Transforming Business from the Inside Out*, Viking, 1996.

5. Steve W. Martin, "What Top Sales Teams Have in Common, in 5 Charts," *Harvard Business Review*, www.hbr.com, January 20, 2015.

Conclusion

1. Ken Blanchard, Patricia Zigarmi, and Drea Zigarmi, *Leadership and the One Minute Manager*, William Morrow and Company, 1985.

Index

C

care for employees
  by bad bosses, 33
  role in trust, 17-18, 20-21
Carr, Thomas H., 195
Carrison, Dan, 207
Cartland, Doug, 167
case studies
  empowerment, 244-247
  finding management style, 46-49
  performance measurement, 267-269
  self-management, 13-16
  servant leadership, 219-221
  team building, 142-146
  teamwork, 209-212
celebrating success, 202-203
challenge-skills balance in flow, 224
challenging goals. *See* goal-setting
challenging oneself, 31-32
Check phase (Deming Cycle), 283-284
Clark, Vern, 227
closes (as metric), 264
cockiness, 171-174
cognitive dissonance, 248-249
cold calls (as metric), 264
collaboration. *See* teamwork
Collins, James, 173
command/control sales hierarchies, 125
commitment, increasing, 197
communication skills
  of bad bosses, 33
  of servant leaders, 222-223
competency, role in trust, 19-20
competitiveness
  gauging via body language, 103
  teamwork versus, 134-136
complimentary skills in No Excuse
  management, 67
concentration in flow, 225
confidence
  building, 138-139
  in mental toughness, 29
conscientiousness
  lack of direction versus, 92-93
  as result of teamwork, 166
  in sales reps, 94-95
consideration as TQM principle, 128
consistency in actions, 141
continuous improvement
  with Deming Cycle, 281-284
  performance measurement versus,
  277-278

sales excellence as goal, 284-286
  with Six Sigma, 278-281
  tips for, 286-288
  as TQM principle, 128
control
  sharing, 229-237
  in Six Sigma, 280-281
criticism in team building, 192
cross-selling (as metric), 264
Csikszentmihalyi, Mihaly, 224, 226
customer engagement in servant
  leadership, 227-228
customer exchange/return desks,
  finding recruitment prospects, 74
customer segmentation, 49-50, 270-276
customers, understanding needs of,
  63-65
custom-made team building, 215-216

D

daily contacts as recruitment prospects,
  72-75
decision making, empowerment and,
  250-251
deference in empathy development, 39
deferred gratification, 10
Define stage (Six Sigma), 279
delegation skills, lack of, 11
Deming, Edward, 125, 232, 281
Deming Cycle, 281-284
dependency on others, 11
DePree, Max, 57
Do phase (Deming Cycle), 283
dominance by bad bosses, 34
dominators (in group dynamics), 159
Drucker, Peter, 232
duplicity of bad bosses, 34
Dutton, Kevin, 127
Dyer, Wayne, 12

E

effective leadership, obstacles to,
  134-137
ego affirmation, 174-176
egotistical actions by bad bosses, 33,
  38-39
Eisenhower, Dwight, 215
emotional stability
  neuroticism versus, 93
  in sales reps, 97
empathy, 39-41
  gauging via body language, 103
  as result of teamwork, 166

employee opinions, *seeking*, 188
empowerment
  benefits of, 247-250
  case study, 244-247
  decision making and, 250-251
  described, 243-244
  fostering ownership, 237-243
  self-managed sales teams
    developing, 251-255
    teamwork benefits of, 256
  sharing control, 229-237
  as TQM principle, 128
engagement
  in ambiverts, 90
  in team building, 167-168
enthusiasm
  in ambiverts, 90
  in extroverts, 89
EQ (emotional quotient) skills
  in sales managers, 40-44
  in sales reps, 108-110
ethics, servant leadership and, 216-217
excitability. *See* enthusiasm
Excuses Begone (Dyer), 12
expectation management, 51-53
expectations
  in servant leadership, 218
  of teamwork, 152-153
external EQ skills, 41-42
extrinsic motivation, intrinsic
  motivation versus, 24, 229-230
extroverts
  characteristics of, 88-91
  gauging via body language, 105
  introverts versus, 92
  as sales reps, 95-96

F

facilitation skills, lack of, 11-12
failure, handling, 205-207
"fake good" answers in interviews,
  81-82
favoritism by bad bosses, 34
feedback in flow, 224
Fernandez, Alvaro, 25
finding management style, 46-49
first team meeting, outline of, 155-158
Flaherty, Karen, 249
flexibility
  in managing millennials, 130
  in mental toughness, 30
  in No Excuse management, 67

Flow
  components of, 223-226
  providing, 54
focus in mental toughness, 29
follow-through, lack of, 33
forming, defined, 155
"forming, storming, norming,
  performing," 154-155
freedom
  loss of, 10
  for salespeople, 54
friend, sales management as, 236-237
frustration, role in burnout, 176

G

Gerstner, Lou, 260
Gioia, Joyce, 238
goal-setting
  in flow, 224
  for oneself, 22-25
  in team building, 170-171
Good to Great (Collins), 173
graciousness in servant leadership,
  218-220
Grant, Adam, 88
gratitude in team building, 183-184
Green, Charles H., 36
Greenleaf, Robert, 213
Gretzky, Wayne, 289
ground rules in team building, 153-154
group dynamics
  in team building, 158-161
  understanding, 63
groupthink, 158-159

H

Helson, Ravenna, 23
Hess, Edward, 214
high expectations in servant leadership,
  218
high-traffic purchase points, finding
  recruitment prospects, 75
Hill, Linda, 236
hiring practices, 45-46, 69-70
  avoiding unknowns, 70-71
  personality types
    analysis of, 91
    "Big Five" personality traits, 91-93
    body language as indicator of,
      101-105
    characteristics of extroverts/
      introverts/ambiverts, 88-91
    honesty-humility factor, 97-99

high expectations, 218
inverted pyramid, 216
problem solving, 221-222
productivity improvement, 226-227
retention rates and customer
engagement, 227-228
shared vision in team building, 124
sharing control, 229-237
Shively, Carol, 195
Shula, Don, 18
Sirota, David, 230
Situational Leadership, 290
Six Sigma, 278-281
skills, traits versus, 87-88
small talk avoidance in introverts, 90
smiling as stress reducer, 173
sociability in extroverts, 88
social perception, 41-42
soft skills training in team building, 185
software sales manager case study (self-management), 13-16
sports background in sales reps, 110
sports teams, sales teams versus, 215-216
spousal support in team building, 182
Stack, Jack, 237
stagnant organizations, 125
A Stake in the Outcome (Stack and Burlingham), 237
Stallard, Michael Lee, 226-227
Stein, Dave, 257
Stockdale, Jim, 173-174
storming, defined, 155
strategy, importance of, 49-50
stress tolerance, 106-108
     in team building, 194-199
stretch goals, creating, 266-267
stuck organizations, 125
success, celebrating, 202-203
Sugars, Bradley J., 188
supportive leadership, 133, 148
synthesis in adaptive leadership, 27

T

talkativeness in extroverts, 89
teaching ability, lack of, 10
teaching moments in team building, 184-185
team building, 123-128
     ambitious vision, creating, 139-140
     case study, 142-146
     confidence priming, 138-139
     consistency in actions, 141

disparate personalities and
     experience, 126-128
effect on sales managers' success, 163
expectations of teamwork, 152-153
first team meeting, 155-158
"forming, storming, norming,
     performing," 154-155
ground rules, 153-154
group dynamics, 158-161
implementing best practices, 149-152
learning environment, 148-149
momentum, 143-147
mutual accountability, 142
obstacles to effective leadership,
     134-137
results of teamwork, 165-167
selflessness, 140-141
sense of ownership, 124-125
shared vision, 124
tips for, 161-162
Total Quality Management (TQM),
     125-126, 128
trust, importance of, 123
Un*see*n Team, 131-134
values, 148
what to expect from team, 164-165
team-player traits in sales reps, 110-114
teamwork. *See also* **sales teams**
benefits of, 122-123
     for self-managed teams, 256
competitiveness versus, 134-136
in customer segmentation, 276
custom-made team building, 215-216
in Deming Cycle, 281-282
expectations of, 152-153
group dynamics, 63
in hiring process, 77-78
intimidation versus, 54-57
maintaining, 167-209
     active involvement, 189
     asking questions, 168-170
     assessments, 189
     basic employee needs, 182-183
     case study, 209-212
     celebrating success, 202-203
     ego affirmation, 174-176
     employee opinions, 188
     engagement, 167-168
     goal-setting, 170-171
     gratitude, 183-184
     handling failure, 205-207